THE RISE OF CHINA AND THE CAPITALIST WORLD ORDER

The International Political Economy of New Regionalisms Series

The International Political Economy of New Regionalisms series presents innovative analyses of a range of novel regional relations and institutions. Going beyond established, formal, interstate economic organizations, this essential series provides informed interdisciplinary and international research and debate about myriad heterogeneous intermediate level interactions.

Reflective of its cosmopolitan and creative orientation, this series is developed by an international editorial team of established and emerging scholars in both the South and North. It reinforces ongoing networks of analysts in both academia and think-tanks as well as international agencies concerned with micro-, meso- and macro-level regionalisms.

Recent titles in the series (continued at the back of the book)

The EU and World Regionalism
The Makability of Regions in the 21st Century
Edited by Philippe De Lombaerde

The Role of the European Union in Asia
China and India as Strategic Partners
Edited by Bart Gaens, Juha Jokela and Eija Limnell

China and the Global Politics of Regionalization
Edited by Emilian Kavalski

The Rise of China and the Capitalist World Order

Edited by
LI XING
Aalborg University, Denmark

ASHGATE

Published by

Ashgate Publishing Limited
Wey Court East
Union Road
Farnham
Surrey, GU9 7PT
England

Ashgate Publishing Company
Suite 420
101 Cherry Street
Burlington
VT 05401-4405
USA

www.ashgate.com

British Library Cataloguing in Publication Data

The rise of China and the capitalist world order. -- (The international political economy of new regionalisms series)
1. China--Economic conditions--2000- 2. China--Economic policy--2000- 3. China--Foreign economic relations.
4. World politics--21st century.
I. Series II. Li, Xing.
330.9'5106-dc22

Library of Congress Cataloging-in-Publication Data

The rise of China and the capitalist world order / edited by Li Xing.
p. cm. -- (International political economy of new regionalisms series)
Includes bibliographical references and index.
ISBN 978-0-7546-7913-4 (hardback) -- ISBN 978-0-7546-9810-4 (ebook)
1. China--Economic conditions--2000- 2. Capitalism--China. 3. China--Foreign economic relations. 4. International economic relations. I. Xing, Li.

HC427.95.R576 2010
330.951--dc22

2009040129

ISBN 9780754679134 (hbk)
ISBN 9780754698104 (ebk)

Mixed Sources
Product group from well-managed forests and other controlled sources
www.fsc.org Cert no. SA-COC-1565
© 1996 Forest Stewardship Council
FSC

Printed and bound in Great Britain by MPG Books Group, UK

Contents

List of Figures and Tables

Figures

Tables

Notes on Contributors

Clemens Stubbe Østergaard is Associate Professor, Department of Political Science, Aarhus University, Denmark.

Jacques Hersh is Professor Emeritus, Department of History, International and Social Studies, Aalborg University, Denmark.

Li Minqi is Assistant Professor, Department of Economics, University of Utah.

Li Xing is Associate Professor, Department of History, International and Social Studies, Aalborg University, Denmark.

Mammo Muchie is Professor, Department of History, International and Social Studies, Aalborg University, Denmark.

Paul Opoku-Mensah is Associate Professor, Department of History, International and Social Studies, Aalborg University, Denmark.

Peer Møller Christensen is Post-doc, Institute of Business Communication and Information Science, University of Southern Denmark, Denmark.

Stig Thøgersen is Professor, Department of History and Area Studies, Aarhus University, Denmark.

Introduction

The Rise of China and the Capitalist World Order: The "Four-China" Nexus

Li Xing

Background

The year 2009 marked the 60th anniversary of the victory of the Chinese Communist Revolution and the founding of the People's Republic of China. From a Chinese perspective, 60 years appears as just a blink of an eye in the long history of Chinese civilization in which many family dynasties had individually ruled China for several hundreds of years. Hence, even though this book attempts to address some issues and find some answers concerning the evolution and development of China during this period, it is still too early to answer many of the questions concerning the internal and external implications and outcomes of China's socio-economic and socio-political development since the Chinese revolution culminated in the political victory in 1949. As one scholar of China studies points out, "Revolutions often do not reveal their true social meaning until many decades, even centuries, after the actual event" (Meisner, 1999: 243).

The re-emergence of China as one of the key world political and economic actors since the end of the 1970s has been globally hailed as one of the most important events in modern world history. China has experienced impressive economic growth over the past 30 years, averaging 9-10 percent real growth per year. The nation has since then lifted 400 million people out of poverty, an achievement that is claimed by the World Bank to be "unprecedented in human history". For many years China has been the engine for East Asian and global economic growth. In 2009 China overtook Germany to become the world's third-largest economy, this occurring earlier than expected.

Today China's economic impact is being felt worldwide. China's market size and its integration with the world economy has contributed to many opportunities and uncertainties: its currency has been a subject of contention; its global trade has raised concerns for workers and companies in both developed and developing countries; its hunger for energy has led to competition and price increase; its policies on finance, currency, trade, security, environment, resource management, food security, raw material and commodity price are increasingly seen as impinging upon with the economies of millions of people outside China's boundary. In some ways China is increasingly seen as being comparable to the erstwhile role of the United States as an "indispensable country".

During the entire 60 years of the People's Republic, the phenomenal rise of China at various momentous historical junctures of dramatic internal and external transformations was characterized by a challenge-and-response dynamism operating in both directions. This has led to a joke quietly circulated on the Internet, "In 1949 only Socialism could save China; in 1979 only Capitalism could save China; in 1989 only China could save Socialism; in 2009 only China can save Capitalism [the current crisis]". This reveals the great expectation from the West during a time of great financial crisis that China, the world's third-biggest economy, will be able to sustain reasonably robust growth and lift the world out of crisis and depression.

Ever since the 1990s the implications of the rise of China have been debated in international relations. What will China eventually become? What impact will the rise of China have on the world? Will China ever be able to fulfill Western expectations? How will the rise of China affect the underlying rules of the game of the existing capitalist world economy? Ever since Napoleon warned the world that it would be better not to wake the "sleeping giant", China has been a source of fascination and opportunities as well as uncertainties and disturbance for the existing world order. The great difficulty facing the West, being the creator and the key stakeholder of the existing world order, is how to respond and adjust to the impact brought about by the rise of China. The failure in forming a comprehensive understanding of China and China-related policies in the West has been periodically translated into a symptom – "*China syndrome*" – which can be characterized by a mixture of psychological anxiety, emotional hysteria and emphatic demonization. In the past decades it is always either fascination or irritation with China that has influenced Western scholarship and journalism, which often produce abrupt sentiments ranging from excessive approval and unqualified optimism to unwarranted revulsion and deep pessimism. Despite Beijing's consistent commitment to embracing economic globalization and improving relations with the rest of the world, especially with western powers, China still finds itself to be a "middle kingdom" surrounded by jealousy, admiration, anxiety, worry and even resentment.

The "Four-China" Nexus Approach

In recent years, the topic of the "rise of China" has caught the global attention. In addition to a vast number of articles, many influential books have been published around the theme of the rise of China and its implication to world order, for example: Goldstein, 2005; Guo, 2005; Kang, 2007; Kurlantzick, 2007; Lampton, 2008; Shambaugh, 2006, and so on. As a further contribution, this introduction and the book as a whole attempt to provide a conceptual and analytical framework for understanding the factors and context of China's persistent struggle in the restoration of global power with a special focus on the historicity of the political economy of China–West relations.

To put it more concretely, it aims to explore the evolutions and dynamics of China's transformation in a combined and mutually dependent and mutually reinforcing "four-China" framework: 1) the historical–cultural China; 2) the revolutionary socialist China; 3) the economic China; and 4) the political China. This "four-China" structure reveals the dialectical nexus between China's internal evolutions and the external influences regarding how the capitalist world system forced the shaping of China's internal transformations and how the opportunities and constraints brought on by China's inner transformations contributed to reshaping the world order.

The "Historical–Cultural China"

The "cultural China" refers to the long period of "historical China", an old civilization whose philosophy and classics have had a worldwide impact and inspired many European intellectuals, both past and present. Western knowledge of "classic China" was largely influenced by the literal studies of its history, literature and cultural philosophy. The vestige of such an influence is still traceable now. However, the image of "cultural China" was often not the real China, but rather an imaginary utopian exotic empire. The image was further mystified by *The Travels of Marco Polo*, which described the Chinese socio-economic formation and gave medieval Europe its first consequential knowledge of China's power and civilization. A more concrete source of knowledge of China came from the "silk road",[1] which was a major route of export of Chinese textile products and porcelain wares to Europe and North Africa.

The historical–cultural China, in the original assumption of "orientalism", represents in the Western imagination a civilizational superiority of non-European pre-capitalist advancement. It must not be forgotten that the leading figures in the age of European Enlightenment such as Leibniz, Voltaire, and Quesnay, among others, found great inspirations from many aspects of Chinese society and political organization. They "looked to China for moral instruction, guidance in institutional development, and supporting evidence for their advocacy of causes such as benevolent absolutism, meritocracy, and an agriculturally based national economy" (Adas, 1989: 79). According to Frank, even Adam Smith had an imagination of China's advance and claimed that "China is a much richer country than any part of Europe" without being aware of the fact that he was writing at the dawning of the European industrial revolution (Smith quoted in Frank, 1998: 13).

However, a real part of historical–cultural China that was less emphasized in Western history textbooks was the achievements and developments of China's pre-modern contributions in science, technology and medicine. Similarly, many other civilizations, such as that of the Arabs, had their due contributions. The

1 This refers to an ancient interconnected network of trade routes across the Asian continent connecting most parts of Asia with North and Northeast Africa and Europe.

Arabs had pioneered in modern mathematics including the use of Arabic numerals, zero, and algebra (the term itself is derived from Arabic). The Arabs also had accomplishment in chemistry (alcohol is another term derived from Arabic). It is historically well-known that the four Chinese ancient inventions, among others,[2] – paper-making, printing, gunpowder, and the magnetic compass – not only had an enormous impact on the development of Chinese civilization but also changed the world on a fundamental level. In 1620 the English philosopher Francis Bacon noted their importance and claimed that "no star seems to have exerted greater power and influence in human affairs than these mechanical discoveries" (Bacon, 1620).

The early European travelers and missionaries to China were surprised and amazed by the prosperity of its major cities and the level of its craftsmanship. China was at the forefront of modernization in the domains of scientific discoveries and their application to the production process. For example, during the Ming Dynasty (1368-1644), the Ming emperors sent seven maritime expeditions probing down into the South Seas and across the Indian Ocean between 1405 and 1433. The Chinese navy had more than 3,800 ships and its fleet was then the world's biggest and most technologically advanced – several times larger than their Portuguese counterparts (Luo, 2007: 3). Led by Admiral Zhen He, the Chinese expedition fleet made seven Indian Ocean voyages and reached the East African coast and as far south as the Mozambique Channel, where the admiral traded with the Africans and took giraffes, animal hides and gold back to China. However, the missions of these expeditions aimed to demonstrate China's organizational capability and technological might, rather than establish international trade or explore overseas markets.

What needs to be particularly emphasized, according to Joseph Needham, is the fact that, aside from those from the ancient Greek tradition, the emergence of modern science in the West owed major debts to many influences and innovations from China (Needham, et al., 1954). Likewise, according to Martin Bernal's research findings (1987), the ancient Greek civilization also derived much of its cultural roots from Afroasiatic (Egyptian and Phoenician) cultures. It is often assumed that since Ancient Greek times Europeans have pioneered their own development, and that the East has been a passive by-stander in the evolution of progressive world history. Some Eurocentric scholars "do not recognize the Chinese contribution to the modern west" and they still "carry the White Man's Burden in Chinese studies – treating 19th century and even contemporary China as a kind of outer space, if not a virtual 'pagandom'" (Tan, 1996: 234).

In a recent influential book by Hobson (2004), he argues that there were two historical processes embedded in the industrial rise of the West. The first was concerned with major development turning-points in the economic take-off in Europe, thanks to the absorption and assimilation of many important inventions from the East in terms of technologies, ideas, and institutions. The second process

2 See the list of ancient Chinese inventions: http://en.wikipedia.org/wiki/List_of_Chinese_inventions.

was driven by European imperialist expansion on the basis of the strength and resources that were appropriated from the East such as land, labour and markets (Hobson, 2004).

In arguing against the ethnocentric interpretation that regards capitalism as an organic outgrowth of Western civilization, Frank (1998) points out the fact that the rise of the West in world economic and demographic terms and the decline of the East coincided around the 19th century. According to his analysis, European powers used the silver extracted from the American colonies to trade with a growing Asian market that already prospered in the world economy. Likewise, it must be recognized, according to one historian, that the history of western industrialization itself could not be properly understood if China were treated as an "outsider" to the modern world:

> China has been a creative force for the modern west. The Industrial Revolution could not have succeeded without the ruthless sale of opium to China and the waging of a dirty war (in the name of opium as Karl Marx saw it) against China, and could not have been carried out so vigorously without Chinese tea. (Tan, 1996: 234)

In the great history book *The Rise of the West*, McNeill stresses the importance of understanding the effect of different world civilizations on one another and the interconnection of factors linking the rise and fall of different civilizations in human history. World civilizations were not independent entities; rather, they were constantly influenced by the diffusion of techniques and ideas between civilizations. In line with this thinking, the rise of the West cannot be separated from the effect of the Chinese supremacy at the time:

> ... historians [have not] yet realized that the rise of Medieval European civilization after AD 1000 coincided with an eastward shift of the world system's [productive] center from the Middle East to China. That is not surprising given the past pre-occupation of our medievalists with the national histories of England and France – implicitly retrospecting upon the entire human past the circumstances of the late nineteenth century, when the French and British empires did cover most of the globe. It requires a real leap of imagination to recognize China's primacy. (McNeill in Hobson, 2004: 50)

However, since China's defeat in the Opium War (1839-42), this mysterious "traditional" and "despotic" civilization became the "sick man of East Asia" and had never been able to compete with the "Western modernity". For some scholars, the milestone of modern history began for the historical–cultural China when the Europeans banged on its door. As Fitzgerald's metaphor goes, "to the amazement of all, within and without, the great structure ... suddenly collapsed, leaving the surprised Europeans still holding the door handle" (Fitzgerld in Cumings, 1996: 29). This abrupt falling of a vast structure perhaps led to Pye's famous saying that China is "a civilization pretending to be a state" (Pye, 1990: 58). Paradoxically, the historical–cultural China was seen to be too stagnant and too far away from the spirit of European enlightenment. Even the contemporary China has been more a metaphor than a nation for Americans (Cumings, 1996).

Since then, the "cultural China" was depicted as *Oriental Despotism* (Wittfogel, 1957), a symbol of traditionalism and backwardness. Hegel, for example, at a time when the Western consciousness of the world created revolutionary history, saw China in the "childhood of history" (Hegel, 1838); and Marx, whose theories and insight inspired the Chinese revolution, described China as a society "vegetating in the teeth of time" and discovered in the Great Wall of China a metaphor for the universal resistance of non-European societies to change (Marx in Dirlik and Meisner, 1989: 17). To put China in the framework of Max Weber's culturalist explanation (Weber, 1958), the failure of China's transition to the stage of capitalism was due to the fact that the value systems of Chinese Confucianism were not receptive to the development of capitalism in terms of creativity, competition and development. Even those Western leftist intellectuals who desired to help to transform China into a west-like modern state often saw themselves as a professorial tutor with moral and cultural superiority.

Thus, since the second half of the 19th century, "not only was world history rewritten wholesale, but 'universal' social 'science' was (new)born, not just as a European, but as a *Eurocentric* invention" (Frank, 1998: 14). However, the dilemma facing the western world today is that many present-day problems and contradictions brought about by the rise of China cannot be understood without going beyond economic statistics and conceptualizing the underlying cultural, philosophical and historical differences between China and West.

The "Revolutionary Socialist China"

Throughout the entire 20th century China was perhaps the only country in the world that had been in constant revolutionary transformations in the midst of great external and internal turbulences: The Republic Revolution, the May 4th Movement, the Anti-Japanese War (the Second World War), the Civil War, the Korea War, the Cold War, the Vietnam War, the Cultural Revolution as well as the great social, economic and political transformations brought about by the economic reform since 1978.

The Chinese communist revolution was an epoch-making historical event – a turning point not only in China's own history but also in that of the world. The historical role and significance of the Chinese revolution including the post-revolution period of Chinese socialism has been constantly rewritten and reinterpreted both at home and abroad. Some Chinese as well as Western elites and academics still have difficulty in recognizing the historical legacy of the Chinese revolution and Chinese socialism of which it was an outcome and in which it had played such an important role. Was the Chinese Revolution really necessary? There are people inside and outside China who suspect the historical imperativeness for the Chinese Revolution and who claim that if China had not adopted the Marxist theory, had not gone through revolutions and had not taken the socialist road, it would have developed more rapidly and might have developed into an advanced nation possessing some of the characteristics of Western democracy. This is actually an ideal image of China for which the West has been longing for ages.

Unfortunately history does not always follow one's will, and it did not grant the time and opportunity that China needed to fulfill such an expectation. The First World War, the Second World War, the anti-Japanese War and the Chinese Civil War totally altered the Chinese development course. It is the combination of the internal turmoils and the external challenges that shaped the development course of the modern Chinese history. Many people have tried to study the modern history of the Chinese revolution from a non-Marxist approach, but they all ended up with a dilemma. As Dirlik describes it, "students of Chinese Communism in the West, the majority of whom do not share a similar conviction in Marxism's truths, have nevertheless found in China's circumstances variegated reasons for radicals' attraction to Marxism and consequently turning to Communist politics, as the only means to resolve the problems of Chinese society" (1989: 255).

Already being burdened by the humiliation of the defeat of the Opium War, the Chinese nation was fully frustrated over another disgrace imposed by the Treaty of Versailles[3] in the aftermath of the First World War. This event led to the May 4th Movement of 1919,[4] during which the appeal of progressive Marxism expanded, and many intellectuals claimed to have discovered a solution to China's social problems from the important teachings of Marxist theories. Marxist class analyses and especially Lenin's theory of imperialism provided Chinese intellectuals with a partial theoretical framework as well as a psychological answer to their difficulties in finding the proper explanations and theories for the failures of traditional Chinese culture and for the humiliation suffered at the hands of the West (Peck, 1975: 73). It was this school that they finally turned to. Marxism and Leninism taught China to see itself as a "proletarian nation" although it did not have a large proletarian working class population and to extend and relate the Chinese revolution to the worldwide proletarian movements against international capitalism and imperialism. Therefore, it is important to know why the Chinese communist revolution could prevail in a society where the cultural heritage had been dominated by Confucianism.

3 This refers to Article 156 of the Treaty of Versailles in 1919 in which all German concessions in China's Shandong peninsula were transferred to Japan rather than being returned to China.

4 This refers to student demonstrations in Beijing on May 4, 1919 protesting against the Chinese government's weak response to the Treaty of Versailles in which the German concessions in China's Shandong peninsula were transferred to Japan rather than being returned to China. These demonstrations sparked anti-imperialist national protests and developed into a progressive socio-political and socio-cultural movement.

When the Chinese Nationalists fled to exile on the island of Taiwan in 1949, Mao Zedong proclaimed the "standing up of the Chinese nation" and the "founding of the People's Republic of China". The "loss of China" (China becoming communist) gave the Western world a tremendous shock. Especially the Americans, from the President and government officials down to the mass of ordinary people, simply could not stand to see how a hopeful nationalist government with a modern military armed to the teeth by the United States could be defeated by the Chinese Communist-led insurrection. The Korean War and the unfolding of the Cold War, along with the expansion of Chinese communist influences in the Third World traumatized China–US relations for decades (Borthwick, 1992). The United States refused to accept the crucial reality in China – the indefinite survival of the communist power, and it rejected to acknowledge the fact that the Chinese revolution was a mass response both to underdevelopment and to unendurable social problems. Revolution does not necessarily have to be communist, but communist ideology was indeed the most attractive and appealing one for any poor agrarian society that sought a fundamental social transformation.

The wishful thinking about the imminent transformation of China into a democratic, capitalist, and Christian nation evaporated into air. Who lost China? This question became the central point of debate in the United States. During the period of the "Red Menace" under McCarthyism,[5] the extended and relentless search for those who were responsible for the alleged "loss of China" targeted any American intellectual who showed the least bit of sympathy for Maoist China. It is argued that such an irrational fear of Chinese communist expansion led to the United States' involvement in the Indo-China War (Madsen, 1998: 55).

The revolutionary China has been in many ways associated with the "socialist China". The socialist China was characterized by carrying out a number of transformative "great-leap-forwards" in the spheres of political, economic and social structures, and cultural traditions in ways that defied conventional ideological and political norms in established capitalist as well as socialist states. The objective of Chinese socialism can be understood as an endeavor to construct a counter-hegemonic project to capitalism. To be more concrete, it was an attempt to "construct a new hegemony around the concept of class at the levels of language, social relations, political and practice, consciousness, and even morality" (Blecher, 1989: 7).

5 McCarthyism is a term that describes the intense anti-communist suspicion in the United States in the 1950s during which hundreds of Americans were accused of being Communists or communist sympathizers and became the subject of aggressive investigations and questioning. Senator Joseph Raymond McCarthy was known for making claims that there were large numbers of Communists and Soviet spies and sympathizers inside the federal government and elsewhere, which led to the sufferings of many who were falsely accused. Today the term is more generally referred to demagogic, irresponsible, and unsupported accusations.

Since 1949, China under Mao had shared with many other developing countries a commitment to economic development. However, being somewhat different from many of them, China took a socialist development path emphasizing human resources, common prosperity, economic equality and balanced development, and social and political mobilization. The socialist China's choice of self-reliance was a response both to the internal constraints of socio-economic backwardness as well to the external pressure of the US-led economic blockage and trade embargo. The self-reliance strategy was particularly the outcome of the harsh experiences of China's external relations with the Soviet Union. No matter how Chinese socialism was assessed later on, the socialist road was in fact the only option at that time if China wanted to sustain its economic development and maintain its independence.

It is historically justified to claim that the period of Chinese socialism, which created tremendous social advances and human development under both political sovereignty and a major change in domestic class relations, laid the *foundation* of the economic progress achieved in the post-Mao era. By the late 1970s, following China's implementation of the "open-door" policy and with major geopolitical transformation and improvement in its relations with the West, the Chinese state was in a position "to define the terms and establish the parameters of interaction" with Western powers.

Indisputably, there were also serious consequences with grave human costs to the dramatic failures during the period of socialist China. But China, after the victory of the communist revolution in 1949, was able to achieve many transformations: from a country plundered and enslaved by Western imperialism, it emerged into an independent and sovereign state; from a fragmented country it coalesced into an unified country (with the exception of Taiwan); from a country characterized by a poor agrarian society it developed into a considerably industrialized state with rapid progress in all fields; and from a country easily bullied by western powers it evolved into a nation enjoying the respect of the international community (Li, Xing, 1999). Even now many developing countries are struggling hard in order to be able to achieve similar great leaps forward. Nevertheless, the crises of the Chinese socialist experiments entailed many theoretical and practical questions to which the post-Mao regimes have been attempting to find the answers.

It is argued here that the revolutionary socialist China cannot be fully understood in isolation from the broader dynamics of the capitalist world system. Chinese socialism was seen as a threat by the US-led capitalist world system because of its projection as a potential development model and its revolutionary ideology. In the past, the central goal of China's communist politics was to overthrow or challenge the unequal hierarchy in the world economic system. However, such an ambition, although threatening, existed more or less *outside* the US-led capitalist world system. Ironically, China's current market capitalism combined with its political authoritarianism is beginning to unleash an awesome "menace" because China's ambitious wealth accumulation driven by high economic growth have increased its access to a larger share of the world's wealth and resources, as well as having created environmental problems. More importantly, such a menace exists *within* the structural mechanism of global capitalism! The "menace" of China's 1.3 billion people engaged in resource consumption and wealth collection seems much more real than Samuel Huntington's notion of a "Clash of Civilizations" (1993). It is a paradox that China's proto-capitalism, compared to its former socialism, is potentially more threatening in realistic terms than in ideological challenges. Some scholars predict that the economic rise of China will eclipse the disintegrating global capitalism and usher in a new world order. As one recent book is provocatively titled: *The Rise of China and The Demise of The Capitalist World Economy* (Li, Minqi, 2008).

The "Economic China"

Capitalism has been regarded as being historically unique to Europe and as an organic development derived from Western civilization. However, according to Frank (2002), the modern capitalist world system with the West as the core, surrounded by semi-periphery and periphery structures, is a relatively contemporary phenomenon. The rise of the West in world economic and demographic terms and the decline of the East (China) occurred around the mid 19th century. Frank predicted that the "center" of the world economy would again be moving back to East Asia with the rise of the "Middle Kingdom" (China) as the key driving force.

In light of this view, the "economic China" refers to the post-Mao period in which China's rapid economic growth began to unleash its worldwide impact in the areas of FDI, commodity price, international trade, regional integration, international relations, etc. China's size, population and its integration in the world economy have contributed to uncertainties about the global inflationary environment; its currency has been a subject of contention; its trade has raised concerns for workers and firms in both developed and developing countries; its demand for energy has led to competition, price rise and conflict; it has rivaled the United States and other developing countries as a destination for foreign direct investment; and the effects of its own overseas investments have begun to be felt across the world. Beijing's economic performance and its policies on finance, currency, trade, security, environment issues, resource management, food security, raw material and commodity prices are bearing worldwide implications and are increasingly seen as impacting the economies of millions of people outside China's boundaries. China's shifts in supply and demand can cause changes in prices, hence leading to adjustment in other countries. Today China has the largest foreign currency reserve in the world.[6]

---

6 According the China's Statistics Bureau, until March 2008 China's foreign currency reserve reached $1.682 billion, and this figure is bigger than the combined number of the G7. See (http://www.chinanews.com.cn/cj/zbjr/news/2008/04-16/1222558.shtml).

China has generated incremental growth in the global economy that has made its success significant for the welfare of other countries. Some scholars and analysts begin to compare the role of the Chinese economy – the workshop of the world – with that of Great Britain in the 19th century and that of the United States in the 20th century (Zakaria, 2006). Consequently, many Westerners begin to ask the crucial questions: "what could happen when China will be able to manufacture nearly everything – computers, cars, jumbo jets, and pharmaceuticals – that the United States and Europe can, at perhaps half the cost?" and "how do these developments reach around the world and straight into the lives of all Americans?"(Fishman, 2005). What particularly worries the West is that the factors behind the Chinese economic successes are in many ways incomprehensible seen in light of some of the established assumptions rooted in Western economic theories. As one observer notices:

> It might be time to admit that we really don't understand China. The country simply does not conform to our most basic beliefs about what makes nations grow. Hernando de Soto, the Peruvian scholar, has argued persuasively that clear and strong property rights are the prerequisite for economic growth. Except that China, the fastest-growing country in human history, has an extremely unclear and weak system of property rights. Alan Greenspan has argued that the rule of law is the linchpin of market economics. Except that China has a patchy set of laws, unevenly enforced. The Washington Consensus that the World Bank and the IMF have peddled across the globe claims that if currencies don't float freely, they will produce huge distortions in the economy. China has declined that advice and yet prospers. So, instead of learning from facts and revising theory, we assume that the facts are wrong, that China is one grand charade. (Zakaria, *Newsweek*, March 12, 2007)

Not only do the basic assumptions of liberal economic theories themselves not seem to be able to explain the Chinese economic success, but also the perceived causal relationships between economic modernization, cultural change, and political democracy are not applicable to the Chinese case either. Contrary to the prophecy that the political rule of the Chinese Communist Party would eventually contradict the outcome of economic logic, and in opposition to the dissident prediction about *The Coming Collapse of China* (Chang, 2001), the political legitimation of the Chinese Communist Party has become more and more strengthened with the number of its membership reaching 74 million by the end of 2007. The Pew Global Attitudes Project[7] has in recent years conducted a series

7 The Pew Global Attitudes Project is one of the research project conducted by Pew Research Centre in Washington DC. It consists of a series of worldwide public opinion surveys that covers a broad array of subjects ranging from people's assessments of their own lives to their views about the current state of the world and important issues of the day. See http://pewglobal.org/.

of worldwide country-based surveys of public opinion, and according to the result a vast majority of Chinese people expressed an extraordinary level of satisfaction with the country's development and economy as well as with many aspects of their own lives, including family life, incomes and jobs. A high percentage of Chinese embraced free markets and modern life following the transformation and growth of the economy.

Today we are witnessing a paradoxical situation: when the Chinese economy is being integrated with the lives of millions of people in the West, the West is becoming eager to talk with China about almost all global socio-economic issues, such as trade balance, exchange rate, energy price, commodity price, environmental protection, unemployment, food security, etc; while at the same time other non-economic issues, such as human rights and democracy, are addressed at random without any consistency. While the West claims to have defeated Chinese communism and socialism in the aftermath of the Cold War, the fact is that these are thriving and creating awesome new contradictions as China's proto-capitalism has begun to influence the global marketplace. In some cases, the West sees China as a renegade state trying to follow its own interests and write its own rules, thus posing strong challenges to the established international system.

While the West is salivating over the purchasing power of 1.3 billion people, it forgets that a nascent ebullient capitalism often takes on rather wild features and may produce unexpected results. The free market economy in China drives people to seek every possible opportunity and means to earn a profit or just to survive. Many of Beijing's "misbehaviors" are actually consequences of the economic marketization process. For instance, the issue of China's disrespect of Western intellectual property rights revealed a typical example of the contradiction that, on the one hand, the West wants to see the capitalist market economy demolish Chinese state authoritarianism; on the other hand, people's rampant profit-seeking practices as a result of a premature capitalist system are highly harmful to Western business interests and must be stopped through the intervention of the state! The fact is that the West is increasingly gaining political bargaining power through China's integration with the world economy but at the same time it is also becoming addicted to the Chinese market (Li, Xing, 1998).

The "Political China"

Largely influenced by the modernization school of thought, the West is convinced that China's economic reform since the end of the 1970s would bring the country into economic marketization, which would inevitably lead it into political liberalization. There were hopeful writings expressing confidence about China's "second revolution"[8] during most of 1980s. However, the June 4th incident in 1989

8 The second revolution refers to China's economic marketization and political liberalization in contrast to its first "communist" revolution.

wiped out the expectation of a west-like democratic China,[9] and made the West deeply antagonistic toward China's resistance to political liberation. In this context, the "political China" implies a strong connotation of political authoritarianism – an undemocratic China and a potential source of instability to the world order.

However, the notion of "political China" is now referred to by the catchphrase: the "Chinese model". It goes beyond the fact that China's success in moving from a plan-economy, owned and controlled by the state, to a market-economy, supervised and regulated by the state in combination with the market mechanism, has itself established a Chinese *model* of development. The "Chinese model", which is embedded with specific historical dimensions, unique cultural elements and assertive ideological discourses, is increasingly becoming attractive to developing countries. It is particularly attractive to many developing countries in terms of how to manage state-market-society relations and international political economy. The Chinese model was recently theorized as the "Beijing Consensus" (Ramo, 2004), a notion coined with distinct attitudes to politics, development and the global balance of power. The formation of such a theoretical notion is driven by China's three-decade success in economic development with relative political stability, by a determinant desire of China to innovate an alternative development path, by a strong belief in state sovereignty and global multilateralism, and by a strategy to accumulate the tools of "asymmetric power projection", i.e. how to achieve and maintain power in an asymmetric power relation to Western superpowers and to transnational capitals.

The Beijing Consensus can also be seen as an outcome of the adjustment and readjustment of China's diplomacy and foreign policy in the past three decades: "good neighbor diplomacy" (1980s and early 1990s), "great power diplomacy" (late 1990s), "energy diplomacy", "soft power diplomacy", "public diplomacy" (2000s) as well as "peaceful rise" and "peaceful development" (Guo, 2006; Zheng, 2005).[10] As a result of these developments and transformations, the "political China" has achieved significant success in international politics. China's membership in the World Trade Organization along with other international involvements, such as contributing troops for United Nations peacekeeping operations, assisting nonproliferation issues, hosting the six-party talks on North Korea's nuclear

9 This refers to a series of demonstrations in Beijing in and near Tiananmen Square led by student and worker activists between the period of April 15 and June 4, 1989. The demonstrations were finally cracked down by the military force. This event caused a short-term pause of China's reform program and deteriorated China–West relations.

10 The word "Rise" (in Chinese "jueqi") can imply a negative connotation of a threat to the existing international order. Therefore, the current Chinese government prefers the phrase "peaceful development" in order to avoid confusions. In introducing the concept of "peaceful development", Chinese Premier Wen Jiabao argued in his speech at Harvard University on December 10, 2003 that while Euro-American powers rose through violent imperial expansion, China is determined to use "scientific and technological progress to solve the problems of resources and the environment. Here lies the essence of China's road of peaceful rise and development".

issue, settling territorial disputes with its neighbors, and participating in a variety of regional and global organizations, has demonstrated Beijing's new style of diplomacy. China intends to couple the new diplomacy with its official slogan of "harmonious world" and to alleviate fears and the likelihood of other countries feeling compelled to form alliances to balance its rising power.

The Beijing Consensus, especially with its emerging "soft power" impact, is perceived by some as a great challenge to the US hegemony (Kurlantzick, 2007; Nye, 2004) as embedded in the "Washington Consensus", here manifested as an ideological discourse and value system. The emergence of China's display of "soft power" depicts the role of a powerful country as a benign hegemon safeguarding a designated national projection or objective through its cultural and political values, foreign policies, and economic interactions as essential components of national strength, thus bestowing the capacity to persuade other nations to willingly to follow suit.

The political China in many ways manifests the modernization process of constructing a unique indigenous political culture and economic system for which it has attained worldwide recognition. Observing the historical interplay of economic and political hegemony in the evolution of the capitalist world system, Arrighi, in his new book (2007), invites people to re-read Adam Smith's *The Wealth of Nations* in a radically different way through a unique interpretation of the economic ascent of China along with its far-reaching *political* implications. He argues that Smith's vision of a world-market-society based on greater equality among the world's civilizations may well be likely, and China may well become what Smith described as a non-neoliberal market-economy that defies the conventional ideological and political norms by the established capitalist hegemony. A potential consequence of this evolution will be a new "beginning of history" rather than the "end of history" envisioned by Fukuyama (1992). In other words, the existing world order will perhaps witness a possible "paradigm shift" brought about by the rise of China.

A paradigm shift refers to a recurrent situation where different ideological paradigms may occupy the dominant position at different times. It also presents a constant conflict between contending ideologies and socio-economic and socio-political systems. It is expected that within the near future Chinese social science theories will gradually emerge to challenge the existing ones which have been historically defined, constructed and dominated by the West. The impact of China's rising influence on the existing theories of the structural and normative dimensions of the international system will influence the development of international relations theory both in the West and within China (Paltiel, 2005). Since ideological cognition/consciousness is discourse-dependent, the construction of new theoretical discourses is loaded with implications for the social–political context of power relations. As one Chinese scholar notices, Chinese schools of "international relations theories" will likely and even inevitably come forward following China's great economic and social achievement (Qin, 2007).

In line with the above framework of understanding, the "political China" also implies the fact that the West does not know how to analyze and deal with China outside of the conceptual frameworks that it feels familiar and comfortable with. On the one hand, the West wishes China to continue its market growth, which can generate enormous business opportunities. On the other hand, to many western politicians and opinion-makers, China simply does not conform to some of the most basic beliefs in the West about what makes nations grow and to the set of mutually dependent relationships between property rights and economic growth, between the rule of law and market economy, between free currency flow and economic order, and, most importantly, and between political system and popular sentiment. Chris Patten, the last British Governor of Hong Kong, explicitly said during a BBC interview that China's success promoted the idea that one could get rich without needing democracy – and such an idea posed a threat to the West. He bluntly admitted that China is "the first example of a country which has done astonishingly well in this international system, but challenges its basic foundations" (BBC on-line, November 23, 2008). Realists, like Mearsheimer, have been categorical in their assertions that China's rise presages an inevitable conflict within the current international system and a challenge to the US hegemony (Mearsheimer, 2006).

The above spells out the uneasiness of the West in dealing with a country that does not readily fit into Western frameworks of understanding. Addressing concepts like democracy, freedom, human rights, liberalism, authoritarianism, dictatorship, etc., one is consciously or unconsciously inserting oneself into a Western intellectual and historical context. No reminder is needed of the important role of the historical milestones in the history of the West, such as the English Revolution, the American Declaration of Independence and the French Revolution, in the formation of the political discourses with which these concepts are associated. Unfortunately the historicity of these events is somehow disembedded from the lens through which the West sees and uses to compare itself with other cultures nowadays. For example, the India model of democracy, which resembles the fundamental features of Western liberal democracy, is perceived to be superior to the Chinese authoritarian system and to eventually outperform China, despite the fact that economically India's decentralized democracy is lagging far behind China's centralized authoritarian system by many social and economic standards (Das, 2005).[11]

What particularly worries the West is the political "uncertainties" generated by the rise of China. Questions like "what will China become?", "what will China want?", "how will China use its power?" are still hanging unanswered in the minds of many Western politicians and mainstream opinion-makers. As Legro points out, "the 'rising China' problem is not just about power, but purpose" (Legro, 2007: 515). China's rapid accumulation of economic and military power

11 There is a global consensus on China's much better economic performance than that of India, although there is a global dispute over the discussion on the relationship between liberal democracy and economic development leading to the debate whether the India electoral liberal democracy will eventually surpass the Chinese one-party authoritarian system.

triggers uncertainty and mistrust about how China will use its power and whether China's application of power is defensive or offensive. Many realists and opinion-makers predict an eventual China–West conflict on the basis of the historical lessons indicating that the rapid growth of the economy of a great country has often triggered enormous, often disruptive, transformations both internally and externally. Thus, the West cannot even bet on China's self-promised "peaceful rise" or "peaceful development" because it is highly influenced by the so-called "democratic peace theory" (Doyle, 1983; Kant, 1957; Ray, 1998), i.e. democracies do not, or rarely, go to war with one another. In line with this type of thinking, the prospect of world peace cannot be assured until China truly becomes a west-like democracy.

One of the central issues determining the gap between an ascendant China, as seen with Chinese eyes, and the existing world system maintained by the West is to which extent China is willing to accept the norms and rules of the existing order and how far the West is willing to accommodate and adjust to the challenges posed by the rise of China. Seen from the Chinese perspective, the rise of China is simply the "rejuvenation of China", partly regaining its lost international status rather than obtaining anything new, and partly restoring fairness rather than taking advantages over others (Yan, 2001: 34). The West is still struggling to envision the hope that China will eventually become a "responsible stakeholder" supporting the existing global system – a system which China is already highly integrated into and which China is seen as enjoying substantial benefits from. It is expected that the rise of China and its development model, no matter how persuasive it is, will unavoidably have to absorb and adjust to the hardcore external challenges and constraints posed by the existing capitalist world system.

The Implications of the "Four-China" Nexus

Ever since its first contact with the West some centuries ago, China has been a source of both attraction and concern for the West, and it has been seen as a nation of puzzle and mystery, remaining unfathomably beyond comprehension. Even now when China has become an integral part of the capitalist world economy, it is still a country that in many ways the major western powers find difficult to accommodate. Thus, the four-China nexus constructs a holistic framework for understanding the synthesis of the complex factors between the rise of China and the existing world system.

The historical relations between China and the West, as reflected by the periodical transitions from the "historical–cultural China" to the "revolutionary socialist China", and subsequently to the "economic China" and then to the "political China", indicate a dialectical process of waxing and waning, rise and decline. Seen from this perspective, the rise of China as a new world hegemonic force vis-à-vis the West as the existing world power will continue to be in a state of flux and reflux, rather than in a purposeful forward or backward movement as

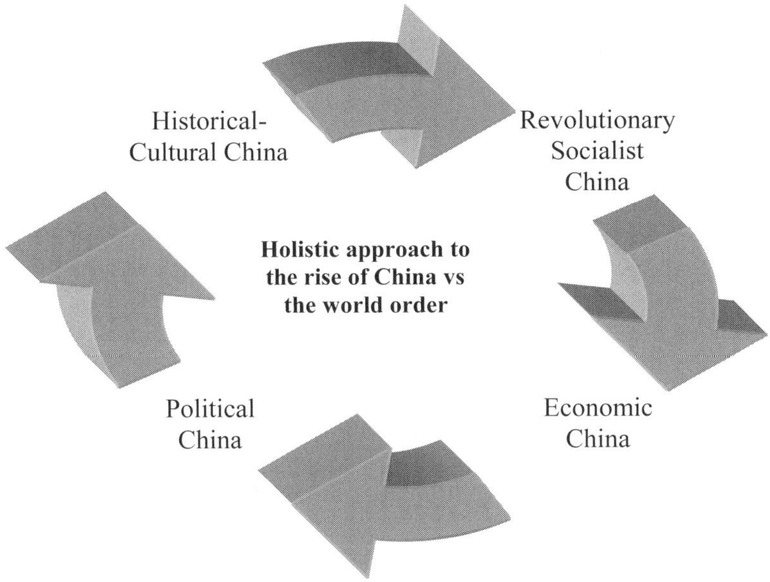

Figure I.1 The dialectical nexus of the four-China framework

deterministic theories imply. The true implication of the rise of China can only be understood through analyzing the historical and interactive combination of the four-Chinas as mutually interdependent entities rather than as independent ones. The interconnection of the mutual generation and mutual influence between the four-Chinas is the key to understand the complexities of modern-day China and the underlying dynamics of the impact brought about by the rise of China to the existing world order.

Western memories of China have their image rooted in the "historical–cultural China" and the "revolutionary socialist China". It has been a tradition for the West to see China by turns either as a great cultural civilization at one time or as an evil communist monster at another. One moment the West views China as the most fascinating and economically vibrant country, and the next moment it depicts China as a vicious police state that is likely to collapse at any time. The result is the same kind of zigzag affected by the mood of the moment, whether euphoria or outrage, that became the basis of China–West relations for the past decades. The West has a strong belief that it can change China, which has resulted in many failures in its China-policies whenever the West has either rejected the internal changes taking place in China or wanted to convert and transform it in a way deemed desirable to western interests. The early Western missionaries had great expectations of converting China into a West-like continent with a Christian religious dominance, but they failed. In China's internal history and civilization, it was once conquered and ruled for centuries by its powerful minority groups such as the Mogols and the Manchus. They tried to change China's fundamental character, but were themselves changed and sinicized. China itself has transformed from time to time over the centuries; but real change can only succeed from within when Chinese themselves want to do so.

The emergence of the "economic China" in the past three decades was seen by the West as the biggest savoir to the capitalist world order because the core of the capitalist world system – the United States and Europe – was also much weakened by the long Cold-War competition with the former Soviet Union. However, if the Maoist self-reliance and self-sufficient path of socialist development was perceived as a threat due to its projection as a potential development model and ideology, and if the central goal of socialist politics was to challenge the unequal hierarchy in the world economic system, such a socialist hegemonic project existed more or less *outside* the US-led capitalist world system. In other words, the "threat of socialism" was more an ideological challenge rather than a project to construct a real alternative world system to replace the capitalist world system. But ironically, China's current economic integration in the world economy, together with the strong role of the state, is strengthening China's comparative advantage and increasing its share of world wealth and resources. More importantly, such a "menace" exists *within* the mechanism of global capitalism!

The "political China" reflects in many ways the Western psychological and sentimental hysteria in the process of their responding and adjusting to the rise of China – a reaction symptom that can be named the *China-syndrome* (Li, Xing, 2008). Advocates of western democracy in general always seem to have difficulties in recognizing China's extraordinary economic growth, a remarkable accomplishment that had been believed impossible to be achieved by an overpopulated and "backward" country under an authoritarian, repressive government. To many western politicians and opinion-makers China simply does not conform to some of the most basic beliefs held in the West about what makes nations grow and about the set of mutually dependent relationships between property rights and economic growth, between the rule of law and market economy, between free currency flow and economic order, and most importantly between political system and popular sentiment. Some western politicians and opinion-makers are still suspicious about the "peaceful rise" of China and about whether China has the intention to use its accumulated power and influence to modify the defined rules and norms toward its desired direction. While some scholars foresee the eventual conflict between the rise of China and the existing powers (Krauthammer, 1995; Mearsheimer, 2006), many others emphasize the fact that China's economic rise is premised on expanding and intensifying integration within the international system, and the internal and external factors of China's economic achievement are so intertwined and mutually dependent. Consequently, as a rising power China's national interests and foreign policy behavior increasingly reflect and embrace the status quo. The reason why China is currently a winner in the era of globalization is precisely because its economic growth and wealth accumulation is generated from within, not from without, the capitalist world system (Ikenberry, 2008). This view is becoming the dominant mainstream view today.

It is expected that within the near future both China as the rising power and the West as the established world ruler will have to find ways to accommodate each other. In order to do so, both will have to go through a considerable period of struggle, adjustment and tension. It is still too early to predict whether the rise of China to challenge the status of the West means a world disorder, a world reorder or a new world order.

The Book's Objectives and the Chapter Contributions

Taking the framework of the four-China nexus as a historical and relational synergy enabling the discussion of a number of issues and challenges presented by the rise of China, this volume intends to contribute to the current China debate and to provide a better understanding of the dynamics and dialectics behind the rise of China with a special reference to the possible impacts and implications – challenges and opportunities – to the existing capitalist world system. In other words, it attempts to promote a better understanding of the complexities of the rise of China through a number of areas of investigation. The chapters included intend to thematically contribute to the China debate from a variety of interdisciplinary approaches and from the perspective of the dynamic interactions between internal and external factors. Some chapters put an emphasis on the historical understanding of the rise of China; some look at the evolution of modern China in the context of China–West relations in connection with the existing world order; some explore the interplay between the internal and external factors and their mutual impact; and others give a special focus on the internal dynamics as factors of explaining the rise of nations, such as the role of the Chinese state and its development strategies as well as the dynamic resiliency of the Chinese Communist Party (the CCP).

Chapter 1 by Jacques Hersh looks at the economic history of the relationship between Europe and China from a developmental perspective and explains the shift that occurred with the European aggressive progress and Chinese regressive decline. The importance of economic nationalism as a determinant in the problematique of catching-up that is encapsulated in the theory of uneven and unequal development deserves greater attention on the part of international political economy. The paradox related to the return of China to its historic status as the global centre of gravity is that this will pose a greater challenge to the West than the Maoist model of development. Whether the rise of China will lead to Realism's zero-sum-game situation or to Liberalism's win-win outcome for all parties concerned is a fundamental issue for the coming decades.

Chapter 2 by Mammo Muchie and Li Xing explores the global effect and impact of the rise of China. It attempts to indicate the fact that, in spite of this growing interdependence, there is an alarmist agitation by some scholars, journalists, policy-makers, and pundits that spreads the view that a looming China threat is what the rise of China means to the world. This chapter attempts to argue that China should not be framed with either a malevolent or benevolent imaging or character. It is an emergent and transitional economy with a very large economy, population, production and market, that can be harnessed for a win-win outcome provided the world is willing to risk engaging with China and understand and respect Chinese patriotism, which has its root in the modern historical evolution of Chinese nationalism.

Chapter 3 by Paul Opoku-Mensah examines the impact of the strong presence of China in Africa on the established international aid system. The international aid system is a historical innovation and a powerful force that reflects and institutionalizes global power relations. Its influence is near absolute as the current international system cannot be properly understood without understanding how the institutionalized politics and policies of aid function on the international, national and local levels. Indeed the aid institutions have formed an evolving international regime, with a set of norms, principles, and procedures that have been designed to defend certain economic and ideological interests and to maintain international stability and consensus around these interests. The entry of China as a major actor in the aid system challenges this international regime of global power relations in very fundamental, but unexplored, ways. This chapter contributes to a much needed process of understanding China's engagement in the international aid system, and it does so through an assessment of the opportunities and dangers China represents to the system.

Chapter 4 by Li Xing and Paul Opoku-Mensah provides a historical and empirical analysis of the role of the Diaspora in the rise of China, and the implications of this for a renascent Africa. In addition, it outlines an analytical framework for understanding the role of Diaspora in the rise of nations. By using Chinese and African Diasporas as its empirical basis under a common analytical template, the chapter provides insights into a) how history shapes the differences affecting Diaspora's identity and relations with the homeland; b) the ways in which the structural positions of Diaspora in their host country determine not only their own economic status but also the role they can play in relation to their homeland; and finally c) how successful the homeland is in systematically incorporating and institutionalizing the role of the Diaspora in its nation building project.

Chapter 5 by Li Minqi evaluates the prospect of energy supply and its impact on economic growth in China and in the world from now to 2100. After considering the potentials of coal, oil, and gas production, as well as the development potentials of renewable and nuclear energy, this chapter finds that the world economy will in effect suffer a permanent depression through the rest of the 21st century. China is likely to face an insurmountable energy crisis beyond 2020. Even with optimistic assumptions, drastic declines of economic growth rate and the eventual end of economic growth cannot be avoided.

Chapter 6 by Li Xing analyzes China's transformation through looking at the interplay between the internal driving forces and the external influences. It proposes to understand the dialectical nexus between China's internal evolutions and the external influences with a focus on the century-long "challenge-response" dynamism. The chapter explores how external factors helped to shape China's internal transformations, i.e. how generations of Chinese have been struggling in responding to the external challenges and attempting to *sinicize* external political ideas in order to change China from within. Likewise, it is equally important to understand how China's inner transformation contributed to reshaping the world and how the capitalist world system has to adjust and readjust itself to the opportunities and constraints brought about by the "China factors".

Chapter 7 by Stig Thøgersen and Clemens Stubbe Østergaard poses and explores two main research questions regarding which external and internal strategies the Chinese state has employed towards the manifold challenges of globalization, and how it has attempted to anchor these strategies in various social groups. China seems to have displayed a particular ability to turn the enormous forces of globalization to its own advantage through a cluster of state strategies. The chapter looks at the process behind the formulation of Chinese globalization policies and delineates seven broad state strategies which together touch on nearly all aspects of Chinese domestic and foreign policy. It also examines the Chinese globalization discourse and how a narrative has been constructed that fully supports China's integration in the world, emphasizing the need for a strong state to defend national interests. One of the chapter's objectives is to discuss and analyze Chinese policies aimed at embedding the party-state more solidly in society through a broad range of political mechanisms. The chapter suggests the appearance of a new, multimodal international system, which may challenge the unipole, the United States, and in which China is one major player.

Chapter 8 by Li Xing and Peer Møller Christensen provide a framework of understanding of the transformative rise of China in connection with the adaptive resilience of the CCP, which has been one of the strongest enduring features of contemporary Chinese political culture both before and after the founding of the People's Republic. It proposes to conceptualize the factors of the historical and social contradictions which shaped China's post-revolution crises in different periods and analyze the systemic behavior of the CCP in combination with its adaptive responses to those emerging social contradictions. The chapter intends to conclude that the CCP's uninterrupted reform and adaptation in the past three decades of economic reform denotes the fact that analysis of Chinese social transformation including the "rise of China" must, therefore, complement the systemic analysis of the CCP as a dynamic institution and a proactive player.

References

Adas, Michel (1989) *Machines as Measure of Men: Science, Technology and Ideologies of Western Dominance.* Ithaca, NY: Cornell University Press.

Arrighi, Giovanni (2007) *Adam Smith in Beijing: Lineages of the Twenty-First Century.* London: Verso.

Bacon, Francis (1620) *Novum Organum – Liber Primus*, CXXIX. Adapted from the 1863 translation, quoted from http://en.wikipedia.org/wiki/Four_Great_Inventions_of_Ancient_China.

Bernal, Martin (1987) *Black Athena: The Afroasiatic Roots of Classical Civilization* (The Fabrication of Ancient Greece 1785-1985, Volume 1). London: Free Association Books.

Blecher, Marc J. (1989) "China's Struggle for a New Hegemony", *Socialist Review*, 19(2): 5-35.

Borthwick, Mark (ed.) (1992) *Pacific Century: The Emergence of Modern Pacific Asia*. Boulder, CO: Westview Press.

Chang, Gordon G. (2001) *The Coming Collapse of China*. New York: Random House Inc.

Cumings, Bruce (1996) "The World Shakes China", *The National Interest*, (43): 28-41.

Das, Dilip K. (2005) "China and India: A Tale of Two Economies", *China and World Economy*, 13(4): 83-97.

Dirlik, Arif (1989) "Revolution Hegemony and the Language of Revolution: Chinese Socialism between Present and Future", in Arif Dirlik and Maurice Meisner (eds) *Marxism and the Chinese Experience.* New York: M.E. Sharpe, Inc.

Dirlik, Arif and Meisner, Maurice (1989) "Politics, Scholarship, and Chinese Socialism", in Arif Dirlik and Maurice Meisner (eds) *Marxism and the Chinese Experience*. New York: M.E. Sharpe, Inc.

Doyle, Michael (1983) "Kant, Liberal Legacies, and Foreign Affairs", *Philosophy and Public Affairs*, 12(3) and (4): 205-235; 323-353.

Fishman, Ted C. (2005) *China, Inc.: How the Rise of the Next Superpower Challenges America and the World.* New York: Scribner.

Frank, Andre G. (1998) *Reorient: Global Economy in the Asian Age*. Berkeley: University of California Press.

Fukuyama, Francis (1992) *The End of History and the Last Man*. New York: Free Press.

Goldstein, Avery (2005) *Rising to the Challenge: China's Grand Strategy and International Security.* Stanford: Stanford University Press.

Guo, Sujian, (ed.) (2005) *China's Peaceful Rise in the 21st Century: Domestic and International Conditions*. Aldershot: Ashgate Publishing.

Hegel, Georg W.F. (1938) *The Philosophy of History*. Available at http://www.btinternet.com/~glynhughes/squashed/hegelhistory.htm.

Hobson, John M. (2004) *Eastern Origins of Western Civilisation.* London: Cambridge University Press.

Huntington, Samuel P. (1993) "The Clash of Civilizations?", *Foreign Affairs*, 72(3): 22-49.

Ikenberry, John G. (2008) "The Rise of China and the Future of the West", *Foreign Affairs*, 87(1): 23-37.

Kang, David C. (2007) *China Rising: Peace, Power, and Order in East Asia.* New York: Columbia University Press.

Kant, Immanuel (1957) *Perpetual Peace* (translated by Lewis White Beck). New York: Liberal Arts Press.

Krauthammer, Charles (1995) "Why We Must Contain China", *Time* Magazine, 146(5): 72.

Kurlantzick, Joshua (2007) *Charm Offensive: How China's Soft Power Is Transforming the World.* New Haven: Yale University Press

Lampton, David (2008) *The Three Faces of Chinese Power.* Berkeley: University of California Press.

Legro, Jeffrey W. (2007) "What China Will Want: The Future Intentions of a Rising Power", *Perspectives on Politics*, 5(3): 515-534.

Li, Minqi (2005) "The Rise of China and the Demise of the Capitalist World-Economy: Exploring Historical Possibilities in the 21st Century", *Science and Society*, 69(3): 420-448.

Li, Minqi (2008) *The Rise of China and The Demise of The Capitalist World Economy*. New York: Pluto Press.

Li, Xing (1998) "Sleeping in the Same Bed with Different Dreams", *Peace Review*, 10(3): 449-454.

Li, Xing (1999) "Socialist Foundations of Market Reforms: Assessing Chinese Past", *Economic and Political Weekly*, 34(49): 3457-3464.

Li, Xing (2008) "Vestens Kina-syndrom" (The West's China Syndrome), *Kritisk Debat*, 42. http://www.kritiskdebat.dk/artikel.php?id=590.

Luo, Chi (2007) *Understanding China's Growth: Forces that Drive China's Economic Future*. London: Palgrave Macmillan.

Madsen, Richard (1998) "China in the American Imagination", *Dissent*, 45(1): 54-59.

McNeill, William H. (1963 [1991]) *The Rise of the West: A History of the Human Community*. Chicago: University of Chicago Press.

Mearsheimer, John (2006) "China's Unpeaceful Rise", *Current History*, 105(690): 160-162.

Meisner, Maurice (1999) "China's Communist Revolution: A Half-century Perspective", *Current History*, 98(629): 243-248.

Needham, Joseph and Wang Ling (1954) *Science and Civilisation in China*, Vol. 1. London: Cambridge University Press.

Nye, Joseph S. (2004) *Soft Power: The Means to Success in World Politics*. New York: Public Affairs.

Paltiel, Jeremy (2005) "The Rise of China as a Challenge to International Relations Theory", a paper Prepared for delivery at International Studies Association Honolulu, Hawaii, March 1-5, available at http://www.allacademic.com/meta/p70638_index.html.

Peck, James (1975) "Revolution Versus Modernization and Revisionism: A Two-Front Struggle", in Victor Nee and James Peck (eds) *China's Uninterrupted Revolution from 1840 to the Present*. New York: Random House.

Pye, Lucian W. (1990) "Erratic State, Frustrated Society", *Foreign Affairs*, 69(4): 56-74.

Qin, Yaqing (2007) "Why is There no Chinese International Relations Theory?", *International Relations of the Asia-Pacific*, 7(3): 313-340.

Ramo, Joshua C. (2004) *The Beijing Consensus*. London: the Foreign Policy Centre.

Ray, Jamee Lee (1998) "Does Democracy Cause Peace?", *Annual Review of Political Science*, 1: 27-46.

Shambaugh, David (2006) *Power Shift: China and Asia's New Dynamics*. Berkeley: University of California Press.

Tan, Chung (1996) "Towards a Holistic Understanding of Chinese History", *China Report*, 32(3): 233-249.

Weber, Max (1958) *The Protestant Ethic and the Spirit of Capitalism*. New York: Scribner's Press.

Wittfogel, Karl (1957) *Oriental Despotism: A Comparative Study of Total Power*. New Haven: Yale University Press.

Yan, Xuetong (2001) "The Rise of China in Chinese Eyes", *Journal of Contemporary China*, 10(26): 33–39.

Zakaria, Fareed (2006) "Does the Future Belong to China?", *Newsweek*, September 2.

Zakaria, Fareed (2007) "The Sky Isn't Falling in China", *Newsweek*, March 12.

Zheng, Bijian (2005) "China's 'Peaceful Rise' to Great-Power Status", *Foreign Affairs*, 84(5): 39-48.

Chapter 1
The Eastern Wind Will Not Subside: China's Long March Back to the Future?

Jacques Hersh

Introduction

The intention of this chapter is to discuss the developing relationship between China and the Western core nations within the context of the capitalist world system. The level of analysis as well as the methodology involved can thus be seen as belonging to the body of social sciences encapsulated by interdisciplinary International Political Economy. In other words, the emphasis on economic history serves to situate the past relationship between "advanced" China and "backward" Europe before the advent of Western capitalism. The search for an explanation to the Chinese societal downturn from the 19th century on to its modern ascendancy cannot be achieved without taking into account the binary historical process of the modernization of Western capitalism as well as what is perceived as its present relative decline vis-à-vis the dynamism of emerging economies as exemplified by China's growth.

To comprehend the significance of the contemporary processes the world is witnessing, the analysis includes a discussion of modernization theory which aims at explaining the development trajectory of Western capitalism as the universal model to be emulated. Seen in this light, the level of analysis in relation to China's ascendancy is its integration into the world economy and the resulting structural consequences this may have for the viability of capitalism and the hierarchical order.

Situating the Historical Experience

Since the demise of "real-existing socialism" the evolution of East Asia has become a primary concern of social sciences and political strategists. Indeed, if there ever were a need to disprove the thesis of "The End of History" (Fukuyama, 1989) a look to this part of the world would be sufficient to convince us that we may be witnessing the beginning of a new historical phase. In other words, a shift of the centre of economic vitality from West to East or as implied by some a return to normalcy in world history (Frank, 1998).

Much thought was devoted in the 1970s and 1980s to the shape of the world capitalist system as a result of the emergence of Japan as a leading economic powerhouse together with the East Asian Newly Industrialized Countries. Regardless of the fact that the Japanese economy is only second to the United States, this challenge was successfully contained by US economic and financial strategy (Hersh, 1993). In recent years, however, the question of East Asia's future position in the world has become of even greater concern for Western strategists.

The reason for this revolves around the impact China is having/will have on the international economic and political system. Because of that nation's size, population and potential this awareness is not only a product of the 20th and 21st century. In the beginning of the 1800s, Napoleon supposedly warned about the potential consequences of a dynamic China: "China is a sickly sleeping giant. But when she wakes the world will tremble" (quoted in Safire, 1993). He is also said to have advised that the best course for the advanced countries would be to "let China sleep".

The 19th century stereotype portrayal of the Chinese socio-economic formation as being in a state of dormancy had the implication of depicting it as anaemic in comparison to the dynamism of the Western capitalist powers. This assumption can be ascribed to the "Orientalism" of Western thought in its appraisal of non-European pre-capitalist societies. But as a matter of fact, prior to the industrial revolution in England and before the "eclipse" of China in the 19th century, Adam Smith had considered China as being ahead of Europe along the path of a similar trajectory. According to Andre Gunder Frank:

> Smith ... was the last major (Western) social theorists to appreciate that Europe was a Johnny-come-lately in the development of the wealth of nations: "China is a much richer country than any part of Europe", Smith remarked in 1776. Smith did not anticipate any change in this comparison and showed no awareness that he was writing at the beginning of what has come to be called the "industrial revolution. (Frank, 1998: 13; see also Arrighi, 2007: 25-26)

It is often forgotten that leading figures of European Enlightenment such as Leibniz, Voltaire, and Quesnay, among others found inspiration in many aspects of Chinese society and political organization. They "looked to China for moral instruction, guidance in institutional development, and supporting evidence for their advocacy of causes such as benevolent absolutism, meritocracy, and an agriculturally based national economy" (Adas, 1989: 79; quoted in Arrighi, 2007: 3). The historical achievements and advances of the Chinese socio-economic formation are essential for understanding the relationship between East and West. In addition such a comprehension contributes also to a critical questioning of the Eurocentric interpretation of the so-called European miracle. Prior to the emergence of the Western world's domination, Asia was central in providing for the largest reproduction of people. Early in the contact between Europe and Asia, "sixteenth-century Europeans had considered Japan and China to be the great hopes of the future", according to the seminal work *Asia in the Making of Europe* by Donald Lach and Edwin van Kley (Lach and van Kley, 1965, in Frank, 1998: 11). The Chinese state – under successive dynasties – developed an administrative system of governance that facilitated the growth of economic resources and population. Before most governments in the world had even conceived of policies for preventing distress and death caused by famines, the Chinese had implemented the strategies of procurement, storage, and distribution of grain in order to protect the population against the eventual ravages of famine through "ever-normal granaries".

During the Qing era, the state was proactively involved through an investment programme in agricultural improvement, irrigation and waterborne food transportation (Bagchi, 2005: 141, 142). Chinese urban centres were more developed than corresponding contemporary European cities. The wealth of major cities and the level of craftsmanship amazed many first-time European travellers to China. In the sphere of scientific discoveries and application to production processes, China was at the forefront of modernization. The three inventions, which according to Francis Bacon changed the world: paper, gunpowder, and the magnetic compass, were of Chinese origin. After a long time lag they spread to Europe and other parts of the world (Needham et al., 1954). Before the growth of machine-based manufacturies in Britain, China and India were the two most important suppliers of manufactured goods to the world. "In 1750 China produced 32.8 percent of world manufactures, India (meaning the subcontinent of South Asia) produced 24.5 percent, and today's developed countries together produced 27.0 percent" (Simmons, 1985: 593-622, in Bagchi, op. cit.: 135). Silk manufacturing from the cocoons to the major silk-working machinery was pioneered by Chinese producers and the country was a major supplier to the world. For more than 2,000 years, the so-called "silk road" had become a major long-distance trade route for export of Chinese textiles and porcelain wares to Europe and North Africa (Ibid.: 137). From the 16th century onwards the Chinese economy became more closely connected to the formation of a global economy through the activities of Portuguese and Spanish merchants with the extension of ocean trade routes.

The accumulation process that resulted from the economic relations established on the world scale after the incorporation of the Americas and Africa was essential to the evolution of European capitalism. Without access to the resources from these continents and the products from Asia, Western capitalist development might have followed a different trajectory. Contrary to the conventional interpretation, industrial capitalism was not an exclusively home-grown phenomenon. From different perspectives, both Adam Smith and Karl Marx recognized the importance of this historical period for the development of the world. In his magnum opus, *The Wealth of Nations*, written in 1776, Smith writes that: "The discovery of America, and that of the passage to the East Indies by the Cape of Good Hope, are the two greatest events recorded in the history of mankind" (Smith, 1937: 557, in Frank, 1998: 13).

Opposite his present-day followers, Adam Smith was somewhat dubious concerning the benefits or misfortunes these great events would have for human kind (Smith, 1937: 189 in Frank 13). Writing after the impact of the industrial revolution had revealed itself, Karl Marx and Friedrich Engels were more explicit about the importance of the geographical extension of economic relations to other continents for the establishment of an international division of labour for the development of capitalism:

> The discovery of America, the rounding of the Cape, opened up fresh ground for the rising bourgeoisie. The East-Indian and Chinese markets, the colonization of America, trade with the colonies, the increase in the means of exchange and in commodities generally, gave to commerce, to navigation, to industry, an impulse never before known, and thereby to the revolutionary element in the tottering feudal society, a rapid development. … Modern industry has established the world-market, for which the discovery of America paved the way. (Marx and Engels, 1958: 35)

Contrary to the Eurocentric interpretation of history, it cannot be emphasized sufficiently that until late in the game Europe was the inferior partner in the relationship to Asia. The trade balance was clearly in favour of the Chinese with the Europeans covering the deficit with the silver mined in the Americas. As Bagchi puts it: "… for two centuries after the discovery of the Americas, the Europeans were unable to compete on equal terms with Asian manufactures" (Bagchi, op.cit.: 142). Consequently, neither Spain nor Portugal, the two powers that gained most immediately from the exploitation of the Amerindians, was able to impinge on the power of the big Asian or Eurasian empires of Ottoman Turkey, China, India, or Persia (Ibid.).

Modern Western social sciences have had difficulties coming to terms with the comparative development of Europe in relation to these non-European entities. It has been difficult for mainstream sciences to admit that the level of development in extra-European regions of the world might earlier have been more advanced than that of the Western socio-economic formations. According to this position, the reasons for the present disparity between developed and underdeveloped nations are to be found in the inherent superiority of European capacities to innovate in relation to the other cultural spheres. In this way of thinking, the "exceptionality" of European civilization is attributed to the internal dynamism of European culture. In recent years, however, the Eurocentric interpretation of world economic history has been challenged by scholars whose aim is to explain the origins and sequencing in time and space of the disparity between Europe and the rest of the world in the context of the divergent paths of development. It has been documented that as far as societal development is concerned, the two most populous entities of the world, India and China, were doing just as well as the best-performing regions of Europe down to the middle of the 18th century. With regard to commercialization, craft production and agricultural growth, China, India and Japan were not behind contemporary major European countries. With the exceptions of England and the Netherlands, there was little to distinguish most of early modern Europe from major states in Asia during the 16th to 18th centuries with regard to economic organization, property rights, or civil society – traits that according to Eurocentric historians had marked Europe out for its "manifest destiny" (Bagchi, 2005: 174; Goldstone, 1998: 249-84).

There cannot be any doubt that the trajectory of Western Europe would have been different had it not been for the discovery of America and the subjugation of its population and that of Africa. In economic terms emerging Europe had been in a catching-up position especially vis-à-vis the Asian centres. The establishment of plantations of sugarcane, cotton and tobacco in the Americas with slave labour imported from Africa was critical for the development of European capitalism. The flow of precious metals extracted from mines in America was essential in settling Western Europe's accounts with Oriental countries. In the words of Bagchi: "... the colonial edge was less a product of initial or technological superiority in civil production than of advantages won on the battlefield" (Bagchi, ibid.: 175). According to this perspective, the industrial revolution in Britain had been contingent on the conquest of India and the reduction of China to a subsidiary position relative to the Western powers.

What is being argued here is that the late development of Western Europe to a large extent came about through the tribute of extra-European regions which contributed to the capital accumulation process of the continent and served to redress the trade imbalances with Asia.

Conceptualization of Capitalist Development

Interpreting the process of "uneven development" is what differentiates the three schools of international political economy that have confronted each other in explication of the development of capitalism in the past few centuries. While liberalism assumes that market relations – with as little state intervention as possible – lead to a harmonious world economy, economic nationalism recognizes that late development is mainly a political project of industrialization which protects the national economy against the interests of the first developers' control of the world market. The dependency school, which is an offshoot of Marxism – with its focus on the creation and division of the surplus under capitalism – and Leninism – with its inclusion of the concept of imperialism, brings in the exploitation of other societies in the conceptualization of capitalism.[1]

Regardless of the fact that Marxism was the most antisystemic approach in the analysis of capitalism, it nevertheless has had difficulties in coming to terms with the Eurocentric perspective. The dilemma is reflected in the fundamental assumption depicting capitalism as the most accomplished socio-economic

1 For a discussion of the different perspectives, see Gilpin, 1987.

formation in the history of mankind. In the pamphlet *Manifesto of the Communist Party*, which was published in London in 1848, K. Marx and F. Engels offered a problematic understanding of the functioning of European capitalism's mode of expansion to other regions of the world:

> The cheap prices of its commodities are the heavy artillery with which it batters down all Chinese walls, with which it forces the barbarians' intensely obstinate hatred of foreigners to capitulate. It compels all nations, on pain of extinction, to adopt the bourgeois mode of production; it compels them to introduce what it calls civilization into their midst, i.e., to become bourgeois themselves. In one word, it creates a world after its own image. (Marx and Engels, 1958: 38)

The supposition that the competitive superiority of capitalist production is the explanation behind the European miracle became axiomatic for Euro-Marxism. This notwithstanding, the fact is that Marx and Engels had actually displayed awareness that the success of capitalism was much more than the functioning of purely economic mechanisms. They recognized that the use of military power had been the midwife to the breaking down of opposition to the expansion of European capitalism. In an article published in 1853 in the *New York Daily Tribune*, Marx touches upon the Opium Wars whereby Britain broke down Chinese resistance to the importation of opium from British India in order to do away with the trade deficit with China. The wars left Chinese society in ruins. He remarks that:

> Up to 1830, the balance of trade being continually in favour of the Chinese, there existed an uninterrupted importation of silver from India, Britain and the United States into China. Since 1833, and especially since 1840, the export of silver from China to India has become almost exhausting for the Celestial Empire. (Marx, n.d: 16)

The narrative utilized by neo-Marxism, especially in the Dependency School version, to describe the ascent of Europe to its world hegemonic position, includes the tribute that non-European social formations paid to the process. In this respect the conquest of the Americas by the Spaniards and Portuguese, following the "discovery" of that part of the world, led to the establishment of plantations of sugarcane, cotton and tobacco utilizing African slave labour. This together with the flow of precious metals, such as silver, extracted from mines in America became crucial in settling Western Europe's trade deficit with Asia. The control of this flow of wealth became a source of contention between the leading contenders for hegemony. The accumulation of capital resulting from this type of triangular trading pattern was critical for the societal transition to European capitalism and its later evolution. In the words of Bagchi: "The role of colonialism did not cease with the end of the phase of merchant capital in Europe. The final conquest of India and the beginning of the reduction of China to a subsidiary of European powers played important roles in facilitating the progress of the industrial revolution in Britain" (Bagchi, op. cit.: 175). It can consequently be argued that the other side of the coin of European industrial capitalism was the strangulation of the industrialization process in Asia. By protecting its own textile industries from cotton goods of Indian origin and denying these exports access to the European continent, British trade policy sheltered the country's cotton mills and enabling them to develop without having to face this competition. Duties on imports of textiles were prohibitive until the end of the 18th century. Not only that, but under British rule Indian domestic producers suffered reverse discrimination: they were made to pay higher duties on Indian exports than on English imports. "India was turned into the biggest consumer of products of the British cotton mills, which for a long time remained the industry employing the largest number of British workers" (Bagch, ibid.: 176).

China was imposed a similar fate after the First Opium War (1839-1842). At the turn of the 19th century, the West imported Chinese silks, porcelain, and tea. China who had a diversified economy was in contrast not seeking to import Western goods. The Western nations – foremost Britain – were, as mentioned above, eager to redress the balance of payment deficit through the export of silver. By forcing China to import Indian opium the outflow of silver was reversed and the British commercial expansion came to depend on this trading relation: "Though the First Opium War was launched to defeat Chinese attempts to ban the opium trade, the British also wanted to 'open' China to Western trade and commerce on terms acceptable to them" (Nee and Peck, 1975: 5). The international division of labour accompanying the expansion and extension of European capitalism was the result of the pattern of trade established during this period. The colonies of European powers became, besides their strategic value, important consumers for the products of the industrialization process in the North Atlantic realm. "Thus colonies played a critical part in the maturing of the first axial age separating Europe and its settler colony extensions from the rest of the world" (Bagchi, op. cit.: 176).

With regard to China, the British victory in the Opium Wars was interwoven with a deepening internal crisis that was aggravated by the Western economic expansion in the country. Compared to previous invaders that could be absorbed in the vast nation, the Western nations not only had superior weapons but commanded a power unleashed by the Industrial Revolution which was able through a combination of military might and economic means to undermine the foundations of China's self-sufficient agricultural economy and burgeoning industrialization as well as the country's traditional culture and values (Lee and Peck, op. cit.: 4).

The development of European capitalism, which enabled it to expand to the rest of the world, is paradoxical when compared to the relative late-development of Asia to the extent that prior to the 19th century at least, the positions were the reverse. In other words it was the West that had been backward in relation to East and South Asia. This observation applies both to the level of economic activity as well as to that of societal organization. The attempt to conceptualize what must have appeared as an anomaly to Eurocentric social sciences, has not been successful in bridging the gap of misunderstanding. The question is of importance and is relevant to understanding the present evolution of the different parts of the world. The divergence of trajectories that characterized the dynamism of European capitalism and the eclipse of the Asian socio-economic formations is still open to discussion and interpretations.

However, evidence suggests that European social scientists of the 18th century were aware of the advanced position of China as compared to that of Europe. When Adam Smith wrote in 1776: "China is a much richer country than any part of Europe" he was echoing David Hume who had appreciated Europe's relative underdevelopment (Smith, in Frank 1998: 13). Nevertheless, following the Industrial Revolution, a new perception of European superiority came to dominate within the scientific community and the accompanying theory building. In the words of Frank:

> The coming of the industrial revolution and the beginning colonialism of Asia had intervened to reshape European minds, and if not to 'invent' all history, then at least to invent a false universalism under European initiation and guidance. Then in the second half of the 19th century, not only was world history rewritten wholesale, but "universal" social "science" was (new)born, not just as a European, but as a *Eurocentric* invention. (Frank, ibid.: 14)

The agenda accompanying the paradigm shift focused on the assumption of a teleological dimension to the development of capitalism for the evolution of humankind. Accordingly, the question to be answered in relation to non-European social formations became one of conceptualizing their inherent propensity to stagnancy and focusing on the conditions preventing the dynamism of capitalist social relations from emerging. The fundamental assumption behind this way of thinking is that capitalism is in greater accordance with human nature. This discourse derives from Adam Smith's often quoted adage that considers the division of labour as being an inescapable consequence of a "certain propensity in human nature … to truck, barter, and exchange one thing for another" (Smith, 1982: 174).

If this axiom of liberalism is applied to world history then, the need arises to explain the reasons why the modern world capitalist economy emerged in Europe and not in other social formations. It is the narrative that sees the rise of capitalism as an exclusive European phenomenon that contributed to creating the foundation of what has been called Eurocentrism whose basic tenet is that this was due to historical conditions generated within Europe itself. Implicitly and explicitly this approach and methodology came to give legitimacy to the followed policies and strategies of European states towards other cultures and civilizations. Biology and implicit racism was one explanation, demography, environment and climate, rationality, technology, societal institutions including the state, religion, universities, and so on were also used to construct an ideologically-determined discourse in relation to non-Europeans.[2] Notwithstanding its emphasis on

2 For a critical discussion of the mythology behind Eurocentrism, see Blaut, 1992.

fundamental divergences between the "West and the rest", as well as diversity among different peoples and social formations, Eurocentrism nevertheless came to project a path of unilinear societal development whereby the rest of the world would duplicate the European experience. As the historical sociologist Barrington Moore put it: "There was a time in the still recent past when many intelligent thinkers believed there was only one main highway to the world of modern industrial society…" (Moore, 1967: 159).

Advanced Europe, Backward Asia!

Two explanations that came to stand out in the body of social sciences with regard to the passage from feudalism to capitalism are 1) the Asiatic Mode of Production and 2) the importance of the cultural dimension in Europe's transition. While the first approach relied on an environmentalist-materialist approach, the second put emphasis on a culturalist explication.

1. Concerning the first, travellers to Asia in the 18th century, such as the physician Francois Bernier and the political thinkers Boulainvillier and Montesquieu portrayed these societies as centres of political despotism. In contrast to Europe, these formations were said to rely on slavery and to be characterized by the non-existence of private property – with the ruler in complete control of the land.[3] The interesting aspect of the conceptualization of the Asiatic Mode of Production was that it appeared to fit in the materialist frame of reference of Marxian societal analysis by combining the natural environment and climatic conditions with the form of political organization.

   In the final analysis, the explication of pre-capitalist Asian societies which arose in the West is based on a notion that places these formations in a status of inferiority relative to European feudalism. In the words of Blaut: "This theory has a number of variants which are known by various names, among them 'the Asiatic Mode of Production', 'hydraulic society', and 'oriental despotism'" (Blaut, 1993: 80-81). The conceptualization is not however entirely coherent to the extent that it seems split between a kind of environmental determinism and the assumption of a developed level of technology. Nevertheless, in an evolutionary perspective, irrigation-based ("hydraulic") societal formations are seen as inhibiting development because of the overbearing state structure and bureaucracies. According to this approach, this type of societal organization was directly related to the need for adjustment to the environment and climate that made irrigation

3 For a critical discussion of the question of the transition to capitalism, see Hersh, 1977.

necessary. Thus the identification of river-valley civilizations, from Egypt to China, with "oriental despotism" was common in 19th century Europe.

Viewed from an evolutionary angle, these types of society were seen as being blocked in their progression towards capitalism. This was the dominating paradigm of the scientific community in the 19th century. The socio-economic model of European capitalism determined the level and the tools of analysis of other type societies following the Industrial Revolution and the rise and increasing use of science together with the spread of the political philosophy of evolution and the notion of progress deriving from the French Revolution. As pointed out by Teodor Shanin, there was general agreement concerning the involved methodology among social scientists: "Central to it was evolutionism – the arch-model of those times, as prominent in the works of Darwin as in the philosophy of Spencer, in Comte's positivism and in the socialism of Fourier and Saint Simon. Evolutionism is, essentially, a combined solution to the problem of heterogeneity and change" (Shanin, 1983: 4). Basically assuming a structurally necessary development as the path to modernity and progress, it was the task of the scientific method to uncover the order and explanation of the various stages through which the diversity of forms, physical, biological and social would go through. In this optic, change was seen as a necessary part of reality while on the other hand it projected a narrative of unwarranted optimism and unilinear determinism according to which "… the progress through stages meant also the universal and necessary ascent to a world more agreeable to the human or even to the 'absolute spirit' or God himself" (Shanin, ibid.).

Although Marx seems to have acquiesced to a certain evolutionism in his schematic periodization of the history of civilization (the typology of societal development going through tribal society, primitive communism, feudalism and capitalism), he was nevertheless disenchanted with the reductionism of the evolutionist scheme. According to Shanin, Marx's position on differentiating feudalism in its European form from the corresponding pre-capitalist formations in the East was an attempt to define the background for the surge of capitalism in Europe. "In consequence and already by 1853 Marx had worked out and put to use the concepts of Oriental Despotism and of the Asiatic Mode of Production, its close synonym, as a major theoretical supplement and alternative to unilinear explanations" (Shanin, ibid.: 5).

This interpretation overlooks the fact that both Marx and Engels were products of their time, meaning that they were both influenced by and in opposition to the social theories in vogue. Besides, their knowledge about the world outside of Europe was rather limited except for what they learned in the press, in books and in official papers representing the colonial point of view. Consequently they did not seriously question the dominant perception of the Orient as being despotic and historically stagnant. However their position was not based on a culturalist approach, but on the consideration of the natural environment as the determining element for the societal form. As Blaut puts it, "… their scepticism about European social theory, with its elitist foundations, immunized them from the usual explanations for Asian despotism and stagnation. Asians were no less rational than Europeans, and no less willing to struggle against economic exploitation" (Blaut, 1993: 82). The theory of the Asiatic Mode of Production was modified by Marx and Engels and altogether rejected by the latter in his late writings. Karl Marx was not exclusively a social scientist who analysed reality, but one that wanted to change it as well. In the article on the revolution in China and in Europe, he touched upon the two ideas that were to constitute the core of the various Marxist imperialism theories a half century later. On the one hand, the development of European capitalism and its expansion on a world scale was creating a single world economic system and on the other, the resulting convulsions would influence the evolution of Europe itself (d'Encausse and Schram, 1965: 16).

Following the establishment of state socialism in the USSR, the notion of the Asiatic Mode of Production disappeared from the Soviet-controlled body of social sciences. However, at the height of the Cold War, a former Komintern specialist on Asian affairs revived the concept. In his book *Oriental Despotism*, Karl Wittfogel not only resuscitated the notion of the Asiatic Mode of Production, but elaborated its scope by maintaining that movement toward capitalist modernization could only be found in feudal societies (such as in Europe and Japan) while Asiatic formations were inadaptable to modern-type transformations because in his words: "Hydraulic society is the outstanding case of societal stagnation" (Wittfogel, 1957: 420). Accordingly, this condition predetermined the political totalitarianism of the state socialist formations, especially that of the USSR and China.

2. The culturalist explanation of the European advance and Asian backwardness owed much to the German sociologist, Max Weber. According to this interpretation of world history and specifically the development of capitalism in Europe, the main reasons are to be found in the cultural realm, and not least in religion. The thesis was expressed clearly in the book *The Protestant Ethic and the Spirit of Capitalism* published in 1905. On the occasion of the 100th anniversary of its publication Francis Fukuyama declared it to be the "most famous sociological tract ever written". In his opinion, whereas the sociology of Marxism was based on a materialist interpretation of social formations, Weber put the emphasis on the cultural background as the most important explicatory element. The difference between the two approaches is in Fukuyama's formulation fundamental: "It was a book that stood Karl Marx on his head. Religion, according to Weber, was not an ideology produced by economic interests (the 'opiate

of the masses,' as Marx had put it); rather, it was what had made modern capitalism possible" (Fukuyama, 2005).

The point of entry for Weber to the understanding of the great divergence between "advanced" European capitalism and Asian underdevelopment was due to the difference in the two cultural backgrounds. The evolution of rationality among Europeans was seen as leading to a kind of "economic ethic" – a set of values, aspirations and logical thought processes that emerged in connection with the Puritanism of Protestantism – nurturing, in the last instance, capitalism. In contrapoint to this interpretation it can however be argued that neither European capitalism nor assumed Asian backwardness can be explained through the prism of an exclusive religious approach. As Blaut puts it: "Weber is not (as some think) explaining capitalism and modernity in terms narrowly of religion. He does invoke religion to explain many aspects of the supposed traditionalism of Asians, but here too a primordial irrationality is seen as underlying religion. (He writes, for instance, of the 'magical traditionalism' of Indians and Chinese)" (Blaut, 1993: 103).

The idea of inherent European rationality has taken an axiomatic position in conventional social sciences such as history in its analysis of the past as well as in Modernization theory, which projects capitalist development as the model to be emulated. A serious criticism of the culturalist perspective arises when one considers the fact that in his study of the economic history of China and Japan, Max Weber concluded that these countries were condemned to remain backward because of their lacking protestant ethic. The culturalist approach thus shows a high degree of inconsistency when applied to the analysis of past and present East Asia. The underdevelopment of these societies was previously ascribed to their cultural background; seemingly unaware of the contradiction the phenomenon of the East Asian Newly Industrialized Countries is likewise ascribed to their shared cultural heritage that combines Buddhism and Confucianism and traditional strong state interventionism in the economy. What was considered to be the explicatory element for the backwardness of these societies in the past was now reversed and put forward as the explanation for their dynamism. This theoretical elasticity undermines the explanatory value of culturalism as the principal factor involved in development.

In the comparative study of different types of societies it is necessary to attempt to develop an understanding of development based on the existing conditions. Perhaps the fact that the conceptual tools of analysis were developed in the European cultural sphere may weaken their application to the analysis of societies with a different background. Seen in this perspective, Gunder Frank's critique of the great social scientists for their lack of inclusion of the concrete societal arrangements outside the Western sphere has a certain validity. This shortcoming may, however, have been related to the lack of knowledge of the concrete cases that were being investigated. Or putting it differently as the saying goes when you have a hammer in your hand, there is a tendency to see nails all over! Writing about the "hammer" of economics, Robert Heilbroner makes the point that "... economics is concerned exclusively with the study of capitalism ... To presume that it applies to societies that do not possess the unique characteristics of capitalism will only lessen its capacity to illuminate the society to which it properly applies". (Heilbroner, 1995: 22, 26). The implication being that economics has no relevance in the study of hunting or gathering tribes nor can it be applied to noncapitalist-stratified societal orders such as kingdoms, empires, feudalities, command societies, or self-styled socialism (Ibid.). The criticism of Eurocentric social sciences is particularly appropriate because of the attempt to project the European experience as the point of departure in the analysis of societal forms of the past as well as of the future. The anthropologist Daniel Thorner makes the following point:

> From our perspective, European feudalism of the high Middle Ages may be seen as embodying a particular form of peasant economy. Nothing is gained by trying to view all peasant economies as variations of that one rather special form. The time has arrived to treat European experience in categories derived from world history, rather than to squeeze world history into Western European categories. (Thorner, 1971: 217)

Development as a Political Process

A related fundamental shortcoming of mainstream Eurocentric development scholarship is related to the failure to give the international dimension of the relationship between the core countries and what is called the periphery its due significance. Thus even though the European experience is offered to the non-European societies as the model to be copied, the theoretical body of the Modernization tradition is oblivious of the nature of the relationship. In other words, the awareness that Western capitalism itself has been a hindrance to the development of non-European capitalism is lacking. Given the fact that European capitalism morphed into imperialism, this advice proved to be more than naïve. Obviously it can be argued that the conceptualization of development and international relations demands an approach that includes all aspects of the processes involved.[4]

---

4 By combining the different aspects of development and international relations International Political Economy seems to have the best suited methodology to break down the "compartmentalization" of social sciences that accompanied the emergence of the modern capitalist state, see Strange, 1970.

Like other parts of Asia, China in the 19th century became prey to the competition between imperialist powers. The unfolding of this systemic force contributed to the forging of the later evolution of this part of the world as political actors turned the imperialist danger into an opportunity for societal change! To a large extent it was the fate of China at the hands of the Western European powers and the emergence of the United States in East Asia that contributed to the surge of economic nationalism and anti-imperialism in the region. In this relation, Japan offers a classic example. The internal crisis of Japanese feudalism combined with the "opening" of the country to the West by Commodore Matthew Perry led to the Meiji Restoration of 1868.[5] The resulting "feudal-merchant" coalition that initiated the downfall of feudalism and the beginning of industrial capitalism grasped the importance of a strong state and intervention in the economy (Norman, 1975). In the transition from feudalism to catching-up Japanese capitalism, industrial strategy, protectionism and other aspects of state interventionism formed what has been called the "capitalist developmental state" (Johnson, 1982).

During the second half of the 20th century, variants of this model were implemented by the Newly Industrialized Countries (NICs) in Eastern Asia (Johnson, 1988; Koo, 1988). As other exemplars of late capitalist development in the world system (such as the United States and Germany) had earlier demonstrated, the Japanese elite realized that economic development was not simply a function of the unfolding of market mechanisms as claimed by the discourse of contemporary British "Cosmopolitan" liberal political economy. Late industrialization required protection of infant industries from the competition of the more industrialized states. For late developers free trade was in fact the protectionism of the strong! The German political economist, Friedrich List, accused England of hypocrisy for having first protected her textile industry from the competition of Indian cotton and silk before achieving supremacy and only thereafter having imposed free trade on the world (List, 1977).

As an important incentive for the implementation of a development strategy based on economic nationalism, the Japanese elite could observe at close range the impact of Western imperialism on China. The project of catching-up was thus dictated by the concern of protecting Japanese society from foreign domination and the fate that befell China. After a period of isolation, a breathing space, from the world economy, the political elites of late developing societies rejoined the capitalist world system from a position of strength and competed for the benefits to be derived from the international division of labour. Thus, far from representing an anti-capitalist force, they in fact gave capitalism an historical dynamism that is encapsulated in the Marxist concept of "uneven development". The upshot of the relationship between first developers and late developers historically led

5 The usual English translation of the Japanese term ishin by "restoration" is somewhat of a misnomer. "Renovation" would be a more accurate translation. According to J.A.A. Stockwin: "Given the root and branch character of the changes which the Japanese people subsequently underwent, the sum total of the changes may well be regarded as revolutionary" (Stockwin, 1999: 14).

to challenges to the existing hierarchical order and changes in the hegemonic position of the system's leadership. The two world wars of the 20th century can be explained as competitive struggles between established imperialist powers and emerging powers. In East Asia, Japan's attempt to conquer the Asian continent that resulted in World War II was an attempt to dominate the region and exclude the Western colonial powers. The confrontation with the United States led to the Pacific War between the two.

The evolution of Chinese domestic politics was not unrelated to the geopolitical processes taking place in East Asia. China's relative isolation from the rest of the world was nearing its end with the emergence of Western imperialism in the area. But far from being a dormant society, Chinese politics were in ebullition. The 19th century had been characterized by widespread corruption within the body politics, the administrative apparatus was deteriorating, peasant rebellions were taking place and the vast public works projects were beginning to break-down. The imperialist intervention following the Opium Wars accentuated the disintegration of Chinese society: growing drug addiction, smuggling and official corruption. The Manchu political establishment was exposed as powerless. Peasant unrest had broken out in dispersed and marginal ways already at the end of the 18th century and culminated with the Taiping Rebellion between 1850 and 1870.

Although peasant uprisings had been part of China's 2000-year history, the Taiping Rebellion was different from previous struggles. Ideas concerning the relative superiority of Western power had penetrated civil society and specifically the awareness of the revolutionaries. The Taiping movement was a revolt against both the ideological hegemony of Confucianism and societal organization. The Manchu's defeat of the Taipings, with Western assistance, weakened the country which was submitted to a number of conflicts including the Sino-Japanese war (1894-1895). While the government collaborated with the Western powers, these gained a vested interest in the survival of the Manchu authority. But below the surface, a debate was going on among traditional Confucian scholar-officials concerning the problem of coping with the imperialist challenge. The dependent development which the country experienced with the foreign intrusion and incorporation in the Western capitalist system led to a paradoxical situation. The imperialist powers advanced their interests by supporting the political conservative elements in China against the forces trying to promote revolutionary change and the growth of indigenous Chinese capitalism. As Nee and Peck put it: "Imperialism, stimulating China's social economy, was producing new groups and social forces which, though essential for its ongoing penetration of Chinese life, were also the basis for a growing opposition to it" (Nee and Peck, op. cit.: 10).

By the early 20th century China had become a semicolony for the competing and colluding imperialist powers (including latecomer Japan!). The unequal treaties reduced the Chinese authorities to the role of a powerless administration. In the wake of the Boxer anti-foreign uprising in 1900, a genuine fear spread among the Chinese people that their country would be partitioned and that they would disappear as an entity. A new political consciousness arose concerning the need to create a modern centralized nation-state in order to force back imperialism and promote the Chinese nation's regeneration. Although there were disputes and dissension among political forces in favour of drastic change, there was general agreement about looking towards the West and Japan as models to be emulated. The idea was that China's modernity would be made in the image of Western capitalism. For the reformers, the predicament was: "how could the country free itself from foreign domination and gain independence while using the reform methods and ideology of Western capitalism?" (Ibid.: 14).

This has been the dilemma all latecomers have had to confront. Seen in this light the lesson of Japan had more value as an example than the Western model. However, even after the establishment of the Chinese Republic, no group or class rose to power, as had been the case with the Japanese Restoration, with the capacity of directing the transformation of the country by regaining national independence and creating a strong state to resist imperialist incursions. The 1911 revolution collapsed and the new republic floundered in the morass of warlord politics and aggressions and occupation by Japanese imperialism. The peace following World War I exerted a political influence on the evolution of Chinese politics. The new generation of Chinese intellectuals and nationalist militants, were dismayed by the results of the Versailles Peace Conference. In order to punish Germany and reward Japan for its participation in the war on the winning side, the German concessions in the Shantung Peninsula were ceded to Japan. This was viewed as a betrayal of China's national sovereignty. For many Chinese, this revealed the hollowness of the idealism of President Woodrow Wilson and the hypocrisy of the Western democracies. Together with the nascent appeal of the October Revolution in Russia this exerted influence on the formation of a new generation of Chinese nationalists and socialists. The May 4th Movement of 1919 unleashed a massive wave of anti-imperialist nationalism culminating in widespread political unrest ie, workers' strikes, demonstrations, riots and nationwide boycotts. The movement became a watershed in Chinese history and would affect the future evolution of the country. The success of the radical intellectuals of the May 4th Movement translated into putting the question of national regeneration on the political agenda.

Both the Kuomintang nationalists and the Communist Party arose out of this movement but were however unable to unite in the anti-Japanese struggle and the building of an independent national economy. Notwithstanding this, the defeat of Japanese imperialism and the victory over the Kuomintang by the Chinese Communist Party (CCP) opened the road to the modernization of China. Perhaps echoing Napoleon's remark concerning the "sleeping giant", Mao Zedong signalled China's resurgence on September 21, 1949 when he declared on Tiananmen Square: "The Chinese people have stood up!"[6] This was also a wake-up call to

6 It is the title of the address by Mao Zedong, Chairman of the Chinese Communist Party, at the First Plenary Session of the Chinese People's Political Consultative Conference, September 21, 1949, available at http://www.international.ucla.edu/eas/documents/mao490921.htm.

the world. The communist victory had political consequences and changed the prospects of global politics. More than anywhere else in the world the failure of the Chinese nationalists under Chiang Kai-shek to gain power was considered as a defeat by the American political class and this affected the Sino–US relationship for decades to come.

The dilemma facing the communist regime upon coming to power concerned the questions of economic development internally and trading relations with the external world in the context of the Cold War. The slogan launched by Mao that "only socialism can save China!" reflected both a choice as well as an adjustment to the imposed realities of international power politics. Paradoxically, the implemented strategy of self-centred development represented a variant of the model of economic nationalism (mobilization of internal resources and isolation from the capitalist world economy). This course together with adherence to an alliance with the USSR and the other socialist countries raised the expectation that the capitalist West could be defeated. During a visit to the Soviet Union, Mao made some remarks to Chinese students in Moscow on November 17, 1957 predicting an end to Western domination of the world. In his view, the balance of forces in the conflict between the two socio-political systems was shifting in favour of socialism. "In the struggle between the socialist and capitalist camps, it was no longer the West wind that prevailed over the East wind, but the East wind that prevailed over the West wind" (Mao, 1957).

As we know of course, the international socialist project didn't materialize as the forces of nationalism truncated the vision and practice of socialism. What took place was that priority in all socialist states was given to their country's national interest. Given the potential and real strength of a nation the size of China, the USSR was not at ease in having such a neighbour whose struggle for independence had culminated in the formation of the People's Republic of China. It is worth mentioning that the Soviet Union had given support to Chiang Kay-shek during the anti-Japanese struggle. With regard to the Chinese Communist Party, it was not a monolithic entity. It comprised two main political projects with each their adherents. The socialist left, around Mao Zedong, was dedicated to the project of socialism, while another tendency envisioned a catching-up project of late development in order to accede to the core status of the world economic system. The coexistence between these two projects exploded with the Great Proletarian Cultural Revolution whose primary intention on the part of Mao had been to purify the party of the so-called "capitalist roaders" and to mobilize the youth. The left in China had recognized that socialism was not predominantly the result of the development of productive forces, as a mechanical understanding of the Marxist vision promoted, but the continuous struggle "between the two lines".

Seen in a historical context, the success of Chinese socialist construction influenced the regional evolution of East Asia, which in turn would come to have an impact on the internal political struggle within the CCP. This aspect is important for understanding the present and future constellation of forces on the world scale. Much literature analysing the so-called East Asian "miracle" has been produced.

The argument can be made that the fear of the spread of socialism outside the Asian socialist countries contributed to the creation of the conditions for the NICs' late-industrialization and the reconstruction of the Japanese economy as a powerhouse in the world market. The revolutionary movement in East Asia predetermined the acceptance by the United States of social reforms and economic nationalism that would lead to late development in the region. Not only did Washington accept this evolution, but it also opened its markets to the exports of these countries in the attempt to isolate China. This was in marked contrast to US policy towards Latin America (Hersh, 1993).

Combined with the internal "two line" political struggle in the CCP, the increasing Soviet antagonism towards Chinese communism leading to the 1969-border military clash between them and the pressures of the United States culminating in the war in Indochina, the modernizing nationalist faction within the party became aware of China's economic weakness relative to the NICs (especially South Korea and Taiwan). The failure of the Cultural Revolution – launched in order to purify the party from rightist influence – resulted in the weakening of the leftwing of the party and after the demise of Chairman Mao, the path was opened for the imposition of a strategy of authoritarian modernization similar to what had been experienced in the cases of the NICs. This opened a new chapter in Chinese history and is affecting the world. The former US ambassador, Chas W. Freeman, describes how the post-Maoist leadership reflected on the evolution of the country:

> In the late summer of 1981, Deng Xiaoping remarked in my presence that when the history of the Twentieth Century was written, Mao's revolution would be described as the prelude to the real Chinese revolution, that which Deng himself had initiated in December 1978. But Deng made it clear that his was a revolution in methodology, not a change in national objectives. (Freeman, 2006)

In this optic, the "real revolution" is thus seen as the reform movement away from the embedded socialism of the Maoist period until the defeat of the leftwing of the Communist party and the introduction of a "socialist market economy". This evolution was not due to internal causes alone (expectation of higher economic growth) but also to a readjustment in the Sino–US relationship. From a felt need to constrain or diminish the power of the Soviet Union, symbolized in the Richard Nixon–Mao Zedong summit in Beijing, the two ruling political elites came to realize that they both could benefit from a less antagonistic relationship. As Immanuel Wallerstein notes: "The US sought to tame China, to bring it out of its Maoist cocoon and into the market whirl of the capitalist world-economy. China sought to buy technology, trade, and above all time in which to strengthen its economy and its military, and enable it to become a superpower" (Wallerstein, 2004). In other words, the two political elites were now willing to sleep in the same bed but were having different dreams!

Influencing the Sino-American relationship were the changes taking place in the world economy with the ascent of China and on the other hand the relative decline of the US hegemonic position in the hierarchical system of nations. Geoeconomics and geopolitics converged in a manner probably not foreseen at the time. Economically speaking the reforms based on the release of market forces in China were impacted by the simultaneous transformation in the world of geoeconomics.

For the Chinese economy, the globalization of neoliberalism opened a window of opportunity for export-led growth which China could take advantage of. As David Harvey notes: "The spectacular emergence of China as a global economic power after 1980 was in part an unintended consequence of the neoliberal turn in the advanced capitalist world" (Harvey, 2005: 121). It is highly improbable that the post-Maoist leadership expected, at the time, China to become a major creditor of the US debt, a large recipient of foreign direct investment (FDI), an important world market actor – both as a leading exporter of cheap finished products and importer of raw materials, a main polluter of the global environment, etc. Not only did the turn to neoliberalism on the part of the leading economies allowed for the surge of Chinese economic growth, but China's integration in the international division of labour contributed in return to making the model of capital accumulation of this phase of capitalism viable. As Minqi Li puts it: "China's transition to capitalism has played an indispensable role in the global triumph of neoliberalism" (Li, 2008: 91). Domestically, Chinese economic growth has contributed to great inequalities between regions and groups. The internal dilemma for the political leadership is to find a way to reduce the negative impacts of the growth model that has been implemented. Although China does have a large potential internal market, the export-led economic development has become dependent on access to the world economy. The way the polity resolves the contradictions will have worldwide consequences. As the economist Andrew Glyn notes: "… there is nothing inevitable about China continuing along its present trajectory. If it does, the problems of adapting to this major shift in the structure of world trade and output will be correspondingly severe" (Glyn, 2006: 90). On the other hand, Chinese failure to resolve the internal contradictions related to its specific model of capitalist growth (based on large export surpluses and a high saving-rate, i.e. underconsumption) will also have worldwide consequences. Either outcome is bound to impact the functioning of the international system. The stakes are high not only for the East Asian region but for the position of the United States as well. The problematique is formulated in the following manner by a Philippino economist: "The global economy has accommodated the NICs by and large, but the full-scale industrialization of the dragon economy will be certain to destabilize the global balance of power. If China fails and plunges into chaos instead, the world will have to deal with the horrors of that failure. Either way, it is the dragon – not the East Asian tigers or the Japanese flying goose or the American eagle – that will spell the future of the Pacific Rim" (Asenario, 1996: 193).

The evolution of China both internally and externally does not take place in a vacuum. Both related and unrelated to China, the disturbances the world is presently experiencing are connected to the ongoing crisis of US hegemony and the formation of a multipolar world system. Whether intentionally or not, China has become a leading actor in the promotion of the new order in gestation. The country's size and the state of its economy are of the utmost significance. At the time of its admittance to the World Trade Organization in 2001, China was rated as the fourth leading economy in the world. Furthermore it is calculated that assuming the Chinese economy continued its dynamism, it could surpass that of the United States and become the first economic power of the world. This could not avert having major geopolitical consequences (Ramonet, 2006: 5).

The fact of the matter is that China has become the "indispensable nation" in the international political economy. As an editorial in the French paper, *Le Monde* put it (July 30, 2009): "China is the only country that is present in the three instances: G2 (US-China), G4 (Brazil, Russia, India, China), G20 (the eight most industrialized countries plus the largest emerging economies). Nothing can be done without China". The ascent of China to the core nation status will inescapably influence the hierarchical order of the world system and especially menace the leadership of the United States. Assuming that the relative decline of the American geoeconomic and geopolitical positions continues, the critical question is whether this transformation will take place peacefully or violently. The only remaining strong American advantage has in recent years been its military power. However, even this card has shown its limitation in dealing with asymmetrical conflicts such as in Iraq or Afghanistan. History shows, as pointed out by imperialism theory, World System Analysis and Realism, that challenges to the hegemonic position of a world power result in conflict.

According to US think-tanks, the ascendancy of China has been considered a strategic menace. It is forgotten that the United States is now involved in the conflicts in Afghanistan and Iraq, and already in the beginning of the 1990s, the influential political scientist Samuel Huntington had warned in his thesis of "The Clash of Civilizations", that a Confucian-Islamic connection could potentially threaten Western interests, values and power. In an interview in *Newsweek* at the time, under the headline "Watch Out for China", Huntington implicitly contradicting his view of culture as the driving force for future conflicts stated that: "History shows that as countries industrialize rapidly they tend to become much more assertive…. The Chinese feel humiliated. So naturally they want to resume what they view as their natural place in the world. And that will have destabilizing consequences" (Huntington, 1994: 62).

Two interesting views on the future of the Sino–US relationship have emerged among American political scientists within the Realism tradition. In a confrontation in the journal *Foreign Policy*, John L. Mearsheimer and Zbiegniew Brzezinski propose two different approaches. The first opines that the only analytical tool we have in the discussion is theory because "we cannot know what political reality is going to look like in the year 2025". Basing himself on the assumption that China will become a military power in the future, Mearsheimer points out that from a theoretical point of view it can be expected that she will "try to push the United States out of Asia, much the way the United States pushed the European powers out of the Western Hemisphere. We should expect China to come up with its own version of the Monroe Doctrine, as Japan did in the 1930s (Mearsheimer, 2006: 162). Based on this conceptualization of China's ascendency as detrimental to American interests he foresees the future whereby the United States will seek "to contain China and ultimately weaken it to the point where it is no longer capable of dominating Asia..." much in the same way as the US behaved toward the Soviet Union during the Cold War (Brzezinski and Mearsheimer, 2005: 2-3).

In contrast, Brzezinski gives priority to the concrete reality over theory arguing that analysis of international relations is mainly retrospective. Nuclear weapons in his opinion have transformed power politics and as in the case with the Soviet Union prevented direct conflict between the two superpowers. Furthermore in contradistinction to Huntington, he finds that "the Chinese leadership appears much more flexible and sophisticated than many previous aspirants to great power status" (Ibid.: 3). While Mearsheimer contends that the growing economic strength of China will morphe into political and military power which can only develop in contradistinction to US interests, Brzezinski on the other hand maintains that China's desire for continued economic growth will make conflict with the United States unlikely (Ibid.: 4 and 3). The weakness of the economistic approach, which Brzezinski seems to project, is that it does not take into consideration the fact that the world will be characterized by increasing competition for access to markets, capital, and raw material in the future.

While US strategists discuss whether the ascendancy of China will lead to conflict or not, their Chinese colleagues also debate whether the United States will "allow" the rise of China and the consequences thereof. Official policy circles attempt to mask present issues and conflicts between the two countries in the interest of a façade of good Sino–US relations (Ramo, 2004: 40). The strategy followed by the Chinese political elite in its external relations lies in the projection of an emerging China as the largest asymmetric superpower. This translates into a foreign policy paradigm based on the example of its development model, strengthening its economic interests in the world, and upholding the Westphalian system of national sovereignty (Ibid.: 37). Defending the international state system is in marked contrast to the strategy of the United States which is pushing for the creation of an American-led post-modern world order of uneven and unequal sovereignty but nevertheless based on the discourse of democracy and neoliberalism.[7]

The guiding principle behind Chinese strategic thinking seems to be based on the historical experience of humiliation imposed on the country by the Opium Wars with nationalism as the modality around which the polity attempts to mobilize the population and promote economic growth as giving it ideological legitimacy.

---

7 For a discussion of the projected differences between the old and the new world order, see Cooper, 1996.

Simultaneously, Chinese foreign affairs planners are positing a new world order. This was conceptualized in the so-called "New Security Concept" introduced at an ASEAN meeting in 1997 and endorsed publicly by President Hu Jintao in 2004. It comprises "the Four No's" and implicitly is a document in favour of multipolarity in the world system: No hegemonism, no power politics, no alliances and no arms races (Ramo, 2004: 41). At the same time, there is a tendency in the academic world in China to project a relationship with the United States based on harmony. Basing themselves on pragmatism as an analytical tool some Chinese experts on the United States operate on what may be called wishful thinking. The vision of a peaceful Sino–US relationship is propagated by Chinese scholars with little understanding of the dynamics of the American system (Liu, 2007).

Conclusion

Scholars belonging to the dependency tradition have in recent times analysed the transformation taking place in the contemporary international political economy as a return to normalcy, i.e. the centrality of Asia after a few centuries of Western dominance of the world. The impact of such a shift is not yet completely grasped in the Western world. One reason may be that the hierarchy of the West over the rest was accompanied by a scientific paradigm in the social sciences in Europe and the United States that proposed an interpretation of this dominance based on Eurocentrism (Arrighi, 2007; Bagchi, 2005; Blaut, 1993; Frank, 1998).

In this contribution the attempt was made to look at the economic history of the relationship between Europe and China from a developmental perspective in order to explain the shift that occurred with the European expansion and the Asian regression. The importance of economic nationalism, as a determinant in the problematique of catching-up that is encapsulated in the theory of uneven and unequal development, deserves greater attention on the part of international political economy. The prophecy of Napoleon concerning the "awakening" of China is in the process of being realized as the preconditions for Western hegemony in the world system are being challenged by the ascendancy of China and other emerging nations. The Eastern wind does seem to be stronger than the Western wind, but not in the way Mao predicted. The paradox related to the return of China to its historic status as the global centre of gravity is that this will pose a greater challenge to the West and to capitalism itself than the Maoist model of development – based on a self-sufficient and self-centred economy – would have been in the short and medium term. From a historical perspective the post-Maoist market orientation – a development welcomed by the capitalist West – cannot but contribute to the transformation of the global economic division of labour as well as the hierarchical order in the nation-state system. In this regard, the US-Sino relationship will dominate world geoeconomics and geopolitics in the coming decades. As of now, the American attempt to weaken the role of the state in all other countries (including China) is counterbalanced by the strategy of the

Chinese leadership to promote nation-state power and the creation of a multipolar state system.

The implication of the ascendancy of China, as well as that of other emerging nations, raises a fundamental issue concerning the *modus operandi* of the capitalist world system itself and the prospect of post-capitalism. While dependency theoreticians see the re-emergence of China as the return to a sino-centric world hierarchy, they do not tell us much concerning the mode of functioning of such a system. Would such hegemony be based on a continuation of the capitalist model or a recreation of the old form of tribute system that existed between old China and its nearer and smaller neighbour states? This is a thesis in a recent book by a British author (Jacques, 2009). On the other hand it is impossible to envisage the imposition of an unequal relationship on countries like Russia, India or Japan. In other words the type and shape of such a world order is still an open-ended question. But from a socialist perspective, the issue at hand is how the emergence of China as a world power will affect the system's mode of functioning.

Of all theoretical approaches only proto-Marxism has conceptualized the importance of the relationship between advanced capitalist nations and the periphery for the process of accumulation of capital and reproduction of capitalism on a world scale. The assumption of early leading theoreticians of the Marxist tradition was that the development of capitalism in the center of the world system necessitated access to "non-capitalist strata and nations". As put by Rosa Luxemburg the inclusion of all these areas in the capitalist mode of production and distribution leads to a blind alley for capitalism itself. According to this understanding of globalization, the capitalist world cannot be flat as the American commentator Thomas Friedman would have us believe that neoliberal globalization can level differences and inequalities between nations. In the words of Rosa Luxemburg:

> The general tendency and final result of this process is the exclusive world rule of capitalist production. Once this is reached, Marx's model becomes valid: accumulation, i.e. further expansion of capital becomes impossible. Capitalism comes to a dead end, it cannot function any more as the historical vehicle for the unfolding of the productive forces, it reaches its objective economic limit. (Luxemburg, 1972: 145-46)

Luxemburg had taken issue with "Das Kapital" for its alleged analysis of the model of capital accumulation as a closed system, that is consisting exclusively of capitalists and labourers and excluding the significance of the phenomena of colonialism and imperialism for the reproduction and accumulation of capital. However, there is evidence that Marx and Engels did in fact show understanding for the dialectics of the expansion of capitalism worldwide and thereby the challenge to its continuous reproduction. With regard to the potential impact of China's inclusion in the capitalist world system both demonstrated awareness that the outcome would be contrary to the normal functioning of capitalism and the expectations of its ruling classes. In an article, written in 1853 Marx made the following point: "Now, England having brought about the revolution of China, the question is how that revolution will in time react on England, and through England on Europe" (Marx, n.d.: 18).

The belief that the defeat of the Maoist model of development would be in the interest of the expansion of the capitalist world system may prove to be relatively short-lived. The paradox of the inclusion of ever larger areas of the world into the sphere of international capitalist relations has not been fully grasped by socialist opinion. The bottom line is that although attractive for capital accumulation in the centres of capitalism in the immediate, the longer term perspectives are still to be felt. Although not the direct cause of the present crisis of world capitalism, the competitive growth of China and emerging economies nevertheless does reflect a historical shift in the balance of forces within the system and will influence the resolution of the difficulties facing capitalism. Seen in this perspective, the insight expressed by Friedrich Engels in 1894 may perhaps prove to be more topical than it was at the time: "It is again the wonderful irony of history: China alone is still to be conquered for capitalist production, and in so doing at long last the latter makes its own existence at home impossible..." (Engels, n.d.: 346).

Whether the "great transformation" the world is going through leads to a zero-sum-game situation, as theorists belonging to the imperialism tradition or Realism predict, or to a win-win outcome for all parties concerned as adherents of (neo)liberalism propose, will be a fundamental issue for the coming decades. What can be said with certainty though is that we are at an open-ended phase of history characterized by potential dangers and new possibilities. As the Chinese saying goes: "Hope for the best and prepare for the worst!"

References

Adas, Michel (1989) *Machines as Measures of Men: Science, Technology and Ideologies of Western Dominance*. Ithaca, NY: Cornell University Press.

Asenario, George (1996) "Asia in the World System", in Sing C. Chew and Robert A. Denemark, *The Underdevelopment of Development.* London: Sage Publications.

Arrighi, Giovani (2007) *Adam Smith in Beijing: Lineages of the Twentieth-First Century.* London and New York: Verso Press.

Bagchi, Amiya Kumar (2005) *Perilous Passage: Mankind and the Global Ascendency of Capital.* London, Boulder, New York, Toronto, Oxford: Rowman & Littlefield Publishers, Inc.

Blaut, James M. (1992) *The Colonizer's Model of the World: Geographical Diffusionism and Eurocentric History.* New York: The Guilford Press.

Brzezinski, Ziegniew and Mearsheimer, John L. (2005) "Clash of the Titans", *Foreign Policy*, (146): 46-49.

Cooper, Robert (1996) *The Post-Modern World Order*. London: Demos, 1996.

d'Encausse, Hélène Carrère and Schram, Stuart (1965) *Le Marxisme et l'Asie 1853-1964.* Paris: Armand Colin.

Engels, Frederick (1853) "Engels to K. Kautsky" in Karl Marx and Friedrich Engels, *On Colonialism*. Moscow: Foreign Languages Publishing House.

Frank, Andre Gunder (1998) *ReOrient: Global Economy in the Asian Age.* Berkeley, CA: University of California Press.

Freeman, Chas W. (2006) "*Mao Zedong: Nationalist In Spite Of Himself*", remarks to the SAIS China Forum, available at http://www.mepc.org/whats/MaoZedong.asp.

Fukuyama, Francis (1989) "The End of History?", *The National Interest*, 16: 3-18.

Fukuyama, Francis (2005) "The Calvinist Manifesto", *The New York Times*, March 5.

Gilpin, Robert (1987) *The Political Economy of International Relations*. Princeton, New Jersey: Princeton University Press.

Glyn, Andrew (2006) *Capitalism Unleashed: Finance, Globalization, and Welfare.* New York: Oxford University Press.

Goldstone, Jack A. (1998) "The Problem of the 'Early Modern' World", *Journal of the Economic and Social History of the Orient*, 41(3): 249-284.

Harvey, David (2005) *A Brief History of Neoliberalism.* New York: Oxford University Press.

Heilbroner, Robert L. (1995) "The Nature of Economics", *Challenge*, 38: 22-26.

Hersh, Jacques (1993) *The USA and the Rise of East Asia Since 1945.* London: Macmillan Press Ltd; New York: St. Martin's Press.

Hersh, Jacques (1977) "Some Problems Concerning the Concept of Asiatic Mode of Production", *Marxistisk Anthropologi*, 3(1): 31-52.

Huntington, Samuel (1994) "Watch Out for China", *Newsweek*, November 21.

Jacques, Martin (2009) *When China Rules the World: The Rise of the Middle Kingdom and the End of the Western World.* London: Allen Lane.

Johnson, Chalmers (1982) *MITI and the Japanese Miracle*. Stanford: Standford University Press.

Johnson, Chalmers (1988) "The Political Institutions and Economic Performance: The Government-Business Relationship in Japan, South Korea and Taiwan", in Deyo, Fredric C. 1988, *The Political Economy of the New Asian Industrialism.* Ithaca and New York: Cornell University Press.

Koo, Hagen (1988) "The Interplay of State, Social Class, and World System in East Asian Development: The Cases of South Korea and Thailand", in Deyo, Fredric 1988, *The Political Economy of the New Asian Industrialism.* Ithaca and New York: Cornell University Press.

Lach, Donald F. and Kley, Edwin J. van (1965) *Asia in the Making of Europe.* Chicago: University of Chicago Press.

Li, Minqi (2008) *The Rise of China and the Demise of the Capitalist World Economy.* London: Pluto Press and New York: Monthly Review Press.

List, Friedrich (1977) *The National System of Political Economy.* Fairfield: Augustus M. Kelly.

Liu, Henry C.K. (2007) "China's Misguided 'Experts' on the US", *Asia Times Online*, May 1, available at http://www.atimes.com/atimes/China/IE02Ad01.html.

Luxemburg, Rosa (1972) *The Accumulation of Capital – An Anti-Critique.* New York: Monthly Review Press.

Mao, Zedong (1957) "The East Wind Prevails Over the West Wind", available at http://www.marxists.org/reference/archive/mao/selected-works/volume-7/mswv7_480.htm.

Marx, Karl and Engels, Friedrich (1958) "Manifesto of the Communist Party", *Selected Works in Two Volumes*, Volume I. Moscow: Foreign Languages Publishing House.

Marx, Karl (n.d.) "Revolution in China and in Europe", in K. Marx and F. Engels, n.d. *On Colonialism.* Moscow: Foreign Language Publishing House.

Mearsheimer, John L. (2006) "China's Unpeaceful Rise", *Current History*, 105(690).

Moore, Barrington, Jr. (1966) *Social Origins of Dictatorship and Democracy.* Boston: Beacon Press Books.

Nee, Victor and Peck, James (eds.) (1975) *China's Uninterrupted Revolution.* New York: Pantheon Books.

Needham, Joseph and Wang Ling (1954) *Science and Civilization in China, Vol. 1.* London: Cambridge University Press.

Norman, E. Herbert (1975) *Origins of the Modern Japanese State: Selected Writings of E.H. Norman*, edited by John W. Dower. New York: Random House.

Ramo, Joshua (2004) *The Beijing Consensus*. London: The Foreign Policy Centre.

Ramonet, Ignacio (2006) "Mégapuissance", *Manière de voir*, 85, February-March.

Safire, William (1993) *Safire's Political Dictionary*. New York: Random House.

Shanin, Teodor (1983) *The Late Marx and the Russian Road – Marx and the 'Peripheries of Capitalism'*. New York: Monthly Review Press.

Simmons, Colin (1985) "'De-Industrialization', Industrialization, and the Indian Economy, c. 1850-1947", *Modern Asian Studies*, 19(3): 593-622.

Smith, Adam (1937) *The Wealth of Nations*. New York: Random House / (1982) *The Wealth of Nations*. Harmondsworth, Middlesex: Penguin Books.

Stockwin, James Arthur A. (1999) *Governing Japan – Divided Politics in a Major Economy*. Malden, MA: Blackwell Publishers.

Strange, Susan (1970) "International Economics and International Relations: A Case of Mutual Neglect", *International Affairs*, 46(2): 304-315.

Thorner, Daniel (1971) "Peasant Economy as a Category in Economic History", in Teodor Shanin (ed.) *Peasants and Peasant Societies*. Harmondsworth: Penguin.

Wallerstein, Immanuel (2004) "China and the US: Competing Geopolitical Strategies", *Commentary* No. 151, December 15, available at http://www.binghamton.edu/fbc/151en.htm.

Wittfogel, Karl (1957) *Oriental Despotism: A Comparative Study of Total Power.* New Haven: Yale University Press.

Chapter 2
The Myths and Realities of the Rising Powers: Is China a Threat to the Existing World Order?

Mammo Muchie and Li Xing

Introduction: The Context and Discussion

Historically world orders have been characterized by a succession of powerful states rising up to reorganize the international system. No world power can last forever, and long-term shift in the accumulation and distribution of power gives rise to new emerging states, that want to translate their newly acquired supremacy into reshaping the established rules of game in the international system in line with their own interests. Throughout the 20th century, the world witnessed the rise and fall of great powers. The endurance of some of world powers was rather short, for example, Germany, Japan, and the Soviet Union. History also shows that the transition of power shift has never been smooth but rather brutal due to the fear of declining powers in losing their control and to their anxiety about the security implications of their weakened position. In the aftermath of the rise of China, the current worldwide debate is on the future of the United States – the superpower and the main architect of the post-war world order.

Since the advent of the 21st century the world is witnessing the emergence of a new great power. China is now recognized as a global rising power. There is a clear indication of a global economic and political power shift brought about by the rise of China, and the awareness is becoming more intense in most recent years in the Western world (Bergsten, et al., 2008; Gu and Frank, 2006; Kynge, 2006; Lampton, 2008; MacDonald, et al., 2009; Möckli, 2007; Ross and Feng, 2008; Shambaugh, 2006). So far China's significant economic success has made its economic impact felt worldwide in a range of areas such as foreign direct investment, commodity price, international trade, regional integration, international relations, etc. Beijing's policies on finance, currency, trade, military security, environment issues, resource management, food security, raw material and commodity prices are connected with the economies and well-being of millions of people outside China's boundary. China's shifts in supply and demand cause changes in prices leading to adjustment in other countries. Most international economic institutions and some analysts project that China will replace the United States and become the leading economy in the span of a couple of decades. As a result, China is increasingly seen as an "indispensable country" like the United States in previous years (Feffer, 2007). Given China's sheer physical, economic and population size as well as its long and rich civilization, the magnitude of the rise of China is viewed with a deep sense of uncertainty and worry.

A global power shift implies some implicit and explicit transformations within the existing world order (Hoge, 2004). As a result, it is assumed that rising powers are demanding more decision-making power in global affairs, and established powers are having difficulties in accommodating the demands. The eventual consequences of these transformations are not easy to predict. Although China's commitment to a peaceful rise has become its national project and ideal, and despite the fact that the rise of China seems to be an indisputable reality, consensus on the approach and future of the nation's ascent has yet to be reached by the world established powers.

This recognition of China's rise has given rise to various debates and disputes regarding possible threats, because in the terminology of international relations, the notion of "rise" entails a potential change of hegemony or transfer of power. In spite of a growing interdependence between China and the rest of the World, there is still an alarmist agitation by some scholars, journalists, policy-makers, and pundits in the West, translating the rise of China into a looming threat for the world order (Bernstein and Munro, 1997; Carpenter, 2005; Kasplan, 2005; Kegan, 1997 and 2005; Krauthammer, 1995; Mearsheimer, 2006). As a result, various "China threat" theories have emerged in the process of China's upsurge, such as ideological threat, economic threat, environmental threat, energy threat, food threat, technological threat, development model threat, and last but not least, the most worrisome, military threat. To many Americans, China represents the central challenge to the core of American hegemony and way of life. China has been described as the "strongest intentional illiberal state on this planet" (White III, 2007: 11). The pessimistic views assert that the rise of China cannot be peaceful or non-threatening to the current status of the established powers of the existing world order. This notion of China-threat instigates containment rather than engagement policy, which if pursued, could become a self fulfilling prophecy.

The various China-threat theories have a common assumption that, when an emerging state becomes economically wealthier and militarily more powerful, it will inevitably seek greater global political influence, which will cause the change of global power structure. Hence, the real challenge to the existing world order is: is there any opportunity open for the 21st century late-comers – growing powers that are emerging largely outside the established post-war Western international order, such as China, Russia, India and Brazil – to gain global economic and political prominence and to join the club of great powers without violence? That possibility exists in theory because historical lessons seem to be less convincing. In reality, it is hard to predict the real calculation of the established powers to the rising powers despite some kinds of symbolic acceptance of international political and economic rearrangements, such as the so-called "G2" or "G20" – formal and informal international dialogue platforms.

The main objective of this chapter is to offer a framework for understanding the regional and global impacts of the rising powers and the economic, political and social implications for the established world order. It aims at getting to the bottom of how the contradictory forces with diverse interests, views and beliefs try to shape the world, and how the ordering, disordering and re-ordering logic is expressed in the dynamics of the rise and fall of great powers. In order to do so it is necessary to gain a good conceptualization of how the existing world order was created, and how it is currently ruled or misruled. The conclusion is that China's emergence will, on the one hand, unavoidably generate power shift and shape the international order in new ways, but on the other hand, help construct a new type of balance of power in world politics based on multilateralism and institutionalism.

The Existing World Order: Hegemony and Discontents

Historically, world orders or reorders have always resulted from the disordering dynamics unleashed in the context and nexus of the rise of new powers and the resistance of established powers. There are still different views regarding whether the power transition from the United Kingdom to the United States was a peaceful one (Feng, 2006), apart from the fact that this power transition took place within the western order. The evolution of a new world order has never been a smooth and peaceful process. Rare are the historical accounts where world hegemonic leadership was attained without some forms of violence injected in the process. As Guo remarks,

> In world history, no major power has risen "peacefully". From the early colonial powers Spain and Britain, to late industrializers, Germany and Japan, all new powers fought their way to their power status. "The history of the United States is the history of confrontation, even conflict, with the other great powers of the earth", first with Britain and France in the 19th century and then with Germany, Japan, and then Russia in the 20th century, not to mention many wars fought by proxy. (Guo, 2006: 3-4)

The Hegemony of the Post-War World Order

In the aftermath of World War II, American objectives were to support the capacity and sustainability of its superpower and hegemony through three global strategies: 1) *the construction of a capitalist world system*: setting up the Bretton Woods system of international trade liberalization, stable currencies, and expanding global economic interdependence; 2) *the creation of a global/regional collective security*: forming an American-European-Asian military alliance to resist and block the expansion of communism; and 3) *the strengthening of international trade regime*: consolidating an Eurasia-centered global trade network.

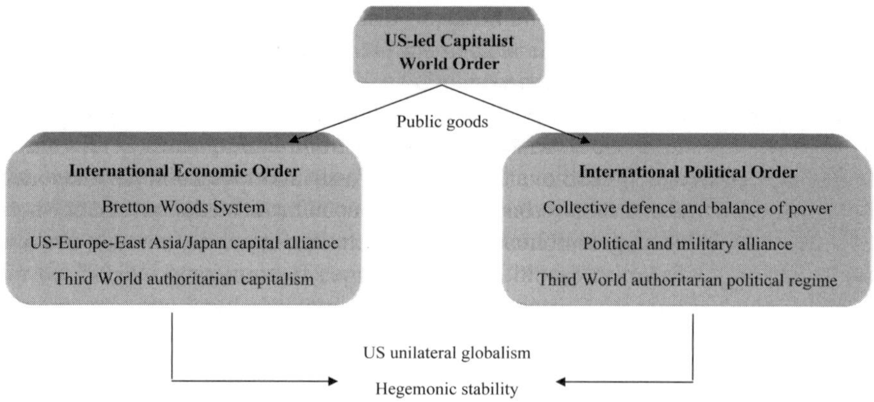

Figure 2.1 The post-war world economic and political order under the US hegemony

The role of the United States during this period was to assume the responsibility of hegemonic stabilizer of the international system and to create the full development of a liberal world market through "providing global public goods in the form of security, opposition to communism, aid for economic development, and the strengthening of international institutions" (Huntington, 1999: 42). This unilateral globalism was later theorized as hegemonic stability theory set out by Charles Kindleberger (1973) and further developed by Robert Gilpin (1987) and substantially reviewed by Julia Schubert (2003).

It is commonly recognized that the United States shaped the post-war world order and had been the benevolent hegemon who bore most of the costs and public goods for maintaining the mode of production of the capitalist world system, and meanwhile who also reaped most of the benefits. Understanding that its own prosperity was tightly bound to the functioning of the global system and the success of its allied countries, the United States was willing to maintain the security and prosperity of other partner nations. This can be seen from the American historical roles in the Bretton Woods System, and so on.

The Post-Cold War "New World Order"

Following the end of the Cold War with the demise of the Soviet Union and with the evolution of China into the logic of capital accumulation becoming "a rationally authoritarian state that observed more or less normal rules of international relations", the Washington-centered alliance system lost both its compelling rationale and legitimacy (Pfaff, 2001: 227). These transformations raised some fundamental questions to the United States: how to maintain the US-centered core structure in the post-Cold War world system (Schwenninger, 1999)?[1] What is the supporting pillar for a continuing United States-led security network in the Triad (North America – Europe – Japan) when the former enemies are disappearing? Which is the new political force after the USSR (including Russia itself) that can be identified as the threat to the US "New World Order"? (Kagan and Kristol, 2000). It can be argued that the United States after the Cold War was facing a world perceived by three different ideologies: 1) the idealism of the "End of history" by Francis Fukuyama (1992), 2) the realism of the "Clash of Civilizations" by Samuel Huntington (1993), and 3) the unilateralism of the "New World Order" by the two Bush Administrations. Their common logic is to perpetuate US global predominance and contain any potential threat.

The real picture was that the United States after the Cold War was confronting a world order in both Kautsky's and Lenin's understanding. Kautsky believed that international relations were determined by what he referred to the "inter-capitalist class", whereas Lenin perceived international relations as competition among states and the relationship between capitalism and international relations was irreconcilably contradictory. Thus, American political and economic policies in the post-Cold War era were aimed at managing global affairs based on a hybrid of Kautsky's and Lenin's analyses: on the one hand, the United States "aimed at the unified, liberalized international capitalist community Kautsky envisioned", and on the other hand, "the global role that the United States has undertaken to sustain that community is determined by a worldview very close to Lenin's (Schwarz, 1996: 100). In the view of Kagan and Kristol the hard-won hegemonic position which the United States enjoyed after the Cold War must be defended at all costs because

> Today's international system is built not around a balance of power but around American hegemony. The international financial institutions were fashioned by Americans and serve American interests. The international security structures are chiefly a collection of American-led alliances. What Americans like to call international "norms" are really reflections of American and West European principles. Since today's relatively benevolent international circumstances are the product of our hegemonic influence, any lessening of that influence will allow others to play a larger part in shaping the world to suit their needs. States such as China and Russia, if given the chance, would configure the international system quite differently. (Kagan and Kristol, 2000: 61)

1 The strategic objective of American foreign policy during the Cold War was not so much to battle a communist threat as to defend gross inequalities in the core–semi-periphery–periphery structure of the capitalist world system and the tremendous privilege and power this global disparity of wealth brought for the United States (Robinson, 1995). The key concern for the United States in the post-Cold War era is how to structurally maintain the key features of the existing world capitalist system.

The United States soon had to engage in two-front economic conflicts with both Europe and East Asia (Bergsten, 2001). The fading of the Soviet threat together with the increasing transnationalization and multipolarization of the world economy largely reduced the vital role of the American security umbrella over Europe and Asia. As a result of these developments, "The security glue that traditionally encouraged the post-war allies to resolve their economic differences no longer exists" (Bergsten, ibid.: 21), and their differences in bilateral or multilateral economic issues as well as global and regional security and environment concerns mattered more than their traditional alliance.[2] The United States intended to, in a gradual unilateral approach, safeguard the new post-Cold War order at any cost including military interventions. Washington's new security paradigm was in close interaction with its global economic interest, and was designed to deter any challenge and resistance, be it popular resistance, state collapse, inter-state and inter-ethnic conflicts, regional instability, economic crisis, "rogue states" and emerging superpowers,[3] that would cause disfunctioning of the existing system.

The coinage of the "new world order" of the two Bush administrations did not entail any essential change in the core features and hierarchies of the post-war international order that were constructed and dominated by the Post-World War II victors with the United States as the hegemonic leader. Put differently, the Cold War stalemate from 1945-1989 did not fundamentally change the world order, so the new world order after the Cold War failed to become any "newer". On the contrary, what appeared to have emerged was the danger to the planet in terms of the possibility of its incineration or extinction that was heightened by the lessening commitment to international norms and regulations by the US hegemonic power. The latter displayed numerous unilateral conducts that can give a license paradoxically to various groups and states that resent American hegemony for a variety of reasons. The manner by which the United States showed disrespect to the UN system and international law by waging war in Iraq can also be seen to imply to others that they can follow suit. This has the unintended consequence of creating ethical anarchy

2 These conflicts cover a number of regional and global issues: America–EU conflict over European import restrictions on American beef and bananas; EU's anger at US sanctions again European firms that trade with Washington's enemies such as Cuba and Iran; America's negative position on European plans for an autonomous military force; EU and Asia's irritation about Washington's antagonistic approach to North Korea and Cuba, its arrogant attitude towards Russia and China, and its unilateral proposals for a missile defense system; and their frustration over Bush Administration's irresponsibility in refusing to sign and implement the global environmental agreement.

3 There is little, if any, evidence in support of such an argument that the NMD is aimed at a nuclear-missile-armed Iran, Iraq or North Korea that might blackmail the United States in the future conflicts. In effect, this mission seeks to deny emerging missile states and especially China's nuclear deterrence against US conventional action. It is widely understood that the NMD is targeted more at China, an emerging superpower, than those so-called "rogue states" (Marshall, 2000: 3).

rather than moral strength to observe norms, rules, procedures and institutional integrity in international public life.

The Post-9/11 "World Disorder"

The post-9/11 world disorder was precisely the consequence of the hostility of the Bush Administration towards the multilateral, rule-based international system that the United States has shaped and led. The Bush Administration shaped world politics in terms of making the pursuit against terrorists become a self-defined feature of global politics: "Our war on terror ... will not end until every terrorist group of global reach has been found, stopped and defeated" (Bush as quoted in Hastedt and Knickrehm, 2003: 9).

It appears that those "terrorists" or "rogue states" that fought US power found the US Government exactly where they wanted it: the country had to continue to be preoccupied with trying to identify any "act of terror". American policy-makers designated terrorist acts as if they were wars waged by states. They declared what they called the global war on terrorism. This escalation provided terrorists with brand names to commit more acts of terror. As a consequence, far from getting a climate of peace and security in the post-Cold War period, the world confronted a peace penalty situation where the whole world turned into a vast guerrilla theatre, and where those individuals or groups, who chose to do so, could operate using the facilities and conveniences of the information and technology revolution. This has changed the norms of war and the places where wars had been fought during the Cold War period. The 9/11 Twin Towers attack in New York showed that no power on earth is immune from terrorism. Global battle arenas can easily be transferred from being fought in the geographical areas of what used to be described as the "Third World" to encompassing literally the whole world including the financial and political hubs of the central hegemonic powers themselves.

Potential Forces for World Re-order

At the moment, there are three possible reordering thrusts that can be identified in the world. The first is reordering world order from below. That is, the World Social Forum and other forms of social movements and civil society organizations, united with similar concerns, would like to claim that another new world order is possible. They argue that the globalization process driven and spearheaded by business, commerce and finance is not inevitable. They mount protests against the global ordering institutions such as WTO, IMF and WB and others. They assert that through anti-globalization actions they wish to reach the poor and the marginalized, and to raise their voice and participation. But this remains yet to be translated into concrete action.

The second is reordering the world through globalization from above, the hegemonic center based in North America and Western Europe with the United

States as the primary leader. The main actors are states, global elite classes and business networks, and they are to seek and form alliance by entering into international arrangements to protect their interests and security, and to create the political economy of reforming, but not disrupting, the existing global order. This state–business alliance appears to support the worldview that through appropriate policies those that are excluded may become included through the provision of the public goods of security and through the benefits of commerce under a liberal global economic system. That is what the World Economic Forum has been advocating as opposed to the World Social Forum.

The third is the rise of China, Russia, India, Brazil and other rising powers with China as the central focus. The controversy has boiled down to this: whether to recognize, engage and accommodate China or fight this rising power by spreading fear, disengagement, surveillance and demonization. Today China cannot be ignored or avoided, and it has an indispensable role in global affairs more so now than at any time in its long history. During the past decade, Russia has also re-emerged as a global power with an ambition to retain its power status by formulating the "near-abroad" policy to keep influence in the former Soviet Union areas. India and Brazil are clearly on their way to becoming the next generation of regional and global powers.

The Rise of China and the Implications for World Order

World history from 1500 to 1945 showed that the rise and fall of the great powers had always been accompanied by rivalries, conflicts and wars (Kennedy, 1989). Seen from the comparative perspective of historical analogy, the rise of China is seen to be equivalent to the late 19th-century rise of Germany (Krauthammer, 1995). Both the rise of Germany and Japan triggered world disorder leading to the two world wars. The rise of China has been interpreted by the realists that China will inevitably try to use its growing influence to reshape the rules and institutions of the international system to meet its own interests; and other declining states will naturally see China as a growing security threat. As some scholars denote the far-reaching significance regarding what they identify as the dramatic transition from a world long dominated by the "Westphalia" system to a forthcoming world dominated by the "Eastphalia", "The question is no longer *if* the rise of China, India, and Asia will affect world politics. The question is *how* the migration of power and influence towards Asia will change global affairs and the nations and people affected by these dramatic shifts" (Kim, et al., 2009: 53).

The Rise of China and its Discontents

In recent years much western media has neatly illustrated an irony admitted by the mainstream opinions and by many western governments: communist China could save capitalism – a desperate wish to expect China's assistance to resolve the world's recession caused by the current global financial crisis.

Thus, what worries the West is not necessarily China's "economic rise" because the rise of the Chinese economy is also seen to bring about potential opportunities. Rather, the "political impact" brought about by the economic rise of China is the issue of concern. The "Chinese model", which is embedded with specific historical dimensions, unique cultural elements and assertive ideological discourses, is increasingly becoming attractive to the developing world. It is particularly attractive to many developing countries in terms of how to manage state–market–society relations and political economy in international relations. The Chinese development model is recently termed as the "Beijing Consensus" (Ramo, 2004), a notion coined with distinct attitudes to politics, development and the global balance of power. It is driven by China's more than three-decade success in economic development with relative political stability, by a determined ambition to find an alternative development path, by maintaining a strong role of the state for development and sovereignty and global multilateralism, and by a strategy to accumulate the tools of "asymmetric power projection", i.e. how to achieve and maintain power in an asymmetric power relation to superpowers and to transnational capitals.

In this context, a recent focus of "China threat" is related to China's active engagement in investment and trade with Africa, Latin America and other developing countries. China's strong presence and engagement in Africa has provoked much debate and discussion (Alden, 2007, 2008; Manji and Marks, 2007; Prah, 2007), and it has sent worrying signals to the United States and the former colonial powers in Europe. What worries them most is the transmission of the "Beijing Consensus" into these regions.

Another negative picture portraying the rise of China is its imminent military threat followed by its increase in military budget and rapid defense modernization. According to the Western source, China's military budget increased by 17.8 percent in 2007 (*BBC*, March 4, 2007) and a similar budget of 17.6 percent rise, which was $59 billion in 2008 (*Washington Post*, March 5, 2008). China's ascendency in military capacities is argued to be a serious menace to the regional balance of power in East Asia and to America's global dominance in military and strategic influence. Analysts and Pentagon sources allege the modernization of the Chinese military is a threat to the USA including China's increasing military expenditure and its producing weapons that give it capability to project global military reach. The most recent assessment by the US Defense Department's on China's military power portrays it as a potential military rival of the United States claiming that Beijing could one day try to dominate Asia or challenge US hegemony (Council on Foreign Relations, 2003, 2006).

Thus, many realists and opinion-makers predict an eventual China–West conflict on the basis of the historical lessons that the rapid growth of the economy of a rising power has often triggered enormous, often disruptive transformations both internally and externally. The established world powers are still struggling to acknowledge the trend that China will eventually become a "responsible stakeholder" in the capitalist world system, a system in which China is already highly integrated, and from which China is seen as enjoying substantial benefits. It is expected that the rise of China and its development model will unavoidably have to absorb and adjust to hardcore external challenges and constraints from the way the world economy undulates periodically with global business, economic and financial cyclical behaviors patterned by upturns and downturns and booms and busts.

A non-mainstream and somewhat radical approach in assessing China's ascent, which is inspired by the Marxist theory on capital accumulation and class struggles and the analysis of the World System Theory, is to see the rise of China in the historical context of the evolution of world systems. According to the view and analysis of Li Minqi (Li 2008), the rise of the European capitalist world economy to global dominance in the 19th century coincided with the decline and demise of the historical supremacy of the Chinese empire. Then, the interesting question is, will the rise of China as a new global power turn out to coincide with the decline and demise of the capitalist world economy in the 21st century? In contrary to the general consensus that China's ascent will help further strengthen and expand the existing capitalist world economy, Li Minqi argues that the rise of China is a recurrent historical process that is contributing to the demise of the existing global capitalist system. According to this interpretation, China is the last paradise on earth for the geographical expansion of the capitalist world economy that will reach its final limit.

The Rise of China and the Existing Superpower

Currently, many unanswered questions are still floating in the minds of many US politicians: what is the implication of the rise of China to the existing world order and the shared norms and values? What will China do with its accumulated capabilities and resources? How will China influence the positions, interests, and policies of the established powers and especially the remaining superpower, the United States? How will such an implication play out in reality?

The American strategic object and policy in the 21st century, which is explicitly expressed in the "Defense Planning Guidance for Fiscal Years 1994-1999", aims to "maintain the mechanisms for deterring potential competitors from even aspiring to a larger regional or global role" (as quoted in Klare, 2000: 10). The willingness and determination to use force to intervene selectively on the basis of American interests is another import component of this report. The original text of the Defense Planning Guidance contains such a formulation, "While the US cannot become the world's 'policeman', assuming responsibility for righting every wrong, we will retain the preeminent responsibility for addressing selectively those wrongs which threaten not only our interests, but those of our allies or friends, or which could seriously unsettle international relations" (as quoted in Klare, 2000: 11).

The above implication is that if American leadership is good for the world, any opposition to it entails opposing what is not only good for America but also for the world; and any new power that appears to contest or is even perceived to contest US authority is likely to be condemned. China threat theories demonizing China's rise with Chinese "malice and dishonesty" have been spawned with hysterical condemnations (Al-Rodhan, 2007). The assumption is that China is unlikely to have a peaceful and benevolent rise to great power status, and if it reaches a superpower status, it will be a threat to the established order. Particularly the Neo-conservatives have been very shrill in portraying the rise of China as a menace to world peace. This is how Robert Kegan puts it: "The Chinese leadership views the world in much the same way Kaiser Wilhelm I did a century ago. Chinese leaders chafe at the constraints on them and worry that they must change the rules of the international system before the international system changes them" (Kegan, 1997: 3).

The American neo-conservative reactions demonstrate the ideological and psychological inability to make US foreign policy open to accommodate late-comers. China threat theories defy the notion of China's possible peaceful rise. Again Robert Kegan claims, "The history of rising powers … and their attempted 'management' by established powers provides little reason for confidence or comfort. Rarely have rising powers risen without sparking a major war that reshaped the international system to reflect new realities of power" (Kegan, 2005). What the neo-conseravatives attempt to imply is that, if the status quo of the existing order is not to be altered, there is no vacancy for any rising powers – America is the occupier. That is why the neo-conservatives are ringing the alarm bells – "the wolf is coming".

In recent years China finds itself to be a "middle kingdom" surrounded by jealousy, admiration, anxiety, worry and even resentment by the neo-conservative forces. China is deeply alert over issues like sovereignty and national unity because it watched how the United States saw off the former USSR by the disintegration of the latter into 15 new states – a similar outcome would have been wished to take place in China as well! It is not only the neo-conservatives, but also senior politicians of different US administrations who corroborate the picture of a possible Chinese threat. Robert Zeoellick, the current President of the World Bank, expressed the fear of American public, "Many Americans worry that the Chinese dragon will prove to be a fire-breather. There is a cauldron of anxiety about China" (quoted in Al-Rodhan, 2007: 43). Condoleezza Rice, the then Secretary of State, also added her voice to the China threat theory, "China is still a potential threat to stability in the Asia Pacific region … China is not a status quo power, but one that would like to alter Asia's balance of power in its own favor. That alone makes it a strategic competitor and not a strategic partner" (Rice, 2000: 56). Selective American public opinions in the past years showed that "China threat" became a focus of national anxiety: in 2005, 31 percent of American people believed that China would soon dominate the world, and 54 percent believed that the emergence of China as a superpower was a threat to world peace (public opinion survey quoted by Al-Rodhan , 2007: 43). In a February 2006 Pew poll, 47 percent of Americans said that China's emergence as a world power was a threat to the well-being of the United States.

It appears that the pendulum may be reversing from neo-conservative distrust and mistrust of China to the democrat willingness to invite China to be a strategic partner. The new Obama Administration is not only bringing back the Clinton doctrine of building strategic partnership with China but also further strengthening the role of the China–US Strategic and Economic Dialogue (S&ED). However, the irony of history also shows that both major conflicts *and* major break-throughs in China–US relations – honeymoons and divorces – took place during some Republican administrations.

The Embedded Rise of China Within the Existing World Order

According to the World System Theory (Wallerstein, 1974a, 1974b), 1) the history of the capitalist world system recurrently exhibits the cyclical rhythms resulted in regular slow-moving but significant geographical shifts in accumulation and power; and 2) the cycles consist of the rise and decline of successive guarantors of global order, each one with its particular pattern of control; 3) the resolution of the systemic crisis of accumulation has often involved a change in the leadership of the world-scale processes of capital accumulation. The rise of China can be interpreted as part of the cyclical rhythms, but is still confined by the system's fundamental logic of capital accumulation.

While the proponents of China-threat theories emphasize the harmful consequence of China's power accumulation, the opponents point out the fact that the rise of China is generated from within and embedded in the existing capitalist world system. The approach of China's economic development and the pattern of its growth increasingly resemble the East Asian NICs model – deepening structural relations with Western industrial countries and dependence on foreign trade, investments and financing. The market-driven growth encourages more concessions to induce capital flows and growth and expansion and more structural changes to meet the demand of the overwhelming pursuit of external markets and resources. In addition, deep integration with the world market is followed by the over-dependence of its productive forces on the fluctuations of the world market. Today the centrality of China's national development policy is to define China's interest largely in terms of social mobility for wealth accumulation within the hierarchy of the world economy, i.e. achieving the production level and approaching the living standard of advanced Western countries. China's criteria for assessing development progress are production, profit, and wealth accumulation rather than class struggle and political ideology. The new national development orientation is redirected at extending and deepening external relations with industrial capitalist states and yielding internal politics to global competition.

To some scholars, it is precisely because the Chinese economy has been fully integrated in the world economy that the country has become a beneficiary of the existing international institutional order, and that it possesses an interest in maintaining and consolidating this order. Accordingly, China's emergence need not lead to a negative struggle for global dominance. If China were to shift the course and seek to undermine the status quo, then it would face a collective resistance from the stakeholders of the system as a whole. The existing international system has some unique resilient and entrenched characteristics based on a set of rules and institutions that is "hard to overturn and easy to join":

> The postwar Western order is historically unique. Any international order dominated by a powerful state is based on a mix of coercion and consent, but the US-led order is distinctive in that it has been more liberal than imperial – and so unusually accessible, legitimate, and durable ... It is expansive, with a wide and widening array of participants and stakeholders. It is capable of generating tremendous economic growth and power while also signaling restraint – all of which make it hard to overturn and easy to join ... [the postwar western order] is built around rules and norms of nondiscrimination and market openness, creating conditions for rising states to advance their expanding economic and political goals within it. ... China has already discovered the massive economic returns that are possible by operating within this open-market system. (Ikenberry, 2008)

The on-going economic relationship between China and the United States in the current era of global financial crisis demonstrates the intense interdependency between the two countries and the imperativeness that the United States must seek to "rebalance relations with China" due to the emerging "paradigm shift" in the Pacific in the last 30 years. In the words of Henry Kissinger, the architect of China–US relations:

> According to conventional wisdom, the world economy will regain its vitality once China consumes more and America consumes less. But as both countries apply that prescription, it will inevitably alter the political framework. As Chinese exports to America decline and China shifts the emphasis of its economy to greater consumption and to increased infrastructure spending, a different economic order will emerge. China will be less dependent on the American market, while the growing dependence of neighboring countries on Chinese markets will increase China's political influence. Political cooperation, in shaping a new world order, must increasingly compensate for the shift in trade patterns. (Kissinger, *Washington Post*, August 19, 2009)

The view that China's success is conditioned and constrained by its deep integration in the global economy is also shared by many other scholars (Shaw and Shaun, 2007), who argue that China's "power" in the global political economy has to be understood from the relationship between China's internal configurations of power and globalized production processes that shape the process and implications of its re-engagement with the global economy and politics. The rise of China is not an easy process, rather, it has been, and will be, highly constrained and shaped by domestic and international contradictions (Hart-Landsberg and Burkett, 2004a, 2004b).

Arguing against the pessimistic views about the rise of China, Chinese government and scholars in recent years are promoting the notion of "peaceful rise" or "peaceful development" in order to emphasize its soft power and characterize China as a responsible world leader (Guo, 2006; PRC, 2005; Zheng, 2005). The Chinese self-claimed "peaceful rise" is arguably winning international recognition on the basis of Beijing's foreign policies and performances in the past decade: its role in promoting regional integration, its involvement in economic development of developing countries, its multilateralism at the United Nations and other international organization, its fight for fairness in the WTO for the developing world, its leadership in promoting regional security through the Shanghai Cooperation Organization in central Asia, its emergence in international aid and development assistance. Despite the China threat theories, China is widely recognized as one of the key contributors to global and regional economic growth, and to international trade and the recovery of the on-going financial crisis.

The basic tenets of the international system today can be traced back to and are rooted in the Westphalian system of international relations – a horizontal system of sovereign states, where balance of power was favored, and the nature of domestic political, economic and social issues was not a concern of international relations. Today, it is generally recognized that China is one of the strongest defenders of the historically West-based Westphalian system. China firmly stands for the principle of sovereign equality and non-intervention in internal affairs despite the "end of history" thesis and the transformation of international political economy in the post-Cold War era.

However, in some international areas, China also sees the imperative trend and transition to a more transnational and multinational features of the post-Cold War order brought about the expansion of capital and economic integration around the world. China has taken a proactive stance on bilateral and multilateral cooperation in both economic and security issues. The WTO is a global rule-setting institution that is being pushed by the new world order to unify global capitalism while dismantling other types of economic system. It is an institution that goes beyond the Westphalian system and has a supranational legal power. But relying on a strong state that has the capacity to control the macro economic stability and policy-making independence, China is seen as a winner benefiting greatly from its WTO membership.

Concluding Remarks: Same Bed, Different Dreams?

The rise of China and other emerging powers represents one of the key driving forces of global political, economic and social change. Given the enormity of their potential impact on global politics and economy, they represent a structural challenge to social scientific understanding with outcomes likely to be of importance to the understanding of world order.

With the onset of globalization and the rise of new powers like the BRIC (Brazil, Russia, India and China), the concern of global reorder has become a hot issue for debate. The question of how rising powers and established powers can co-evolve and accommodate each other is part of the on-going discourse of the time. Established powers stress threats from rising powers, while conversely rising powers may feel slighted that they are not taken seriously by established powers. Albeit some of the constructive voices of promoting partnership, the dominant narrative nevertheless remains, emphasizing threat and mistrust.

The voices from the rising powers are mixed, but they also have similarities. The new rising powers would like to construct a global governance system that recognizes and acknowledges their status. They argue and call for a "new world order" founded on multilateralism and the functioning of the UN while avoiding the temptation to create "coalitions of the willing" based on unilateral actions by the established powers.

The possible evolutions of world order are three-fold: 1) the continuation of the existing order with the established powers resisting the inclusion of new rising powers. This option is likely to exacerbate conflict possibilities; 2) the rising powers recognize the fact that the established powers will not permit their inclusion to shape a global reorder and then they will have to go their own way by establishing their own alliances. This is likely to trigger strong resistance by the established powers; 3) the acceptance of co-evolution where rising and established powers agree to uphold global governance as paramount.

The rise of China will inevitably set up a "China wing" of the new world order. Those who fear China's ascent project a malevolent dragon out to beat and swallow the eagle. If such a threatening image became policy-making rationale by the established powers, China could be cornered into a position where it may have no option but to resist this constraint on its desire to grow prosperous and join the community of developed economies. China should not be framed with either malevolent or benevolent imaging or character. Both of China's hard and soft powers must not be either demonized or exaggerated (Jiang, 2002). It is an emergent and transitional economy with a very large economic size, population, production and market sizes, that can be harnessed to a win-win outcome provided the world is willing to risk engaging with China and understand and respect Chinese patriotism as clearly expressed by the modern founder of Chinese nationalism Dr. Sun Yatsen. There is no doubt as Sun-Yat-Sen said that China could become a superpower if it were not distracted by other concerns. Sun was convinced that China would not do what others did when it achieved power and prosperity, i.e., become imperialistic and militaristic. He also said that China should share its prosperity with those that went through historical humiliation like itself before (Sun, 1999).

It seems the Chinese leadership is doing what their first nationalist leader envisioned – a united and prosperous nation. What should be received positively by the established power is the fact that China has been continuing to advocate and stick to "peaceful rise". Some American strategists see the trend of China's development and suggest a China–US G2 structure, a special relationship like the UK-USA alliance. That is a very noble ambition, but the reality is that for that to take place, the imagination for the future world order should first require building and storing a mutual recognition of equal co-existence.

Given the interdependence of China with the rest of the world, it is not containment but engagement with China that can stabilize a new world order. The established powers should support reconfiguration of the global power architecture to incorporate China into the arrangement of both the development of shared international rules. China cannot be only a rule-follower, and it must be a rule-settler as well. There is a need for wisdom to change strategic confrontation into networks of renewed strategic partnerships across the globe, and China and other rising powers should be invited and welcomed to shaping this partnership for sustaining long-term global governance architecture. World order must be founded not only on balance of power with suspicion and mistrust remaining undiluted and in fact exacerbated, but also on a balance of justice and fairness in the rules of game of international relations.

It is still too early to predict whether China, the rising power, and the US and Europe, the existing powers, can not only sleep together but also have the same dream. Within the near future both will have to find a regional and global role which the other will accept and support. In order to do so both will have to go through a considerable period of struggle, adjustment and tension.

References

Alden, Christopher (2007) *China in Africa*. New York: Zed Books.

Alden, Chrisopher, Daniel Large and Ricardo Soares de Oliveira (2008) *China Returns to Africa: A Rising Power and a Continent Embrace: A Superpower and a Continent Embrace*. London: HURST Publishers Ltd.

Al-Rodhan, Khalid R. (2007) "A Critique of the China Threat Theory: A Systematic Analysis", *Asian Perspective*, 31(3): 41-66.

Bergsten, Fred C. (2001) "America's Two-Front Economic Conflict", *Foreign Affairs*, 80(2): 16-27.

Bergsten, Fred C., Charles Freeman, Nicholas R. Lardy and Derek J. Mitchell (2008) *China's Rise: Challenges and Opportunities*. Washington, D.C.: Peterson Institute for International Economics.

Bernstein, Richard and Munro, Ross H. (1997) *The Coming Conflict With China*. New York: Alfred A. Knopf.

Carpenter, Ted Galen (2005) *America's Coming War with China: A Collision Course over Taiwan*. New York: Palgrave Macmillan.

Council on Foreign Relations (2003) *Chinese Military Power*. Washington: Council on Foreign Relations Press

Council on Foreign Relations (2006) *The Scope of China's Military Threat*. Washington: Council on Foreign Relations Press, available at http://www.cfr.org/publication/10824/.

Feffer, John (2007) "China the Indispensable?" *Foreign Policy In Focus*, March 9, available at http://www.fpif.org/fpiftxt/4070.

Feng, Yongping (2006) "The Peaceful Transition of Power from the UK to the US", *The Chinese Journal of International Politics*, 1(1): 83-108.

Gilpin, Robert (1987) *The Political Economy of International Relations*. Princeton: Princeton University Press.

Gu, George Zhibin and Frank, Andre Gunder (2006) *China's Global Reach: Markets, Multinationals, and Globalization*. Palo Alto, CA: Fultus Corporation.

Guo, Sujian (2006) "Introduction: Challenges and Opportunities for China's 'Peaceful Rise'", in Guo Sujian (ed.) (2006) *China's Peaceful Rise in the 21st Century: Domestic and International Conditions*. Aldershot: Ashgate Publishing.

Guo, Sujian (ed.) (2006) *China's Peaceful Rise in the 21st Century: Domestic and International Conditions*. Aldershot: Ashgate Publishing.

Hart-Landsberg, Martin and Burkett, Paul (2004) "Contradictions of China's Transformation: Domestic", *Monthly Review*, 56(3): 55-79.

Hart-Landsberg, Martin and Burkett, Paul (2004) "Contradictions of China's Transformation: International", *Monthly Review*, 56(3): 81-108.

Hastedt, Glenn P. and Knickrehm, Kay M. (eds.) (2003) *International Politics in a Changing World*. New York: Longman Publishers.

He, Wenping (2007) "All-Weather Friend: The Evolution of China's Africa Policy", in Kwsi Kwaa Prah (ed.) *Afro-Chinese Relations: Past, Present and Future*. Cape Town: The Centre for Advanced Studies of African Society (CASAS).

Hoge, Jr James F. (2004) "Global Power Shift in the Making", *Foreign Affairs*, 83(4): 2-7.

Huntington, Samuel P. (1993) "The Clash of Civilizations?", *Foreign Affairs*, 72(3): 22-49.

Huntington, Samuel P. (1999) "The Lonely Superpower", *Foreign Affairs*, 78(2): 35-49.

Ikenberry, John G. (2008) "The Rise of China and the Future of the West", *Foreign Affairs*, 87(1): 23-37, available at http://www.foreignaffairs.com/articles/63042/g-john-ikenberry/the-rise-of-china-and-the-future-of-the-west.

Jiang, Ye (2002) "Will China be a "Threat" to Its Neighbors and the World in the Twenty-First Century?", *Ritsumeikan Annual Review of International Studies*, 1: 55-68.

Kasplan, Robert (2005) "How would we Fight China", *The Atlantic Monthly*, 295(5): 49-64.

Kegan, Robert (1997) "What China Knows that We Don't: The Case for a New Strategy of Containment", *The Weekly Standard*, January 20: 3.

Kagan, Robert and Kristol, William (2000) "The Present Danger", *The National Interest*, (59): 57-69.

Kegan, Robert (2005) "The Illusion of 'Managing' China", *Washington Post*, May 15.

Kennedy, Paul (1989) *The Rise and Fall of the Great Powers*. New York: Vintage Books.

Kim, Sung Won, David P. Fidler and Sumit Ganguly (2009) "Eastphalia Rising? Asian Influence and the Fate of Human Security", *World Policy Journal*, 26(2): 53-64.

Kindelberger, Charles P. (1973) *The World in Depression, 1919-1939*. Berkeley: University of California Press.

Kissinger, Henry (2009) "Rebalancing Relations with China", *Washington Post*, August 19, 2009, available at http://www.washingtonpost.com/wp-dyn/content/article/2009/08/18/AR2009081802850.html.

Klare, Michael T. (2000) "Permanent Preeminence: US Strategic Policy for the 21st Century", *NACLA Report on the Americas*, 34(3): 8-15.

Krauthammer, Charles (1995) "Why We Must Contain China", *Time* Magazine, 146(5): 72.

Kynge, James (2006) *China Shakes the World: A Titan's Rise and Troubled Future – and the Challenge for America*. New York: Houghton Mifflin Company.

Lampton, David M. (2008) *The Three Faces of Chinese Power: Might, Money, and Minds*. Berkeley: University of California Press.

Li, Minqi (2008) *The Rise of China and the Demise of the Capitalist World Economy*. New York: Monthly Review.

MacDonald, Greg and Yow, Yit-Seng and Li, Xing (2009) *Innovation in China: The Dawning of the Asian Century*. London: Adonis & Abbey Publishers Ltd.

Manji, Firoze and Marks, Stephen (eds) (2007) *African Perspectives on China in Africa*. Oxford: Fahamu.

Mearsheimer, John (2006) "China's Unpeaceful Rise", *Current History*, 105(690): 160-162.

Möckli, Daniel (2007) "The Rise of China: Regional and Global Power Shifts", *CSS Analyses in Security Policy*, 2(8): 1-3.

Pfaff, William (2001) "The Question of Hegemony", *Foreign Affairs*, 80(1): 221-232.

Prah, Kwesi K. (ed.) (2007) *Afro-Chinese Relations, Past, Present and Future*. Cape Town: The Centre for Advanced Studies of African Society (CASAS)

PRC (2005) *White Paper on China's Peaceful Development Road*. Beijing: State Council of the Chinese People's Republic, Information Office.

Ramo, Joshua C. (2004) *The Beijing Consensus*. London: The Foreign Policy Centre.

Rice, Condaleezza (2000) "Campaign 2000: Promoting the National Interest", *Foreign Affairs*, 75(1): 45-62.

Robinson, William I. (1995) "Pushing Polyarchy: the US-Cuba Case and the Third World", *Third World Quarterly*, 16(4): 643-659.

Ross, Robert S. and Zhu, Feng (eds) (2008) *China's Ascent: Power, Security, and the Future of International Politics*. Ithaca, NY: Cornell University Press.

Schubert, Julia (2003) *Hegemonic Stability Theory: The Rise and Fall of the US-Leadership in World Economic Relations*. On-line publisher: GRIN Publishing.

Schwarz, Benjamin (1996) "Why America Thinks it Has to Run the World", *Atlantic Monthly*, 277(6): 92-102.

Schwenninger, Sherle R. (1999) "World Order Lost: American Foreign Policy in the Post-Cold War World", *World Policy Journal*, 16(2): 42-71.

Shambaugh, David (2006) *Power Shift: China and Asia's New Dynamics*. Berkeley: University of California Press.

Shaw, Timothy M. and Breslin, Shaun (2007) *China and the Global Political Economy*. London: Palgrave Macmillan.

Sun, Yat-sen (1999) "National Morale and World Tranquillity", in Lewis Copeland, Lawrence W. Lamm and Stephen J. McKenna (eds.) *The World Great Speeches*. New York: Dover Publications.

Wallerstein, Immanuel (1974a) "The Rise and Future Demise of the World Capitalist System: Concepts for Comparative Analysis", *Comparative Studies in Society and History*, 16(4): 387-415.

Wallerstein, Immanuel (1974b) *The Modern World System I: Capitalist Agriculture and the Origins of the European World-Economy in the Sixteenth Century*. New York: Academic Press.

White III, Lynn T. (2007) "America at the Taiwan Strait: Five Scenarios", *Asia Perspective*, 3(3): 5-40.

Zheng, Bijian (2005) "China's 'Peaceful Rise' to Great-Power Status", *Foreign Affairs*, 84(5): 39-48.

Chapter 3

China and the International Aid System: Transformation or Cooptation?

Paul Opoku-Mensah

Introduction

A recent increase in Chinese activity within development aid, as in many areas of the international system, is raising increasing concerns especially from the West about China's role and impact in this international system of power and development. From a purely technical appraisal by a bureaucrat within the aid system, China's aid activity has systemic ramifications: "Here comes a very large new player on the block that has the potential of changing the landscape of overseas development assistance".[1] From a critical politico-moral-ideological standpoint, the view is less sanguine: "China is effectively pricing responsible and well-meaning aid organizations out of the market in the very places where they are needed most. If they continue to succeed in pushing their alternative development model, they will succeed in underwriting a world that is more corrupt, chaotic, and authoritarian".[2] From official China, however, the noise about Chinese aid is much ado about nothing: "China is attracting external capital, and as a balance China wants to help developing countries by financing infrastructure projects. Helping your neighbours to have a good life is no sin".[3]

These three authors no doubt bring three different and relevant perspectives to Chinese aid activity. What is common to all these three, however, is the recognition that while in the recent past aid politics was discussed without reference to China, current discussions cannot ignore China. Indeed any analysis that seeks to provide understanding of aid, necessarily, has to integrate the role of China and its impact on this international system of power relations as well as the system's underlying structures of ideologies, norms and values.

This is the objective of this chapter. It seeks to understand China's involvement as an actor in the aid system, and its implications for restructuring the nature of the aid system itself. Is China fundamentally redefining the nature of the aid system

1 Tom Crouch, Country director for the Philippines at the Asian Development Bank (cited in Perlez, Jane, 2006).

2 Moisés Naím, editor in chief of Foreign Policy (cited in Naim, 2007: 2).

3 Liqun Jin, vice president of the Asian Development Bank and a former vice minister of finance in Beijing (cited in Perlez, Jane, 2006).

in ways that effectively price out other players, and challenge the normative principles underlying the system? Or is it simply an actor helping poor neighbours with no systemic ramifications on the aid system? This chapter provides answers to these questions. Specifically, through using the case of Chinese aid to Africa, it seeks to understand and assess the nature of Chinese aid, and its effect – if any – on the international aid system. The chapter is structured as follows: this introduction is followed by a discussion on the international aid system and its role in the international system of power relations in general and African development in particular. This is followed by a discussion on the Chinese aid system with an emphasis on its history, characteristics, and influence in African development. Following this empirical analysis, the next section compares the dominant aid system with that of the Chinese. Following this comparison, the final section brings the discussions together in an assessment of China's impact on the nature of the aid. The objective is to assess if China is radically transforming the aid system, or rather been integrated into this international system of power relations.

The Aid System: An International System of Power Relations

The international development aid system remains, undoubtedly, the most powerful and enduring structural force influencing development worldwide. Established after WWII to facilitate the development of the poor countries of the "South", it has become a distinct, very powerful and new type of international system, reflecting global power relations, and continuously developing and framing regional, national and local subsystems and organizational landscapes all over the world. As a system, it is premised on both accelerating and directing a country's development through the transfer of, mainly concessional resources. Disbursing billions of dollars, and with immense conceptual and institutional power, it shapes institutions and policies across the world.

It is a system that comprises donor and receiver nations. The donor side includes most of the advanced countries of the OECD. On the recipient side over 160 countries around the world received aid in 2001. The bulk of this aid was concentrated on the poorest countries in Asia and sub-Saharan Africa, but with a substantial contribution also to middle-income countries, especially in Central and Eastern Europe (Fowler, 2000). As was indicated in the previous chapter, what primarily produces and reproduces this system and defines its borders vis-à-vis the rest of the world and the rest of the organizational landscape is the flow and transfer of funds, and the character of this resource transfer. Thus, understanding this resource transfer becomes a prerequisite to gauging the power relations, and indeed the overall impact of the system on its various actors (Tvedt, 2002). The primary sources of international assistance are from official aid – and from private donations and investment income – i.e. private aid. In 1998, $47.9 billion of tax funds were allocated as official overseas development assistance (ODA) (World Bank, 1999: 68). The major institutions providing official aid can be divided between bilateral donors – that is the specialized development agencies of Northern countries, and the multilateral agencies of the United Nations system. In 1997, 70 percent of official aid was allocated bilaterally, the remainder through multilateral channels. By and large, the international financial institutions (IFIs) within this system – the International Monetary Fund (IMF), the World Bank Group and its sister regional development banks – provide loans for financial stabilization and reform as well as for development investment. United Nations agencies typically employ grant funding. The private aid system (of foundations, charities and international NGOs) also works on a grant basis (Fowler, 2000). The resource transfers, however goes both ways. For instance, over the period 1985-1992, developing countries transferred more in repayments and interest than they received from the North. During these years, the average annual flow of resources from South to North was US$44.39 billion. The figure became positive again in 1993 with a net flow to the South of US$11.4 billion (Microsoft Encarta, 2002).

It is a hierarchical system, even if the rhetoric sometimes is to the contrary, with donors at the helm because of their financial resources, conceptual dominance, and the unequal distribution of sanctionary instruments (Tvedt, 1998: 224; Fowler, 2000). The system is made up of sub-systems at all levels, each with its own history, logic and internal dynamics. In most countries, the system is relatively autonomous and insulated with its own developments, norm systems and value orientations (Tvedt, 1998: 62). Nonetheless all these subsystems form one part of a bigger multinational, together with and mingling with other subsystems where donor states are at the core of the system. There is *always* a dominant discourse, appropriated by the major actors: donors, recipient states and NGOs. This powerful development discourse may change over time, but for the period it dominates, it shapes the policy responses of the actors in the system (Tvedt, 2002). The actors in this system are structurally integrated primarily via resource transfers and communication-exchange. These actors – public and private donors, recipient governments, international NGOs, local NGOs – can be conceptualized as a river and its "feeders". A river system consists of both channels (rivers) and reservoirs. The system can be seen as consisting of different subsystems, or different tributaries or deltaic streams. The point with the river system analogy is that this social system consists of both recipient governments and NGOs as diversion channels and the donor-offices and funding sources as reservoirs.

It is a system that encourages and institutionalizes different forms of social integration, but despite the use of the word integration there is no assumption that the relationships so described are harmonious. The terms social integration and system integration as used here embrace both order and conflict.[4] Indeed it

4 In a further elaboration, Tvedt (1998) argues that in the literature on social integration and system integration it is often noted how conflict theorists emphasize the conflict between groups of actors as the motor of social change, while normative functionalists downplay the role of actors and seek to emphasize the (functional or dysfunctional) relationships between the institutions of society. Neither approach is of course adequate, precisely because each

has evolved into an international regime, with a set of norms, principles, and procedures that have been designed to defend certain economic and ideological interests and to promote international stability (van de Walle, 2001).

The influence of the aid system is structured around financial transfers, institutional arrangements, and policy frameworks. The 1990s in particular saw the particular influence of the aid system through the imposition of policy instruments like the SAPS, ERPs. The nature of interventions has also undergone change with a focus on process. Thus processes like the PRSPs become central the aid effectiveness debate, and the use of non-state channels. An understanding of these different channels becomes important to understanding the nature of international aid system, and the nature of power in the system. The influence of the aid system on Africa is near absolute, as it remains a very powerful and enduring structural force impacting institutional and policy development in African countries. In many African countries it finances the bulk of development interventions, shapes institutional arrangements, frames policy alternatives, as well as provides mediating structure(s) for societal processes. In other countries the aid system's influence is more marginal. Nevertheless; its concepts, institutions, administrative arrangements and fiscal resources help shape the most critical aspects of development and politics on the African continent.

Chinese Aid to Africa: Continuities and Discontinuities

As a rising actor, the Chinese Aid system lacks the institutionalized and well developed support services made up of the numerous aid research institutions, evaluation departments of official aid agencies, and the entire consultancy industry that has developed around the Western aid system (Lancaster, 2007). Consequently, not as much information and/or knowledge is known about the Chinese aid system. Yet an outline of the system is gradually emerging, which a study of Chinese aid to Africa helps unravel.

A study of Chinese aid to Africa indicates, first, that Chinese aid is not new. Indeed Chinese aid to African countries was founded, in part, on a logic and motivation articulated in the 1950s by Mao Zedong that although China is a poor nation, it should take the responsibility of helping those in need, those smaller and powerless nations (Hu, 2003). Africa was identified by Mao as the key part

---

deals with only one side of the agency versus structure problem. The task should be to overcome this dualism, but the micro versus macro distinction cannot be overcome by regarding social integration as something which should only refer to situations where actors are physically *co-present* and system integration to where they are not. This is unsatisfactory because face-to-face interactions are not confined to micro-processes, and macro-processes may be organized as face-to-face interactions.

of the "Third World" revolutionary forces in his famous "Three World Theory".[5] But beyond helping poor Africa countries, Chinese aid also had other motivations, including neutralizing assistance from rival countries, which were being helped by Taiwan. In the 1960s and 1970s, for example, China aided Angola while Taiwan helped neighbouring South Africa (Perlez, 2006). The modalities of Chinese aid, more so, include grants, investment/tied aid, concessional loans, and government guarantees for investment.

The historiography of Chinese aid to Africa can be disaggregated into three distinct phases, stretching from the late 1940s to the present era. The first phase, dating from the late 1940s to the end of the 1970s, was characterized by the use of aid as a moral, ideological, and foreign policy tool with aid being used by China to support other socialist countries and liberation movements. Beyond this, it also had a strategic purpose aimed at countering the Society Union's influence in Africa, as well as promoting its one China policy through granting aid only to those African states that refused to recognize an independent and sovereign Taiwan. Practically the relations with Africa were through a two-pronged strategy of courting the newly independent African countries, while encouraging and supporting the liberation struggles of those still under colonial rule. A landmark event in the evolution of Chinese aid occurred in 1964 during the then Premier Zhou en Lai's visit to Mali and Ghana where he launched what has become known as "China's Eight Principles of Economic and Technical Aid". These eight principles fully give expression to the desire of China to conduct economic and cultural cooperation with the newly-emerged countries of Asia, Africa and Latin America (China, Ministry of Foreign Affairs 2000).[6]

---

5 Mao's *Three World Theory* of international relations divides the world into three political and economic blocs: the US and the Soviet Union belong to the *First World;* the middle elements, such as Japan, Europe, Australia, and Canada, belong to the *Second World*; China and the vast majority of developing countries belong to the *Third World.*

6 The eight principles are:

a. The Chinese Government always bases itself on the principle of equality and mutual benefit in providing aid to other countries. It never regards such aid as a kind of unilateral alm [sic] but as something mutual.

b. In providing aid to other countries, the Chinese Government strictly respects the sovereignty of the recipient countries, and never attaches any conditions or asks for any privileges.

c. China provides economic aid in the form of interest-free or low-interest loans and extends the time limit for repayment when necessary so as to lighten the burden of the recipient countries as far as possible.

d. In providing aid to other countries, the purpose of the Chinese Government is not to make the recipient countries dependent on China but to help them embark step by step on the road of self-reliance and independent economic development.

e. The Chinese Government tries its best to help the recipient countries build projects which require less investment while yielding quicker results, so that the recipient governments may increase their income and accumulate capital.

By the end of 1965, 17 of the 38 African states had recognized China (compared to 14 who continued diplomatic relations with Taiwan), and linkages had been established with at least a dozen African liberation movements. However, with the outbreak of the Cultural Revolution in 1966 the direction of China's policy and behaviour changed. Similar to its foreign policy globally, China's relations with Africa were curtailed. But even though operational activities were reduced and relations even suspended or terminated in a few instances, relations were intensified with select African states such as e.g. Congo (Brazzaville), Tanzania and Zambia (Yu, 1988). From 1975-1978 Chinese aid projects in Africa were seen in the light industry, agriculture, health and transport where the latter was especially seen in the construction of the TAZARA[7] Railway. The railroad was a key project financed and executed by China. Construction was started in 1970 and operation commenced six years later. At that time, it was the largest foreign-aid project ever undertaken by China. It was built to serve the landlocked Zambia as an alternative to rail lines via Rhodesia and South Africa. The Chinese government sponsored the construction of the railway specifically to eliminate Zambia's economic dependence on Rhodesia and South Africa (Robinson and Shambaugh, 1994).

The second phase of China's aid to Africa, the first decade under Deng Xiaoping (1978-1989), was marked by the end of ideology, the start of economic pragmatism, and declining aid to Africa. This was a period marked by the end of the ideological framework that had characterized the first, and the start of economic pragmatism. While the conception and rhetoric generally did not change, this phase nonetheless was characterized by a reduction in Chinese aid due to changing relations with Moscow and Washington, and an internal reorganization of the Chinese economy which was also ailing. Focus was now on mutual benefits and economic sustainability. By 1988, only 13 African countries received Chinese aid, while trade relations increased. For example, between 1976 and 1980, Chinese exports to Nigeria rose from $128 million to $378 million; and overall trade with Africa rose by 70 percent in this period. Aid pledges fell, although China's aid commitments of $258.9m in 1984 still made it Africa's sixth largest donor.

The current and third phase, the post-Tiananmen Square era (from 1989), is marked by unparalleled institutionalized relations, with the establishment of the

f. The Chinese Government provides the best-quality equipment and material of its own manufacture at international market prices. If the equipment and material provided by the Chinese Government are not up to the agreed specifications and quality, the Chinese Government undertakes to replace them.

g. In providing any technical assistance, the Chinese Government will see to it that the personnel of the recipient country fully master such technique.

h. The experts dispatched by China to help in construction in the recipient countries will have the same standard of living as the experts of the recipient country. The Chinese experts are not allowed to make any special demands or enjoy any special amenities (China, Ministry of Foreign Affairs, 2000).

7 Tanzania–Zambia Railway Authority.

Forum on China–Africa Cooperation (FOCAC) in 2000, and the development of a *China Africa Policy*[8] in 2006. In general this phase is characterized by a twin process of increasing the volume of Aid, as well as institutionalizing the aid relations between China and Africa. Conceptually aid to Africa was still discussed in terms of South–South cooperation, rather than the North–South conception that defines traditional aid between the West and Africa. As will be shown later, this has implications for understating the nature of the relations, and China's potential impact in the aid system. This period also marked a period of renewed interest in Africa with an increase in aid from US $60 million in 1988 to US $375 million in 1990. An expansion of collaboration was necessary due to China's demand for resources, markets and investment possibilities, and these circumstances led to the establishment of the China–Africa Forum in order to have a means to increase political power by providing an alternative to the orthodox development route for African governments. China's Africa Policy of 2006 and the development of the *Beijing Action Plan* 2007-2009 show that China's interest in Africa is increasing. In the context of this institutionalization of the relations, Chinese Premier Wen Jiabao, speaking at FOCAC committed China to the following:

- Double its 2006 assistance to Africa by 2009.
- Provide US$3 billion of preferential loans and US$2 billion of preferential buyer's credits to Africa in the next three years.
- Set up a China–Africa development fund, which would reach US$5 billion, to encourage Chinese companies to invest in Africa and provide support to them.
- Cancel debt in the form of all the interest-free government loans that matured at the end of 2005 owed by the heavily indebted poor countries and the least developed countries in Africa that have diplomatic relations with China.
- Increase from 190 to over 440 the number of export items to China receiving zero-tariff treatment from the least developed countries in Africa with diplomatic ties with China.
- Establish three to five trade and economic cooperation zones in Africa in the next three years.
- Over the next three years, train 15,000 African professionals; send 100 senior agricultural experts to Africa; set up 10 special agricultural technology demonstration centres in Africa; build 30 hospitals in Africa and provide a grant of RMB 300 million for providing artemisinin-2 and build 30 malaria prevention and treatment centres to fight malaria in Africa; dispatch 300 youth volunteers to Africa; build 100 rural schools in Africa; and increase the number of Chinese government scholarships to African students from the current 2,000 per year to 4,000 per year by 2009 (Manji, 2007: 2).

---

8 The full text is available at http://www.gov.cn/misc/2006-01/12/content_156490.htm.

The extent to which the list of commitments has been met, the motivations for China's commitment – whether indeed Chinese aid is good or detrimental to overall African development – are still debated. In the midst of these debates, the fact still remains that these commitments *per se* represent a new phase of China's relations with Africa – an era of institutionalized and enlarged Chinese aid engagement in Africa.

Besides the general historiography, the second aspect of Chinese aid vis-à-vis the dominant Western model of aid relates to conception, delivery and relational aspects of Chinese aid – that is, the praxis of aid. In deed Chinese aid to Africa, and elsewhere, is not important only in terms of its volume and historical development. To the contrary, its importance is gauged when its aid praxis is compared to the praxis of the Western aid system. The first such difference is the conception for aid. Conceptually, China's aid is framed in terms of a developing country helping another developing country, thus negating the conceptual order of the aid system as a system of relations between the developed North and the undeveloped South. This has substantive as well as symbolic implications, as will be discussed later. In addition, Chinese aid is conceived as a two way process, defined in terms of mutual benefit to China and aid recipient countries. Indeed it is official Chinese policy to disburse aid in ways that benefits China economically, i.e. tied aid in kind, technical assistance and infrastructure construction for initiatives that favour Chinese investment. Thus, a very important dimension of Chinese aid as it relates to the economic pragmatism of the post-Deng years, is the rhetoric of a "win-win" economic cooperation and trade relations, rather than poverty reduction. This is a departure from the traditional aid which is conceived in terms of the giver helping the recipient, even if the rhetoric is not always borne out in practice.

But perhaps one of the most important differences relates to the channel of aid delivery. Traditional Western aid relies on various channels including multilateral channels (e.g. World Bank, UN agencies, EU Aid); bilateral channels (Danida, USAID; CIDA, NORAD etc); private organizations (NGOs, PVOs, CSOs). Indeed for Western aid the NGO channel, in particular, became a very important channel in the 1980s, a period referred to as the "NGO Decade" in development discourse because of the importance NGOs assumed in development. The delivery of Chinese aid, on the other hand, relies exclusively on bilateral state channels. To the extent that non-state actors are involved, they are normally private companies used in the implementation of infrastructural projects. Chinese aid is thus delivered through private-sector or state-owned enterprises. Thus the NGO channel in aid that was established since the 1980s, and has become important to Western aid, plays no role in the implementation of Chinese aid. Absent, too, are the other multiplicity of supporting actors and institutions that service, and are part of traditional Western aid. This includes the consultancy firms, the development institutes, and the "development diplomats" that are essential parts of traditional aid. For instance in a comparison to World Bank practice, Jane Perlez argues that China's aid "rarely include the extra freight of expensive consultants, provisions that are common to World Bank projects" (Perlez, 2006: para. 8).

There are other remaining areas, such as the intersection of aid and migration, aid and trade, in which the Chinese aid model differs from its Western counterpart (Sautman, 2006).

Restructuring Power Relations in the Aid System

This examination of Chinese aid in Africa certainly shows that in a Western-led system dominated by North–South relations and powerful countries, China is now a visible actor. And in the case of Africa, this engagement is becoming important to the continent's development, particularly in the areas of infrastructure development (Prah, 2007; Manji and Marks, 2007; Kaplinsky et al., 2007). But is this visibility indicative of fundamental change in the structural relations of power and the rules of game in the aid system? In other words is China restructuring power in the aid system, or has it become a new actor with a different modus operandi but who will gradually be incorporated into the system. Put differently, will China be a transformer or rather be caught by the isomorphism that has characterized the aid system?

To answer the question, a recap of how power is structured and influenced in the aid system. At the time of its establishment in the years immediately after WWII, the aid system reflected the state of power relations in the global system. At the head of the system was the United States – albeit challenged by the USSR – followed by the colonial powers. Besides this fact that the establishment of the aid system reflected and institutionalized a system of power relations, as a system, it has its modes of exercising influence. Concretely the aid system exercises power through its financial transfers, institutional dominance, conceptual dominance, and sanctionary instruments. An assessment of China's role in the system does have to take cognizance of this reality.

First, although China is not the dominant power in the international system, its place in the hierarchy has changed substantively. Irrespective of the standard of measurement, and areas of influence, the power of China is increasingly visible in the international hierarchy of power. This is more so reflected, particularly, in the global economic system. Within the aid system itself, the size and volume of Chinese aid, and the expectations that this will increase, is a major indicator that financially the power of the actors in the aid system has changed. For instance in terms of volume, in the course of the past 50 years China has given 44.4 billion in aid to African countries. Since 2000, China has cancelled more than US$10bilion debt owed it by 31 African countries, and established a US$ 5.5 billion fund to support African development. Beyond the volume, however, the overall implications of Chinese aid in Africa can be gauged when it is compared to Western aid. In 2005, for instance, Chinese loans to three African countries: Nigeria, Angola and Mozambique was US$8.0 billion, exceeding total World Bank loans to the whole of Africa, which was US$2.3 billion. Similarly, in 2006 the amount of Chinese aid in the form of loans to Africa was thrice the total sum of loans given by all OECD member countries to African countries during the same period; and 25 times of the aid from the American Import and Export Bank (Xiaoyun, Li, 2008; Lyakurwa, 2008).

Chinese aid is also distinguished by its practical focus, and direct impact: As William Lyakurwa, the Executive Director of the African Economic Research Consortium based in Nairobi, Kenya puts it:

> Initially, Beijing's aid was concentrated on national stadiums and "People's Palaces". This has given way to a more practical focus: constructing roads, dams and government buildings; upgrading power distribution systems; installing methane generating plants; and so on. The sending of medical teams and agricultural specialists continues to be a mainstay of Chinese assistance to Africa. Chinese foreign aid has tended to concentrate on these basic infrastructures and education, areas where Western donors have cut back substantially. (Lyakurwa, 2008: 17)

Similarly Sautman argues that while China's aid to Africa is not entirely untied, it is distinct from Western aid in a key way:

> Chinese aid is often dispensed in such a way that corrupt rulers cannot somehow use it to buy Mercedes Benzes ... [It] is often in the form of infrastructure, such as a railroad network in Nigeria or roads in Kenya and Rwanda. Or in the form of doctors and nurses to provide health care to people who otherwise would not have access ... In addition, China provides scholarships for African students to study in its universities and, increasingly, funds to encourage its businessmen to invest in Africa. (Sautman, 2007: 27)

The overall effect of this approach is captured by Sierra Leone's ambassador to China who argues that while Chinese aid leads to visible results and impact in Africa, "the G-8 countries are putting in huge sums of money and they don't see very much" (ibid). Some of these results include newly constructed roads in Ethiopia, the renovation of the railway system in Nigeria, and the construction of a US$562 million hydro electric power plant at Bui in Ghana.

It needs to be emphasized that it is not the volume of Chinese aid resources *per se* that makes China an important actor in the aid system. Rather it is the fact that its resources is increasingly pricing out actors who a decade ago were indisputable leaders in the field. And this aid had become an important tool in African development, itself reflected by the ease with which China is able to routinely convene meetings of African leaders. To be sure, this does not mean that China has rendered the traditional actors irrelevant and powerless, as it has not. What is stressed therefore is the fact that within the past decade China is increasingly becoming important in an international policy area where it was an insignificant player just two decades ago.

But the power of the aid system does not reside, solely, in its financial resources. Indeed the aid system remains the major arena within which the dominant ideas in development are developed, implemented and contested (Abrahamsen, 2000; Tvedt, 2006; Opoku-Mensah, 2007; 2009; Opoku-Mensah, Lewis and Tvedt, 2007). This is an acknowledgment that politically, the powerful actors in the aid system – the World Bank, the UN, the major donor states and the biggest and most influential development NGOs – dominate the development and implementation of the most influential ideas and strategies of development. As Abrahamsen argues, the aid system and its most powerful institutional actors:

> ... constantly update and refine knowledge about how best to achieve development, and it is also through these myriad organizations that the decrees of development filter down from the various expert offices to the local settings in Africa, Asia and Latin America. (Abrahamsen, 2000: 20-21. See also Tvedt, 2006; Wallace et al., 2006)

From this persepctive, both the World Bank (Washington Consesus) and the UNDP (the New York Dissent) are part of the same aid system within which the dominant ideas in development are created, adopted, negated, distorted and/or implemented, and where different actors compete for hegemonic control over development ideas and practices. The conceptual power of the aid system to define what is good and bad development, and to impose these definitions on recipient countries, has been perhaps the most effective and vexatious exercise of the power of aid actors, as it affects the sovereignty of aid recipients. In the case of Africa some commentators argue that this definitional power of the aid system has had the most far reaching impact on the continent, as unlike other aid practices, they seek to shape the development route *itself* (Kankwenda, 2004).

The entry of China into the aid system is changing this power of the traditional aid system to shape the development route, as it offers a new set of ideas and practices that, first, is breaking the monopoly of Western aid to define, and second, is also proving attractive to aid recipient countries, particularly in Africa. These new set of ideas and practices, subsumed under what is increasingly called the "Beijing Consensus" (Ramo, C.J., 2004; Xing, 2007), departs in some substantive ways from the aid system's consensus on policy and practice. While the Beijing consensus, and China in general, is nowhere near replacing the institutions of the aid system as the dominant developers of development ideas, some of these practices – including the right to self determination by states, non interference in domestic political and governance issues, the leadership role of the state in development – challenge the prevailing development orthodoxy of the past two decades. But more important, the Beijing consensus gives to aid recipients to exercise choice in what the past decade has been an array of conditionalities, including vexatious political ones. The issue is not that Chinese aid does not involve conditionality. It does as it is official Chinese policy to disburse aid in ways that benefits China economically, i.e. tied aid in kind, technical assistance and infrastructure construction for initiatives that favour Chinese investment. What is different, however, is that these conditionalities do not relate to the touchy issue of sovereignty that has been at the heart of the criticisms levelled at traditional Western aid by a number of African countries (Kankwenda, 2004).

But perhaps the most important effect of Chinese aid relates to the opportunity it gives aid recipients, particularly African countries, to rethink their relations with Western aid actors who have exercised substantive power in African development. Thus for instance, in a recent interview, the Senegalese President Abdoulaye Wade argues that the continent can ignore Europe and look to China for its needs, as China offers Africa the same thing that Europe has been offering at a better price with excellent conditions.[9] And these "better conditions" include the absence of intrusive conditionalities often associated with Western aid. As a number of analysts argue, China's aid to Africa, while not disinterested, is not used as a political tool in the same way as aid from Western political actors in Africa. Indeed, in contrast to most other donors (especially the United States and the United Kingdom, with France much less so), China does not impose political and economic conditionality requirements. This makes the country an attractive source of aid, especially when, as in Angola and Zimbabwe, the international financial institutions like the International Monetary Fund (IMF) or World Bank are trying to alter the behaviours of governments by imposing political conditions (Lyakurwa, William, 2008: 17. See also Sautman, 2007; Prah, 2008). Perhaps this is best captured by Julius Nyerere, Tanzania's first leader, in a comment on China's grant for building the Tanzania-Zambia railways (Tazara):

> The Chinese people have not asked us to become communists in order to qualify for this loan ... they have never at any point suggested that we should change any of our policies – internal or external (Nyerere, 1974: 235).

To be sure, this in itself does not indicate a permanent restructuring of power relations in aid. But it does indicate that change is certainly in the making in the international aid system of power relations.

Conclusion

Exactly a decade ago, in a seminal and provocative article in *Foreign Affairs* titled "Does China Matter?" Gerald Segal argued that the purported influence of China is often greatly exaggerated, indeed the effect of a carefully managed theatrical performance by China itself. The Chinese involvement in aid is certainly not a theatrical performance, but one that poses a challenge to the existing international system in fundamental, unexplored, and unknown ways.

---

9 It is available at http://blog.taragana.com/n/africa-looking-towards-india-china-senegal-president-91009/.

Will China's engagement lead to long-term and permanent realignment of power relations in the aid system? Or in line with the institutional isomorphism that has characterized the aid system in the past, will China ultimately be co-opted into the established practise and consensus in the aid system? Put differently, are we going to witness a sinization of the aid system, or simply the inclusion of an actors, even this actor sometimes operates differetenly?

Like most things about China's recent rise, definitive conclusions do not exist, as we are still in the midst of the process we seek to assess. Yet contradictory tendencies can be observed. On the one hand, and as has already been argued, China's presence in the aid system has *already* changed the system. The aid system and its operations cannot be adequately understood outside an analytical integration of the activities of China in this system. But similarly, Chinese aid is also *already* undergoing change as it interacts with the already established Western aid system (Guérin, 2008).

In the final analyses, however, perhaps the most critical question should not be the extent to which China has changed the system, or is itself changed by the aid system. Indeed the debate should not be framed as a zero-sum game. Rather the focus should be on the implications of China's entry on the *purpose* of the aid system: to assist the development of the developing countries. Perhaps the question ought to be rephrased in terms of the implications of China's recent involvement in the aid system for the purpose of aid. Concretely, the entry of China into the aid system, and the challenge it poses to the Westen aid project, should be used as an entry point to reconstitute power in the system on behalf of those who, traditionally, have been dictated to. Perhaps it offers the opportunity to rationally rethink, and address the pathologies that have characterized the operandi of the Western aid system, including the sometimes paternalistic intrusion into the affairs of aid recipient countries, the imposition of one-size-fits-all development models, and the lack of effectiveness. If China's engagement in the aid system can achieve this, it would have played a far greater role in restructuring the system than in simply changing the power relations in her interests.

References

Abrahamsen, Rita (2000) *Disciplining Democracy: Development Discourse and Good Governance in Africa.* London and New York: Zed Books.

Carlsson, Jerker, Somolekae, Gloria and van de Walle, Nicholas (eds) (1997) *Foreign Aid in Africa: Learning from Country Experiences.* The Nordic Africa Institute.

Fowler, Alan (ed.) (2000) *Questioning Partnership: The Reality of Aid and NGO Relations.* IDS Bulletin, 31(3).

Gill, Bates and Reilly, James (2007) "The Tenuous Hold of China Inc. in Africa", *The Washington Quarterly*, 30(3): 37-52.

Guérin, Émmanuel (2008) *Emerging Donors and Global Governance of Development Aid: What is China's Role in Africa*?. No. 03/2008 GLOBAL GOVERNANCE.

Hu, Wenping (2003) *China–Africa Relations Facing the 21st Century*. Beijing: Chinese Academy of Social Sciences.

Kankwenda, Mbaya (2004) "Forty Years of Development Illusions: Revisiting Development Policies and Practices in Africa", in Onimode, Bade et al. *African Development and Governance Strategies in the 21st Century: Looking Back to Move Forward: Essays in honour of Adebayo Adedeji at Seventy.* London: Zed Books.

Kaplinsky, Raphael; McCormick, Dorothy and Morris, Mike (2007) "The Impact of China on Sub Saharan Africa", Paper prepared with support from the DFID China Office <http://www.uneca.org/eca_programmes/acgd/Overview_Report.pdf>.

Kissling, Sandra (2009) *Made in China? The Challenge of Chinese Imports on the Private Sector: A Case Study on the Furniture Industry in Accra, Ghana*. Masters theses in Development and International Relations, Aalborg University.

Lancaster, Carol (2007) *The Chinese Aid System.* Center for Global Development, Georgetown, available at http://www.cgdev.org/content/general/detail/13953.

Lyakurwa, William (2008) *American and Chinese Activities in Africa – and African Priorities for the Future,* BRENTHURST DISCUSSION PAPER 6/2008, The Brenthurst Foundation.

Li, Xiaoyun (2008) *China's Foreign Aid to Africa: Overview* (paper). College of Humanities and Development, China Agricultural University, Beijing.

Li, Xing (2007) "Paradigm Shift: From 'Washington Consnsus' to 'Beijing Consensus'", in Prah, Kwesi (ed.) *Afro-Chinese Relations: Past, Present and Future.* The Centre for Advanced Studies of African Society (CASAS).

Manji, Firoze, (2007) "Preface" in Manji, Firoze and Marks, Stephen (eds) *African Perspectives on China in Africa*. Oxford/Nairobi: Fahamu.

Manji, Firoze and Marks, Stephen (eds.) (2007) *African Perspectives On China In Africa*, Oxford/Nairobi: Fahamu.

Marks, Stephen (2007) "Introduction", in Manji, Fironze and Marks, Stephen (eds.) *African Perspectives on China in Africa.* Oxford/Nairobi: Fahamu.

Naím, Moisés (2007) "Rogue Aid", in *Foreign Policy*, March/April 2007, available at < http://www.foreignpolicy.com/story/cms.php?story_id=3732>.

Nyerere, Julius (1974) *Freedom and Development.* Dar Es Salaam: Oxford University Press.

Onimode, Bade et al. (2004) *African Development and Governance Strategies in the 21st Century: Looking Back to Move Forward: Essays in Honour of Adebayo Adedeji at Seventy*. London: Zed Books.

Opoku-Mensah, Paul (2007) "Can NGOs Make a Difference? Revisiting and Reframing a 20-year Debate", *Forum for Development Studies*, 34(2): 311-322.

Opoku-Mensah, Paul (2009) *NGOs and the Politics of African Development: The Ghanaian Experience*. Saarbrucken: VDM Verlag.

Opoku-Mensah, Paul, Lewis, David and Tvedt, Terje (eds) (2007) *Reconceptualising NGOs and their Roles in Development: NGOs, Civil Society and the International Aid System.* Aalborg, Denmark: Aalborg University Press.

Prah, Kwesi (ed.) (2007) *Afro-Chinese Relations: Past, Present and Future.* Cape Town: The Centre for Advanced Studies of African Society (CASAS).

Perlez, Jane (2006) "China Competes With West in Aid to its Neighbors", *New York Times*, September 18. Availabe at: www.nytimes.com/2006/09/18/world/asia/18iht-web.0918aid.2845121.html.

Ramo, Joshua C. (2004) *The Beijing Consensus*. London: The Foreign Policy Centre.

Robinson, Thomas W. and Shambaugh, David L. (1994) *Chinese Foreign Policy: Theory and Practice*. Oxford: Clarendon Press.

Segal, Gerald (1999) "Does China Matter?", *Foreign Affairs*, 78(5): 24-36.

Sautman, Barry V. (2006) "Friends and Interests: China's distinctive links with Africa", *Working Paper No. 12*, The Hong Kong University of Science and Technology: Center on China's Transnational Relation.

Tvedt, Terje (1998) *Angels of Mercy or Development Diplomats? NGOs and Foreign Aid.* Trenton, NJ: James Currey Publishers, Oxford and Africa World Press (Reprinted in 2003).

Tvedt, Terje (2002) "Development NGOs: Actors in a Global Civil Society or in a New International Social System?", *Voluntas: International Journal of Voluntary and Nonprofit Organizations*, 13(4): 363-375.

Tvedt, Terje (2006) "The International Aid System and the Non-Governmental Organizations: A New Research Agenda", *Journal of International Development*, 18: 677–690.

Van de Walle, Nicholas (2001) *African Economies and the Politics of Permanent Crisis: 1979-1999*. New York: Cambridge University Press.

Wallace, Tina; Lisa Bornstein and Chapman, Jennifer (2006) *Coercion and Commitment: Development Ngos and the Aid Chain*, Rugby: ITDG Publishing.

Yu, George T. (1988) "Africa in Chinese Foreign Policy", *Asian Survey*, 28(8): 849-862.

Chapter 4

The Diaspora and the Rise of Nations: China and Africa Compared

Li Xing and Paul Opoku-Mensah

Introduction

At a time when the rise of China is a reality *sui generis* on the international economic, political and social landscape, African countries have also made bold to declare an African renaissance. Central to both China's rise, and Africa's desire for a renaissance, is a rediscovery of the Diaspora, regarded as crucial to the imperatives of national reconstruction and development. To be sure, this "discovery" or "awareness" of the Diaspora is itself the product of a historical period where transnational relations are integral to the workings of the international system and to the mobility of individual nations. Notwithstanding the diversities of the historical factors of migration for each country and region, the current reality is that people are more transnational today than at any other time in history, and successful economic development and integration increasingly depends on human capital crossing borders. Diaspora is inherently transnational, characterized by both opportunities and constraints in a mixture of paradox of distance and closeness.

Despite this general recognition of the importance of the role of the Diaspora to China's economic rise, analytical works on how the Diaspora has actually contributed to China's development, the organic interplay between the Diaspora and their home countries, and the comparative relevance of the Chinese Diaspora experience for others, including Africa, hardly exist. This results, in part, from a lack of comparative empirical information. But equally responsible for the underdevelopment of analysis, perhaps more so, is the lack of a common, shared frame for comparative analysis.

This chapter seeks to address this gap in knowledge through a historical and empirical analysis of the role of the Diaspora in the rise of China, and its implications for a renascent Africa. The chapter also has analytical ambitions in that it specifically seeks to contribute to the search for conceptual frameworks for understanding the role of Diaspora, as an analytical variable, in nation building. This template builds on three pillars, namely 1) the historical evolution (making) of each Diaspora, including its structural location in the host country; 2) its historical and contemporary roles, in particular those related to political and economic integration with the homeland; and finally 3) the homeland state's institutional response to its Diaspora. The essence of this comparative template is to generate insights regarding a) how history shapes the differences affecting a Diaspora's identity and relations with the homeland; b) the ways in which the structural position of a Diaspora in its host country determines not only its own economic status but also the role that it can play in relation to its homeland; and finally c) how successful the homeland is in systematically incorporating and institutionalizing the role of the Diaspora in its rise. The primary objective of the chapter, therefore, is *not* to compare China and Africa *per se*. Rather it is to use the case of the Chinese and African Diasporas as an entry point to understand the processes and factors influencing Diaspora's contribution to the rise of nations.

The chapter is structured as follows: this introduction is followed by an analysis of the Chinese Diaspora and its contributions to China's development, using the common analytical template outlined above. This is followed by an analysis of the African Diaspora and its contributions to African development and integration. Building on insights from the previous two sections, in particular the Chinese experience, the third section discusses the comparative implications of the study. The objective of this comparative assessment is not the comparison and sharing of experiences *per se*. Rather, it is to highlight analytically the important variables that are crucial to understanding any Diaspora's developmental linkages to and roles in its homeland.

The Chinese Diaspora in China's Development

The generally applied English term for "Chinese Diaspora" is "overseas Chinese". For various purposes "overseas Chinese" is often used by the government of People's Republic of China to refer to people of Chinese ethnicities who live outside the mainland China, regardless of citizenship.

However, this literal term "overseas China" consists of three different connotations in Chinese language expression: Huáqiáo (华侨), huárén (华人), Huáyì (华裔). The notion of "Hua Qiao" refers to those Chinese nationals living abroad and still holding Chinese passport, but it does not include people of the following categories, such as those working for diplomatic missions and resident organizations, contract workers, travellers and students studying abroad. More importantly, it does not include citizens from Hong Kong, Marco and Taiwan because politically these territories are not "foreign" but are part of one China (the Great China). However, due to the historical reasons, the notion of "Chinese Diaspora" often includes populations from these three territories.

The notion of "Hua Ren" refers to those Chinese who not only live in foreign countries on a permanent basis but also obtain foreign nationalities (holding a foreign passport). The notion of "Hua Yi" refers to descendents of both Hua Qiao and Hua Ren (second generation and onward), and it implies that they are foreign nationals and have already been integrated in host countries.

Early Migration

The Chinese Diaspora in its current form results from centuries of migration. Sporadic migration led to an early trade or merchant Diaspora in Southeast Asia, but it was during the decline of the Qing Dynasty (1644-1911) that the endless internal and external conflicts following the *Opium War* and the *Taiping Rebellion* triggered the rapid rise of the emigration of ordinary Chinese migrants by the mid 19th century. Most of the early emigrants were from the southeastern Guangdong and Fujian provinces and they were illiterate or poorly educated peasants who hoped to earn a living abroad and to send a surplus income as a remittance to support their families in the homeland. They were regarded as *coolies* (Chinese: 苦力), i.e. hard labour, who were sent or migrated to countries in North America, Australia, Africa, Southeast Asia, and other places. Many of these coolies flocked to America in search of opportunities and worked in labour-intensive mining and railway projects under extremely harsh conditions, as in the development of America's Transcontinental Railroad (Yin, 2001). The life of these coolies was miserable and they faced serious discrimination; many did not survive. All the early Chinese emigrants to the United States suffered from anti-Chinese sentiment, which took its most concrete form in the Chinese Exclusion Act.[1] Despite barriers and interruptions, emigration continued and today, the population of the Chinese Diaspora has reached 35 million, making it the largest migrant group in the world, according to a report by the Chinese Academy of Social Sciences (CASS).[2]

The World's Most Economically Successful Diasporas

According to *World Business*, a leading world economic and management journal, Chinese Diasporas in the East and Southeast Asian region were once labeled by a former king of Thailand as the "Jews of Asia". However, in the view of this journal, Chinese Diasporas have been far more successful in achieving economic hegemony in many Southeast Asian economies than the Jews were in Europe in the past (*World Business*, April 3, 2007). The regional economic power of Chinese Disappears is described in the following way:

> In south-east Asia, they dominate business despite forming only a small minority of the population. Approximately 6 percent of the combined population of the five main south-east Asian economies (Indonesia, Malaysia, the Philippines, Singapore and Thailand) is ethnically Chinese, but that 6 percent controlled around 60 percent of the region's private corporate wealth. … The dominance is perhaps at its most extreme in Indonesia. Three quarters of the country's

1 A federal discrimination law of the United States passed on May 6, 1882, which banned Chinese immigration. It was abolished in 1943.

2 *China Daily*, http://www.chinadaily.com.cn/china/2007-02/12/content_807738.htm.

top 300 big business groups are either wholly or partly owned by Indonesian Chinese businesspeople – not a bad result for an ethnic group that comprises just 3 percent of the population. (*World Business*, April 3, 2007)

Some researchers estimate that overseas Chinese (all those living outside mainland China) control more than $2.5 trillion of wealth. This figure looks impressive even when compared with Japan's 1995 GNP of $5.1 trillion, or with United States' 1995 GNP of $7.2 trillion (Koo, 1995; Kwong, 1996) More understandably, if we use this figure to make population-based across-country comparisons, then this figure is indeed impressive because it is larger than the GNP of many countries of 35 million, for example, India $793 billon, Mexico $753 billon, Brazil $644 billon, Russia $639 billon.[3]

It is internationally recognized that overseas Chinese enterprises and business networks in East and Southeast Asia have been the driving force behind the region's economic explosion and integration. On the basis of some scholars' research studies, it is argued that the distinctiveness of the Chinese Diaspora capitalism and the homeland's attracting and regulating Diaspora capital has made it possible for the transnational Chinese Diaspora capital and business networks to play an indispensable role in the economic rise of China and in connecting China with the rest of the region and the world (Bolt, 1996; 1997). One distinctive feature about the Diaspora capital can be seen from the crucial synergy it brings about between overseas investors and markets and China's local development. Chinese Diaspora create the most dynamic linkages between Diaspora capitalism and entrepreneurship and the booming economies of the towns and villages of the coastal regions (Lever-Tracy, et al., 1996a, 1996b).

Historical Roles

During certain periods of China's modern history, overseas Chinese Diasporas played an important role in shaping the direction of China's internal politics. In particular, they were political and economic pioneers with an important role in domestic evolution and especially in domestic revolution. Many of the funds supporting China's domestic reforms and revolutions came from the Diaspora. Most importantly, Sun Yat-sen (孙中山, Sūn Zhōngshān, 1866-1925), the "father of modern China" and the first revolutionary political leader, was also in important ways a Chinese Diaspora. At the age of 13, Sun migrated to Honolulu and lived with his elder brother for 5 years. In 1904 he became a citizen of the United States and was issued an American passport. He led the first Chinese Revolution of 1911-1912,[4] which led to the collapse of the imperial Qing Dynasty. He was both the

3 2005 data from *Student of the World*, available at http://www.studentsoftheworld.info/infopays/rank/PNB2.html.

4 It is also known as the *1911 Revolution* or the *Chinese Republic Revolution*, which overthrew the last dynasty – Qing Dynasty (1644-1911) and turned China into a republic. It

first provisional president of the Republic of China (ROC) in 1912 and one of the co-founders of the nationalist party Kuomintang (KMT); he served as its first leader. In these years of crucial transformation, most of the funding supporting Sun's 1911 Revolution came from overseas Chinese (Damon, 1991).

During the 1950s and 1960s, due to the internal turmoil of political struggle and the Cultural Revolution, overseas Chinese were viewed with suspicion as possible capitalist or counter-revolution infiltrators. Relations with overseas Chinese were politicized, addressed with an embellished revolutionary lexicon that insisted on a class-based patriotism and international solidarity with other revolutionary movements. As a result, the politicization of dealing with overseas Chinese issues, such as the question identity, the paradox of nationality and loyalty, according to need and changes in domestic revolutionary politics alienated many Diaspora Chinese who were attracted to Taiwan. Although Taiwan is not covered in this chapter, the struggles between Mainland China and Taiwan have historically divided the Diaspora communities shaping the political development of the US Chinese Diasporas for decades.

Since the implementation of market reforms at the end of 1970s, the attitude of the Chinese party-state toward overseas Chinese *has* changed fundamentally. The late Chinese leader Deng Xiaoping regarded tens of millions of Chinese Diasporas as one of the resources that the PRC might be able to use in development. The Diaspora was and is no longer regarded with the same distrust. Rather, its members are viewed as political and economic assets, endowed with professional skills and economic capital which could play a vital role in China's industrialization and overall development. Starting in the 1980s, the Chinese government was actively engaged in courting the support of its Diaspora by a variety of means, including returning properties that were confiscated since 1949.

In recent years, as students, scholars and professionals seeking advanced education and positions in high-level research have emigrated to the West in large numbers, the Chinese government has initiated new favourable policies designed to attract the support of the new emigrants of the 1990s. Apart from providing FDI and financial resources to feed China's economic growth, many Chinese Diasporas are playing leading roles in promoting China's social, cultural, scientific and academic development.

Chinese Diaspora in the Economic Rise of China

There is increased recognition and consensus that the Chinese Diaspora is one of the main economic and financial resources sustaining China's economic growth since China started its economic reform at the end of 1970s. The overseas remittances sent back home account for a substantial proportion of China's growth as well as the investments contributed by Chinese Diaspora. It is not an

---

is also called *Xinhai Revolution* in Chinese because the year 1911 was a Xinhai Year in the sexagenary cycle of the Chinese calendar.

exaggeration to claim that Chinese Diasporas are a vital key to China's economic miracle and its sustainable success of the economic reform in the past decades (Constance, et al., 1996).

Since the reform started in the early period, they have played an indispensable role in China's efforts to exchange and cooperate with foreign markets, to introduce international capitals, to enter the global market, and to sell domestic commodities to all over the world. For example, FDI is seen as one of the key driving elements behind China's rapid growth, and by 1993, 69 percent of direct foreign investment in China – $47.5 billion – came from ethnic Chinese in Hong Kong; and the investment from Taiwan (still no official direct economic and trade links with mainland China), reached up to $6.4 billion by 1993, which was 9.3 percent of total foreign investment according to China's statistics (Kwong, 1996). According to *OECD Observer* (No. 237, May 2003) China has since 1996 attracted more FDI than other developing countries; and in 2002 it received a record US$52.7 billion FDI surpassing all OECD member countries and became one of the largest FDI recipients. What is interesting in this regard is that fact that almost half of cumulative realized FDI China received came from the Chinese Diaspora-centred countries and regions, such as Hong Kong, Taiwan.

The first wave of foreign direct investment was primarily from the overseas Chinese who took a pioneering step into China's premature market in face of regulatory uncertainty and political sensitivity towards "capitalism" in the 1970s and 1980s. After the late 1990s and since 2000 there was a rise of flow of FDI from North American and European corporations. Following China's membership of the WTO, China has to reduce the preferential treatment to those overseas Chinese pioneers who were willing to take the risks of the lack of property law and unclear political systems.

Another distinctive feature about the Diaspora capital is the crucial synergy between overseas Chinese investors and China's local governments, one not found to the same extent or in the same form with non-Chinese FDI (Smart, Alan and Hsu, Jinn-Yuh, 2004). The Diaspora capitals paved the most dynamic linkages established between Diaspora capitalism and entrepreneurship and the booming economies of the towns and villages of the coastal regions (Constance, et al., 1996).

China's Multiple Channels of Interaction with its Diaspora

Comprehensive Strategic Policies on Overseas Diaspora Since the Economic Reform

Recognizing the fact that the 30 million Chinese Diasporas and their family members are an important force in China's economic development and modernization drive, national reunification and rejuvenation, the Chinese party-state has effectively set up multiple official, semi-official and grass-root mechanisms for incorporating the Chinese Diaspora into the modernization and globalization strategy so as

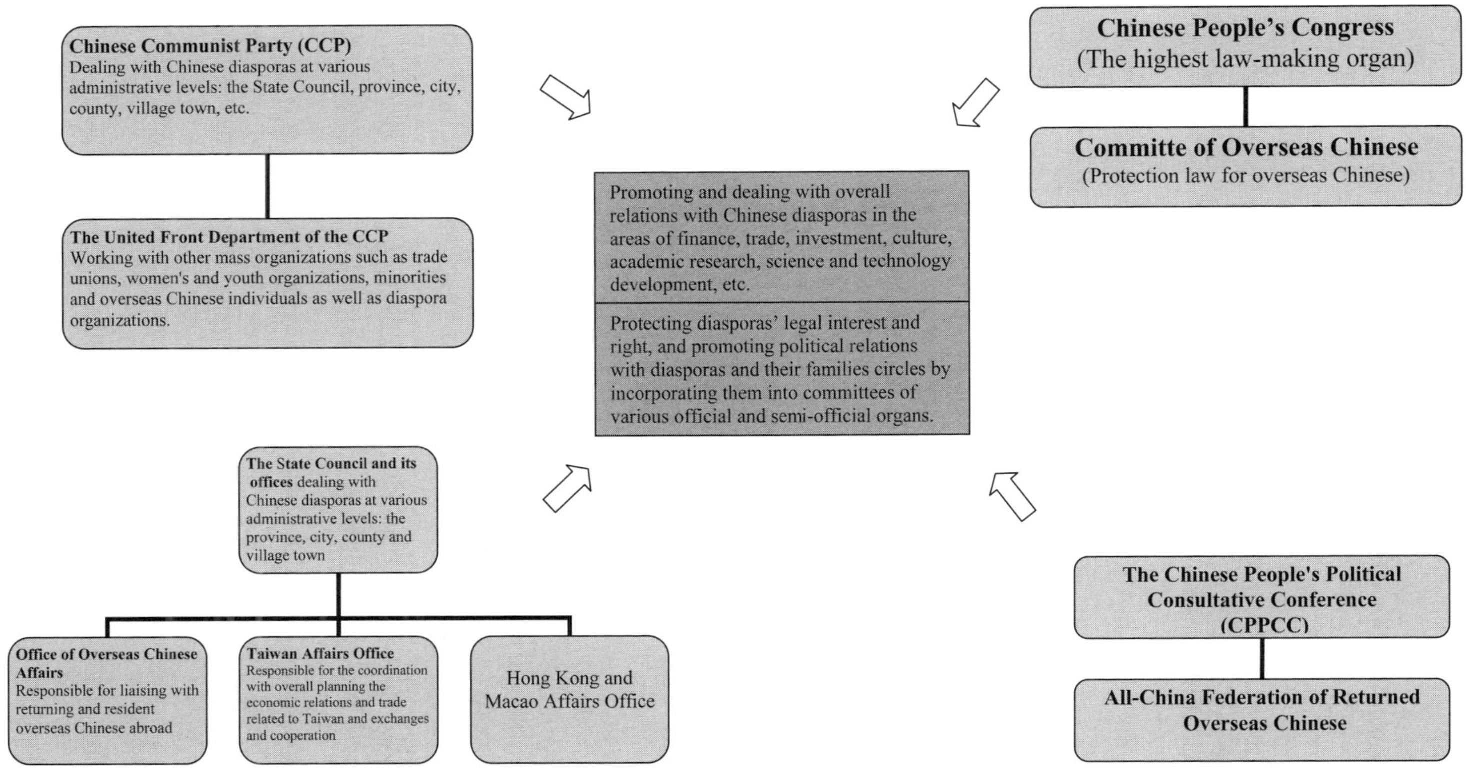

Figure 4.1 China's multiple institutional approaches in promoting and managing relations with its Diaspora

to reach a broad party-state political legitimacy, to serve the interest of China's economic development and to expand China's political influence. The strategy has been designated and implemented under a broad historical bloc around the notion of "Chineseness", i.e. Chinese culture and Chinese nation. Such a strategy is clearly reflected in both the policies and practical implementation of the relevant government institutions and the organization of the overseas Chinese affairs throughout the central and local governments (see Figure 4.1).

Legal Protection of Chinese Diaspora

In order to legally guarantee the protection of Chinese Diaspora and their overall interests in China, the National People's Congress on September 7, 1990, promulgated by Order No. 33 of the President of the People's Republic of China on September 7, 1990, passed the Law of the People's Republic of China on the Protection of the Rights and Interests of Returned Overseas Chinese and the Family Members of Overseas Chinese. This law began to be effective as of January 1, 1991. According to *China Daily* (November 17, 2000[5]), since 1990, government offices in charge of the overseas Chinese affairs at various levels across the country had treated more than 700,000 cases relating to rights and interests protection. This law was further amended in 2001 after it was practised for a decade. It aimed to create practical and preferential measures in order to provide overseas Chinese investments with efficient and privileged services on issues such as project approval, business registration, and approval of land requisition.

Overseas Diaspora as China's "State Affairs"

Administratively the affairs of Chinese Diaspora are governed by the Overseas Chinese Affairs Office. This office is placed at all administrative levels (state council, province, city, county and village-based town). At the highest level – the state council – the main objective of this office is to design and formulate national guidelines, policies and regulations regarding all works in connection with overseas Chinese affairs including supervising and checking the implementation of them at various local administrative levels. The office also conducts researches in studying the overseas Chinese affairs both at home and abroad. It provides the information and recommendation to the Central Committee of the Chinese Communist Party (CCP) and the government on development plan for overseas Chinese affairs works[6] (see Figure 4.1).

5 *China Daily*, http://english.peopledaily.com.cn/english/200011/17/eng20001117_55494.html.

6 The institutional functions of this office can be accessed in the Chinese website http://www.gqb.gov.cn/node2/node3/node22/node23//index.html.

In concrete terms, the office is to carry out a few practical tasks: 1) assisting the Premier in the administration of the overseas Chinese affairs and reviewing policies which directly concern the overseas Chinese affairs initiated by relevant ministries or local governments; 2) conducting necessary management and coordination for the overseas Chinese affairs works in connection with other relevant departments and social organizations; 3) protecting the legitimate rights and interests of the overseas Chinese; to enhance the unity and friendship in the overseas Chinese communities; 4) keeping contact with and support overseas Chinese medias and Chinese language schools; To accelerate the cooperation and exchanges of the overseas Chinese with China in terms of economy, science, culture and education (Chinese State Council, 2005).

The United-Front Strategy of the Chinese Communist Party (CCP)

One of the key departments of the Chinese Communist Party is the United Front Work Department. The original idea of "united front" was established during the period of the anti-Japanese War and the Civil War. Its strategy of the "mass line"[7] during the Chinese Revolution in the 1930s and 1940s was consistent with what Gramsci describes as the "national-popular" and the "war of position". The Chinese Communist Party, which assumed the vanguard role of the proletarian class,[8] achieved success in transforming itself into a hegemonic class. This was done by building an alliance with all social forces and combining them into the class struggle to create a collective will to achieve national independence and build a prosperous and equal society.

In the economic reform period, the united front strategy of the Chinese Communist Party after the economic reform is to unite all social forces both domestic and international to serve China's economic development. When Deng Xiaoping revived the united front activities at the Third Plenary Session of the 11th CCP Central Committee in 1978, he emphasized the vital role the investment of China's overseas Diaspora would play in bringing capital and technology to its modernization project. Without the economic investment and political support of the Chinese Diaspora, Deng maintained, China would never be able to live up to its full economic potential. Promotion of a sense of patriotism among overseas Diaspora by the united front strategy can be misread by many Western

7 During the war period, the Chinese Communist Party showed a deep understanding of the possible obstacles to draw peasants' participation in the communist revolution. Mao also made concrete investigations on this issue. The strategy of the "mass line" was developed in order to overcome the hindrances.

8 The original power of the Chinese Communist Party came from the peasant's movements in the countryside rather than from urban-based proletarian struggles, although there were some urban uprisings.

powers as a "fifth column"[9] and can be misguided by the suspicions over the potential emergence of a worldwide "Chinese Commonwealth" of entrepreneurial relationships under Chinese patriotism.

Organized Civil Society Networks for the Chinese Diaspora

Under the leadership of The Chinese People's Political Consultative Conference (CPC),[10] the *All-China Federation of Returned Overseas Chinese* is a mass organization formed by returned overseas Chinese and their relatives. Its main purpose is to function as a bridge linking the CPC and the government with returned overseas Chinese, their relatives and Chinese Diaspora residing abroad. Apart from actively participating in daily political, economic, cultural and social affairs of the country, its main task is to conduct consultation and supervision as a co-player in administration of Diaspora-related matters in order to unleash the full potential of overseas Diaspora to contribute to promoting economic and social development as well as national unity.

In concrete terms, the organization's practical tasks also include involvement in a number of direct areas:[11] 1) strengthening the relationship with the overseas Chinese and their relations and unleashing their enthusiasm for serving China; 2) playing the role of supervision and voicing the concerns and wishes of the Diaspora; 3) protecting the interests and rights concerning overseas Diaspora, such as supervising the implementation of Law of the Peoples Republic of China on the protection of the Rights and Interests of Returned or Returned Overseas Chinese and the Family Members of Overseas Chinese as well as improving the service quality; 4) strengthening relationship with new generation of overseas Chinese and their associations, building up strong links with international and regional organizations of overseas Chinese as well as actively participating in the grass-root activities.

In a word, through the last three decades we are witnessing the successful convergence of a dual process – Chinese Diaspora's active role in contributing to the homeland's economic success and enhancing China's integration with regional and global economy together with the homeland's systematic incorporating and institutionalizing the role of Diaspora in its development project. This dual process is driven by mutual interest and is continuously reinforcing both sides

9 The concept derived from the Spanish Civil War (1936-39). It refers to any clandestine group or faction of subversive agents who attempt to undermine a nation's solidarity.

10 *The Chinese People's Political Consultative Conference* is a united front organization under the leadership of the Communist Party of China and an organ for various other political parties, mass organizations and personages of various social circles to play an active consultative role in state affairs. See the website of the Central People's Government of People's Republic of China. http://english.gov.cn/links/cppcc.htm.

11 See the introductory article on "All-China Federation of Returned Overseas Chinese", available at http://knows.jongo.com/res/article/3595.

in a coordinated and institutionalized manner. What needs to be emphasized is that fact that China has built an effective institutional infrastructure assisted with preferential policies which networks the financial and skilled Diasporas and reaps the benefits.

The Making of the African Diaspora: A Tale of Two Boats

One of the remarkable features of the global institutional landscape is the presence of Africans all over the world, resulting in what is increasingly called a global Africa. The roots of this spread of Africans lie in two historically distinct movements, or two boats – one involuntary and the other voluntary – that left Africa at different historical periods. The first of these two boats, and the major cause of the making of the African Diaspora, is the result of the transatlantic slave trade. As Prah argues:

> Except for the migration, mainly to Europe and North America which have taken place over the last century, in almost all these parts of the world where Africans find themselves today, they have, for the most part, been taken there in bondage and pain. During the era of the Atlantic slave trade, so many Africans were taken out of the continent that by 1850, about a third of the people of African descent lived outside Africa. For almost four and half centuries (1441-1888) the transatlantic slave trade created an African Diaspora of about 15-20 million people, from many parts of Africa, particularly the West coast. (Prah, 2006: 232-233)

This Atlantic slave trade ensured that the African Diaspora today is spread and can be found in diverse places as Brazil, Peru, Colombia, the whole of Middle America, Mexico, the United States, Canada and the whole of the West Indies. Similarly others have ended up in Western Asia, with a "steady trickle" finding its way into India, Central Asia, the Balkans and beyond (Prah, 1996: 232). This first boat, largely involuntary, movement of Africans represents the old historical Diaspora, whose presence outside African laid the foundation for what can now be legitimately described as Global Africa.

While the Diaspora forged out of the slave trade represent the first Diaspora, a recent movement of Africans, particularly since the 1970s – the second boat – has resulted in Africa's second or postcolonial Diaspora. This second movement of Africans, largely voluntary – but sometimes involuntary in the sense of resulting from dislocation of wars and political upheavals on the continent – is a post slave trade phenomenon, and has become the bedrock of the remaking of the African Diaspora. This voluntary migration more so is to Europe as well as North America. Explaining the making of this second Diaspora in North America, Zeleza argues that after the staggered abolitions of the European and American slave trades and the end of African forced migration, only small numbers of Africans left the continent to settle in North America as compared to other immigrant groups. Indeed data covering the period 1850 to 1990 shows that the number of African born migrants in the US population rose from 2,538 in 1900, climbing to 18,326 in 1930, 35,355 in 1960, and 363,819 in 1990, an indication that more than three-quarters of the African migrants in 1990 entered the US since 1970 (Zeleza, 2002. See also El-Nur, 2002; Harris, 2003).

African post slave trade migration to Europe also followed the same pattern. In terms of destination these migrations reflected the colonial ties, making the UK and France the popular destinations for African migrants. This pattern, however changed with the inclusion of other European destinations like Germany and the Netherlands, Italy, Spain, and Portugal, which had until the 1970s themselves been countries of emigration (ibid.).

Together the first and second movement of Africans has ensured that there is a Global Africa, spread across the face of the world, in varying sizes and with diverse crosscutting linkages with the continent. For definitional purposes, this spread of Africans, or the African Diaspora, is conceptualized as consisting of the following:

> The global dispersion (voluntary and involuntary) of Africans throughout history; the emergence of a cultural identity abroad based on origin and social condition; and the psychological or physical return to the homeland, Africa. Thus viewed, the African Diaspora assumes the character of a dynamic, continuous, and complex phenomenon stretching across time, geography, class, and gender. (Alpers, 2001: 8)

In statistical terms, this global Africa is said to be made up of nearly 800 million Africans on the continent and up to another 100 million persons of African descent living in other parts of world, most in the United States but with significant communities in Brazil, the Caribbean, Canada, and parts of Western Europe (Bridgwater, 2003). For instance, according to the 2000 United States census, there are 34,658,190 African-Americans in the United States. Of the 35 million people that claimed Hispanic heritage in the 2000 US census, at least one third are likely to have African ancestry. Nearly 1.8 million people from the Caribbean lived in the United States in 2000. About 0.6 percent of all people living in United States (1,781,877) identified themselves as Sub-Saharan Africans. Conservatively, in the United States alone, at least 50 million individuals have African ancestry. Most people in the Caribbean and significant proportions of individuals in Latin America have African ancestry. The International Office of Migration (IOM), a United Nations agency, estimates that the African Diaspora population in France is 1,633,142 and another 1.5 million Diaspora Africans live in other European countries.

The IOM also provides a picture of an affluent Diaspora Africans. About 22 percent of Diaspora Africans are in the teaching, education and research professions; 20 percent in finance, investments and economics; 20 percent in public health; 15 percent in engineering; 9 percent in agriculture; 5 percent in information technology; 5 percent in legal sciences; 3 percent in administration, and; 1 percent in natural sciences. The 2000 US census indicates that foreign-born Sub-Saharan Africans (recent immigrants) have the highest proportion of foreign-born individuals 25 years and over who have bachelors degrees (49.3 percent) compared to Europe (32.9 percent) and Asia (44.9 percent). At least 38.2 percent of Sub-Saharan householders in the US own their own homes. The average median household income of foreign-born households headed by Sub-Saharan Africans was $36,371, according to the 2000 US census. For the period 2000 through 2002, the median household income for African Americans was $29,483 according to the US Census. Home-ownership for African Americans was 48 percent in 2003. Black-owned business in 1997, the latest period for which data is available, employed 718,300 persons and generated US$71 billion in revenues, according to the US Census (cited in Opoku-Mensah, 2006).

The Diaspora and the African Renaissance Imperatives of Development and Integration

The roles of the African Diaspora largely conflate with the nature of its evolution and structural location in the host countries. The recent upsurge and popularity of the Diaspora discourse is premised on the assumption that the African Diaspora has immense capacities, indeed it is a historical resource that can be mobilized in the service of African integration and development (Mbeki, 2003; World Bank, 2007; Asante, 2004). How has the African Diaspora responded to this twin call, and with what effect?

The African Diaspora and African Political Integration

An analysis of the African unification project indicates the critical role of the African Diaspora. Indeed in an exercise historicizing the political integration project, Kwesi Prah argues that the very notion of African unity and integration is a Diaspora construct:

> The roots of the idea of African Unity are buried in the mid-19th century. Together and enmeshed with the related ideas of nationalism and pan-Africanism, they emerged as the articulate response of people of African descent in Africa and its Diaspora to the continuing experience of western domination and exploitation. (Prah, 2000: 2)

He is emphatic that the primary reason for the emergence of the idea of African integration was, and is, the Diaspora inspiration forged out of the alienation from the continent, the detribalization and homogenization of Africans taken across the Atlantic, and their longing and reference for what is captured in spirit by Aimé

Césaire's extended poem (1939) called "Notes on a Return to the Native Country" (ibid).

A direct route of the Diaspora to African Integration, and the inauguration of the African Union in July 2002, is given by Thabo Mbeki, who in an address at the University of the West Indies argues that the stirrings and fermentation of the notions of decolonization and freedom on the African continent were significantly inspired by the courageous pioneers of African freedom in the Diaspora:

> It was in the year 1900 when the Trinidadian barrister Henry Sylvester Williams initiated the first Pan-African conference, in London. That conference was seminal to the political and philosophical movement of Pan-Africanism throughout the world, the catalyst that has ultimately led to the formation of the African Union, at the beginning of the 21st century. (Mbeki, 2003: 4)

This initiative of the Diaspora, and the inspiration it gave to the freedom fighters on the continent, he argues, was the decisive factor in the final onslaught against colonial domination on the African continent. He remains convinced that the 1945 5th Pan-African Congress in Manchester, England which featured anti-colonial thinkers and activists such as George Padmore and W.E.B. Du Bois, again impacted on the young African freedom fighters and intellectuals such as Kwame Nkrumah, and gave sustenance to the struggles which finally saw the realization of the process of African independence and freedom that started with the liberation of Ghana (ibid. See also Drake, 2003).

In sum, to the effect that African political integration is concerned, the Diaspora has provided the ideological and motivational basis for the project. Yet its role(s) in the practical realization of this ideal has, until recently, not been recognized. Indeed the Organization of African Unity (OAU), established in 1963 as the institutional architecture and framework for promoting African integration adopted a continental approach, conceiving African integration in purely geographic terms, largely conflating it with the integration of Africa states, excluding the Diaspora (Opoku-Mensah, 2006; 2007). The establishment of the African Union (AU) in 2002 has significantly shifted the terms of debating Africa's integration, with the process conceived as one involving Africa and its Diaspora. This shift in conception was given practical expression in a change to the constitutive act of the African Union (AU) in February 2003 to include the participation of the African Diaspora in the activities of the AU, and in the processes of African integration. As will be explained later, this has resulted in the legitimization of the role of the Diaspora in the unification project, although its exact roles remain to be largely gauged and accessed.

The African Diaspora and African Economic Development

Discussions on the African Diaspora and the continent's development, which have gained momentum in recent years, take place against the backdrop of recent efforts to highlight the increasing economic power of the Diaspora. For instance, Kwesi Prah argues that central to any program of African renewal is the process of accumulation, which necessarily will result from massive investment and capitalization. For this accumulation, Africans would have to be able to attract capital especially from within Africa and the African Diaspora in much the same way as China and India have been able to over the past few decades (Prah, 2007: 76. See also Opoku-Mensah and Banjoko, 2009). In sum, the African Diaspora is said to have significant human and economic resources to commit to the improvement of the African continent. Thus in relating this to the American context, the former US Assistant Secretary for State for African Affairs (and now US Ambassador to Ghana) Pamela Bridgewater, argues that

> There are now roughly 35 million citizens of African descent in the US with a collective purchasing power of about $450 billion per annum – a sum that if represented by a single country would make it one of the 15 largest economies in the world. (Bridgewater, 2003)

Thus with this yearly spending power of about $500 billion, African Americans are exhorted to expand their cultural linkages to Africa into economic linkages (Veney, 2002). Similar sentiments are raised for the African Diaspora in Europe, whose increasing economic purchasing power and contributions to African development is touted. In general the African Diaspora, like other Diaspora groups, is said to contribute to African Development in various ways including the provision of financial support to family and communities, establishing small businesses, building private transportation systems, stimulating new home constructions and artisan enterprise development, serving as cultural ambassadors, helping to extend and maintain public infrastructure such as schools and hospitals, and through their networks are beginning to delivering services in the health and education sectors in particular (World Bank, 2007: 16).

While there are increasing attempts to tap into this Diaspora economic resource through the establishment of African Diaspora investment forums, there is a lack of concrete data on how much of the growing economic power of the African Diaspora actually finds its way into Africa as investment capital. Anecdotal evidence of these contributions abound, although empirical verification is lacking. What is increasingly documented are remittances, which the World Bank argues amounted to $4 billion for Sub-Saharan Africa alone, surpassing the official development assistance received by these countries (World Bank, 2007). According to the IOM, Nigerians in the Diaspora remitted US$1.3 billion in 1999, equivalent to 3.7 percent of the country's GDP and 55 percent of overseas development assistance. Remittances from African Diasporas that identify Eritrea as their country of origin, accounted for 19.7 percent of the country's GDP and 85.8 percent of the overseas development assistance. It is important to note that these remittances do not include informal transactions that may be higher than data in official records (Opoku-Mensah, 2006).

For a continent that depends mostly on foreign aid, these contributions by the Diaspora are critically important for African countries. However, from a comparative perspective, more specifically in a comparison with the Chinese Diaspora, the economic roles of the African Diaspora raises questions as to the extent to which these remittances can constitute the type of foreign investment necessary for African development. To be sure, remittances provide much-needed finances for ensuring household security and alleviating poverty. Remittances also help siblings, kin, and friends to start or expand businesses; build houses, and undertake self-financed projects and investments (World Bank, 2007).

Yet these are far from the massive investments that are fuelling China's rapid economic growth and development. In general the contributions of the African Diaspora, while substantive and still increasing, have hardly concentrated on long-term investment projects. This has implications for the discussions on the role of the African Diaspora and its contribution to African development. These discussions have often been divorced from a discussion of the actual capacity and contributions the Diaspora can make. Akin to discussions on NGOs in the early 1990s, the African Diaspora is increasingly perceived as a "magic bullet", able and willing to contribute to the development integration of the African continent. Yet the available, or rather unavailable data, points to the limits of the African Diaspora's potential in African development.

This limitation, more so, is related to the structural location of the African Diaspora in the host countries. Indeed, one distinctive character of African Diasporas, wherever they are found, is that they share national and social marginalities in the global racialized hierarchies of power and privilege. Nowhere does the African Diaspora, both the historical and contemporary, dominate economic life. Indeed in Brazil, which is reputed to have the highest concentration of Africans outside the continent, Brazilian Africans are said to be the "invincible citizens" in economic life. This is true for most parts of the Western hemisphere with large concentrations of Africans. Haiti for instance remains "one of the poorest and most wretched counties in the Western hemisphere" (Prah, 2006: 253).

A notable exception might be the case of African Americans, who have witnessed some remarkable changes to their structural position in American society. This relates in particular to the arts and politics where names like Armstrong, Coltrane, Michael Jackson and Mohammed Ali are global households names. Their growing economic clout, as well as their entry into the high echelons of American political power, exemplified by the fact that there has been two African American US secretaries of State in succession – Colin Powell and Condoleezza Rice – as well as the recent election of Barack Obama as US President – is adequate indication of a change in their structural location. Yet, even here; "there are still enormous discrepancies and difficulties, and they remain an under class in American society" (Prah, 2006: 265).

Despite incremental changes, the African Diaspora occupies a similar place in Europe. In fact in the European case, one author argues that the Europeanization project has created a transnational space where migrants and African migrants in particular are especially marginalized, and on the lower rungs of the society (Zeleza, 2002: 7). This is not to discount, or even downplay, the contributions of the African Diaspora to African economic development, but to locate it within its limits, and perhaps to refocus it in areas where it can and have the capacity to make a difference, as in the case of higher education (Zeleza, 2002; Opoku-Mensah, 2006; 2007).

In sum, despite some progress, both the first and second African Diasporas remain politically and economically fragile. Discussions on their roles must therefore be tempered by this reality of their structural location in their host countries.

The African Diaspora and the African State

Historically the relation between the African state and the Diaspora has gone from ad-hoc communion, through indifference and outright hostility to the current period of rapprochement and organized institutionalized relations. But overall institutionalized relations between the African Diaspora and African governments remain weak:

> Although African Governments have begun to recognize the potential contributions of their Diasporas to home country development, serious efforts on the part of government in terms of strategies and instruments to harness these potentials are lacking, beyond the use of catchphrases (Africa news media are replete with phrases such as "turning brain drain to brain gain") or creating ministerial positions in cabinet or within the Presidency to be responsible for Diaspora affairs but without strategies that engage the Diaspora. As a result, institutional relationships between home country and Diasporas are weak. (World Bank, 2007: 17).

This notwithstanding some evidence of a desire for institutionalized mechanisms for relating to the African Diaspora is emerging at the regional level. As has been indicated earlier, the establishment of the African Union in 2002 has set in motion a number of efforts to institutionalize relations with the African Diaspora. Concrete initiatives in this respect have been established, beginning with the inclusion of Diaspora representatives in two major OAU-Civil Society Conferences on June 11-14, 2001 and June 11-15, 2002 respectively as part of the process of transforming the OAU into the AU. Indeed the genesis of the current efforts at incorporating the Diaspora took place at the second Conference in 2002, which focused on the contribution of the Civil Society to the establishment of the African Union, and which included Diaspora representatives. That Conference also elected a Provisional Working Group to work with the AU Commission on a continuous basis in between larger assemblies to be held on bi-annual basis. The Diaspora was given two representatives on this working Group – one for Europe and one for the Western Hemisphere including the US and other parts of the Americas.

Following its formal inauguration the AU has sought to establish a framework through which the African Diaspora would be mainstreamed in the activities of the new AU. For instance, the AU Commission made plans to launch AU Diaspora Forums in Europe and the Western Hemisphere. Consequently, the First AU–Western Hemisphere Diaspora Forum was convened in Washington DC from December 17-19, 2002. The Forum began the process of institutional links between the African Diaspora and Continental Africans in an effort to establish the Union project as a truly global African effort. As a result of this initial meeting, a Western Hemisphere Diaspora Network (WHADN) was established to interface with the AU Commission in this regard and the Network set up permanent working groups made up of Experts and Resource persons in each area. The Working Group has put up proposals for effective collaboration in each of these domains. These proposals have been refined by the Commission in consultation with the nascent WHADN Secretariat to allow for effective programme support and to feed into the policy demands of the Commission. The Network has also decided on the establishment of an AU Education Endowment Fund and an AU Trade and Economic Development Forum for the US Diaspora and agreed on a series of measures for contribution to these funds including elements of salary deductions.

By far the most important and far-reaching measure taken by the AU on the incorporation of the Diaspora took place at the Extra-Ordinary Summit of the Assembly of Heads of States and Governments held in Addis Ababa, Ethiopia on February 3, 2003 to deliberate on proposed amendments to the Constitutive Act. At the meeting of the Executive Council that preceded the Summit, Senegal proposed an amendment to formally integrate the Diaspora in the policy framework of the Union. The proposed amendment was refined and adopted by the Summit in a new Article 3 (q) that would "invite and encourage the full participation of the African Diaspora as an important part of our continent, in the building of the African Union". The amendment constitutes a milestone in the bid to incorporate the Diaspora into the policy-making and policy support processes of the AU. In a further demonstration of commitment, the AU has allocated the Diaspora representation in the Economic Social and Cultural Council (ECOSOCC). Of a total of 150 civil society organizations allocated representation, 20 of these must come from the African Diaspora.

Finally there is a series of regional consultative meetings being organized across the globe in preparation for an Africa Union–African Diaspora summit in South Africa in 2008. The Summit, whose theme: "Towards the realization of a united and integrated Africa and its Diaspora: A shared vision for sustainable development to address common challenges", ultimately seeks to produce a practical programme of action for institutionalized co-operation between Africa and its Diaspora.

Similar efforts are been undertaken at the national level where Ministries for Diaspora affairs are being established, as is the case of Ghana and Nigeria. In the

Ghanaian case, for instance, a concerted effort is being made by the state to establish institutionalized links with the Ghanaian Diaspora through the establishment of a Ministry for Diaspora relations; the passing of a law for dual citizenship; as well as a law paving the way for the Diaspora to vote. Similarly, in a proactive bid to reach out to the historical or first Diaspora, the Ghanaian government has established a so-called Joseph project – a reference to the biblical story of Joseph – to encourage the return of the historical Diaspora to the continent. For this purpose, it intends to introduce a permanent Diaspora visa that allows descendants of the historical Diaspora to visit Ghana without visas after their first visit. Similarly, and the first African country to do so, it has supported the establishment of a Diaspora Africa Forum in Ghana, the first diplomatic mission established by the African Union to deal with Diaspora issues.

Since 2001, an annual "homecoming summit" has also been organized for the Ghanaian government, private sector and civil society to interact with members of the Ghanaian Diaspora. In effect, while institutionalized relations between have been non-existent the past few years have seen activities to establish these mechanisms. It is too early, however, to assess the extent to which this will lead to a better structuring of the relations between African and her Diasporas.

The Chinese and African Diaspora in a Comparative Perspective

As a methodological approach in social sciences especially in the areas of development research, cross-country comparison, a method which is largely inspired by the modernization school of thought, becomes a tradition to apply a country or region as a contrasting model in comparing with other countries or regions that differ profoundly in history, tradition, values, and organization.

Very often problems of conceptualization and measurement followed by causal theorizing and causal conclusion are not taken into serious consideration in many development literatures influenced by the modernization paradigm. For example, it is a fashion in development research to compare the economic success of East Asia with the underdevelopment of Africa, and often the conclusion goes: most Asian dragons were at the same level as Kenya among other African countries including Ghana in the 1960s, and the factors that East Asia has developed into a developed semi-core status whereas African countries are now among the poorest of the poor are due to the fact that East Asia has shown superior performance in some key areas, such as the role of the state, cultural values, government policies, democratic politics, and issues of governance (Evans, 1995; Jones, 1980; Tu, 1989; Wade, 1990; World Bank 1993, etc.) However, what is neglected is the international political economy of East Asian dynamism (Borthwick, 1992; Deyo, 1988).

Without taking into consideration the extent of the capitalist world system especially American historical, political and economic influence in the region, it would be meaningless to discuss the economic success and the historical development path of East Asia (Hersh, 1993; Li, 2007). The post-war United States as the dominant political, economic and military power in the international system played a significant part in structuring post-war world development. This fear of Communism due to the deep sentiment of the "loss of China" made America take part in two perhaps entirely avoidable wars in Korean Peninsula and Southeast Asia. The "loss of China" also attributed to the political economy of the emergence of East Asian developmental states under the American parenthood in terms of market access, military and financial aid as well as national security. Before generating any conclusion when comparing East Asia with Africa, these important external factors cannot be ignored!

Another comparison in a dichotomy of East Asia/China versus Africa is within the lines of discussion of norms and values promoted by the culturalist approach. Today, the East Asian and Chinese economic success is portrayed as a model for the developing world, and the Chinese Confucian tradition is considered by the culturalist interpretation as having made a contribution in terms of its emphasis on knowledge, education, diligence, self-sacrifice and delayed gratification to social stability as well as its acceptance of bureaucratic governance at both governmental and enterprise levels. However, it should not be forgotten that the relative decline of China in the mid-19th century was seen by the culturalist school as attributable to its cultural stagnation. The views of the culturalist school were understandable because these perceptions of China, although premature, were a product of a comparison between the immobility of non-Western cultures and the revolutionary Europe. What was behind the viewpoint was to establish a European model for other cultures to follow. To put China in the framework of the Weberian explanation, the failure of China's transition to the stage of capitalism is due to the fact that Chinese Confucian cultural values are not receptive to the development of capitalism in terms of creativity, competition and entrepreneurship.

In sum, despite the value of comparative studies of the Chinese and African Diaspora, it is imperative to be aware of the limitations and dangers of such comparative exercise, as a basis to avoid misinterpretations and misconceptualizations. Similarly, it needs to be stressed from the outset that the aim of this comparison is not a wholesale transference of the Chinese experience to Africa, or vice versa. Rather the objective of the comparison is to understand some of the major determinants of the nature and strength of Diaspora links and contributions to the homeland.

With this caveat in mind, the discussions so far indicate that both the Chinese and African Diasporas maintain active links with the homeland, playing various roles in the development and integration of the homeland. Indeed both the Chinese and the African Diasporas have played varying roles in the quest for regional unity, with different effect. Yet these roles, and the effectiveness with which they are played, are critically mediated by a number of factors, which are discussed below. These factors relate to the role of history, the contemporary structural location of the Diaspora, and the nature of state response. Specifically, the analyses indicate that the roles(s) of the Diaspora are a function of its historical evolution; composition and structural location in the host land; and the institutional response of the homeland. These are discussed below:

History and Nation Matters!

Understanding the historicity behind our comparative studies, this chapter intends to point out the fact that the discussions on the Diaspora and their contributions to the homeland cannot be divorced from the historical making of various Diasporas, as is often done. These discussions have often been normative and adopted a prescriptive posture, with the Diaspora called upon to support the development of the homeland. Yet despite these increasing calls, the comparative evidence however does not support a one-to-one correlation between the existence of a Diaspora and its support for the homeland (Brinkerhoff, 2004).

In the African discussions, for instance, the African Diaspora is admonished to aid the renaissance of the continent in similar terms to the Chinese Diaspora contributions to the rise of China (Zeleza, 2002; World Bank, 2007; Prah, 2007). Our analyses indicate that such discussions are problematic because they fail to place these roles in the context of the historical evolution, and making, of specific Diasporas. For instance, the history of the Chinese historical dispersion and its relations to a single homeland makes the relations of the overseas Chinese to the homeland straightforward. On the other hand the African historical Diaspora deterritorialized and without links to a specific African country influences its ability to link to a homeland, which more or less is simply imagined. Similarly, the historical circumstances under which those who left with Africa's second boat – whether they left under economic or political "persecution" – will determine the *dominant nature* of their links to the homeland.

Analytically this raises questions about the validity of this homogenizing discourse on the roles of the Diaspora which brands disparate Diasporas together. In this frame, the African Diaspora is challenged to live up to the Chinese and the Jewish Diaspora, and their contributions to China and Israel respectively (Prah, 2007; Opoku-Mensah and Banjoko, 2009). A historicization of the process of Diaspora formation might caution against such prescriptive discussions, as the roles of the African Diaspora must be a function of its history. This argument supports Robin Cohen's analytical schema that distinguishes among various Diasporas, such as the "victim Diasporas" (Africans and Armenians), "labor Diasporas" (Indians), "imperial Diasporas" (British), "trade Diasporas" (Chinese and Lebanese), or "cultural Diasporas" (the Caribbean) (Cohen, 1997: 26). Although this schema has been criticized, among others, on the grounds that these Diasporas are not mutually exclusive, it nevertheless lends credence to this need for historical origins as a first step to understanding the nature of the Diasporas links to the homeland. Seen in this light, the dominance of cultural relations in the links between Africa's historic first Diaspora and the continent can be understood as a function of its cultural dislocation from the continent.

Similarly, the dominance of economic relations in overseas Chinese links to the homeland makes sense in the light of its historical evolution as a labouring or trading Diaspora. This is not to generalize, or essentialize across the board, but to stress that history does matter in understanding the Diaspora and its links to the homeland.

In a sense, the centrality of differences in understanding the role of Chinese and African Diaspora and their linkage to the homeland is the "haves" and "have-nots" of national identity. The concept of Diaspora implies those people who live outside their "home country" and their reflective identity cannot be separate from their roots of origin. Identity is understood to be a process based on positive identifications with a number of ingredients of self-formation at different levels, such as nation, language, family, ethnicity, gender, class and so on. Often, sentimental feelings like "nostalgia" and "melancholy" are closely associated with Diaspora's cultural identity which is central to the construction of subjectivity, the formation of self-image, and the delineation of social boundaries. Therefore, national identity is often equated with cultural identity, and a nation-state is the precondition for articulating a coherent and independent cultural identity. The relationship between history, nation-state and cultural identity is dynamic because rapid and dramatic transformation can generate a dislocation of identity and problems of identity fragmentation.

Within the last century China has undergone more transformative changes than any other country in the world. This history of Chinese overseas migration was closely connected with these transformations. The Chinese state and society transformed from an imperial monarchy to a short-lived republic, and from a weak and decentralized warlord authoritarianism to a centralized revolutionary socialist state; economically it went from a state-led industrialization based on planned economy and socialist egalitarianism to an all-round structural reform based on market mechanisms, and its economy underwent repeated shift from crisis and failure to very rapid growth and modernization; politically Chinese society and people experienced imperialism and warlordism as well as dictatorship and class struggle; ideologically Chinese value systems underwent transformations from feudalism to socialism and from collectivism to individualism. In recent decades economic growth has torn down much of the physical symbols of China's cultural history, but Chinese people still remain an intensely historical nation with strong and popular *nationalism*. Chinese nationalism connotes a cohesive history, a united people and a shared cultural tradition under a unified country known as China. To Chinese Diaspora, regardless of the historical period in which they left China, homeland identity is always significant to their own identity. The homeland's political fate and international status has profound implications for them. The rise of China in recent decades has without doubt a positive impact on the position and role of Chinese Diaspora communities.

On the contrary, the memory of early generations of African Diaspora is the one associated with slavery, and the history of African Diaspora is a history of racial conflict without any national embodiment and without any cultural, linguistic and social reference for the formation of the Diaspora identity. The identity of African Diaspora is not historically embedded and needs to be created and negotiated in a continuous process of defining the Diaspora themselves and negotiating their identity and belonging.

Structural Location Matters!

The analysis shows that if history is important to understand the evolution, composition and Diaspora attitudes to the homeland, their present structural location in the host country provides an indication to the *ability* and *capacity* with which the Diaspora can be a resource for the development of the homeland. The logic is rather straightforward. A Chinese Diaspora that controls 60 percent of the private economy of a country like Indonesia is more likely to play meaningful economic roles in the homeland than the African Diaspora whose members remain at the bottom of the economic ladder of their host countries. The Chinese Diaspora is a powerful economic force anywhere it is located. The African Diaspora remains a fragile actor in almost all the places where it is located. Even in the United States where the African Diaspora is most wealthy, as a group it still remains an underclass. This has implications for the roles they can play in African development. To be sure, this does not mean they do not play any roles at all, as the evidence indicates multiple and sustained roles. What is being stressed is that, based on their current structural locations, both the historical and the current Diaspora, although actively involved in Africa, nevertheless cannot be expected to be a major source of investment capital. On the other hand, it does have the potential to play other roles, including knowledge transfer and political mobilization.

Being an economic class armed with capital and technology overseas Chinese commercial capitalism operates on a form of social interaction that is built through kinship network and ethnic relationship (social capital with national reference and cultural root originated and connected with the homeland) making it independent from the local system of political economy. The organization of business transactions through cultural affinitive networks gives Chinese Diaspora entrepreneurs a comparative advantage in which economic calculation is well combined with cultural trust, thus reducing the transaction cost. Ethnic Chinese are the prime sources of capital and entrepreneurship not only in mainland China but also in most of the Southeast Asian countries. The spill-over effect of the regional network-based capitalism driven by the Chinese Diaspora can be partly illustrated by the role of the hundreds of successful ethnic Chinese family business and networks connecting and interlocking medium-sized businesses in many countries in the region. Overseas Chinese entrepreneurs, business executives, traders and financiers are the major players linking local economies with that of the region.

The lack of the development of such an economic class prevents the kinds of organised structured interventions in the economies of Africa. Although there is gradual development of African Diaspora investment forums in Europe and North

America, these remain fragile, and to date there is a lack of documentation on what their exact contributions have been to African economies.

State Response Matters!

Beyond history and structural location, the response of the home country is the final indicator of the ability of the Diaspora to make meaningful contributions. Ultimately the efficacy with which the Diaspora can play developmental roles in the homeland is fundamentally related to the response of the homeland state. The extensive and multiple institutional responses of the Chinese state to its Diaspora, is in sharp contrasts to the undeveloped, non institutionalized mechanisms for Africa's relations with its Diaspora. Indeed the activist and proactive role of the Chinese state towards its Diaspora contrasts to the lackadaisical, and in some instances almost non-existent, institutional mechanism for Africa's relations its Diasporas. This in turn, determines the effectiveness with which the Chinese Diaspora, the so-called Overseas Chinese, have participated in China's development over the years. The corollary is that the state becomes the anchor around which the transnational activities of the Diaspora can be made effective. This brings the state into the transnational discussions on the Diaspora – once again!

Since the late 1970s, China has had a new overseas Chinese policy in place aiming at actively supporting overseas Chinese abroad as well as creating mechanisms for incorporating the Chinese Diaspora into China's modernization strategy. This strategy is clearly inbuilt in the organization of Chinese Diaspora, which is clearly reflected in the work and the practices of the relevant party, legislation and government institutions including civil society-based associations (see Figure 4.1). The new development strategy raises the overseas Chinese affairs to such a high level that they have come to be regarded as a matter of Chinese national interests, and as one scholar observes, this demonstrates that "the PRC's authorities make considerable efforts to win the loyalty of the overseas Chinese and to organise them in a strong and loyal ethnically conscious and politically sympathetic pro-Beijing front of Chinese people who are concentrated outside the sovereignty of the PRC" (Barabantseva, 2005: 27). The Chinese state seems to understand Chinese Diaspora as a uniting factor and an indispensable intermediate to pursue China's national interests and exercise Beijing's logocentric and ideological presence in transnational localities. Reviewing the evolution of China's Diaspora policy, it can be argued that overseas Chinese Diasporas are current not only identified by the Chinese state and government as an integral part of Chinese patriotic nationalism, but also increasingly incorporated in line with the current Chinese national project of modernization (Nyíri 2001 and 2002). As a result, Chinese Diasporas have actually become a "national asset" enjoying an active support from the state both politically, legislatively and economically.

At both the continental and country levels, African countries are gradually waking up to the need to harness the resources of their Diaspora. Thus incentives and institutional mechanisms are being put in place. At the continental level, the recognition of the Diaspora as the sixth region, and the establishment of a Directorate for Diaspora affairs, provides the motivational and institutional platform for Diaspora–Africa relations. Indeed this represents by far the most significant response of the African state to the need for a collective African response to its Diaspora. At the country level, and as has been indicated earlier, various African states are also enacting policies, providing incentives and enabling environments for harnessing the potential of their Diasporas. This has taken the form of dual citizenship laws, and in some countries, like Ghana, the granting of voting rights to the Diaspora. One such law has been a Diaspora visa introduced by the Ghana to the historical Diaspora. This is part of a so-called Joseph Project being spearheaded by Ghana, on behalf of for Africa, to bring back the descendants of Africans taken out of the continent during the slave trade, and who have no links to a particular African country. This has led to a constant flow of Diaspora visitors to the country resulting in the establishment of a Diaspora Africa Forum (DAF) in Accra, the first official mission established by the African Union to formalize its relations with the African Diaspora.

Together these developments show the increasing proactive role of the state, and its recognition of the strategic importance of the Diaspora. The extent to which these developments can be sustained as part of long term institutionalized links is difficult to tell. What is certain, however, is that the increasing attention by both the Chinese and African states to their Diasporas is, *ipso facto*, an indication of the growing importance of the Diaspora in an era characterised by transnational flows and linkages.

Conclusion

In an era characterized by globalization and transnational relations, discussions on the rise of nations cannot afford to ignore the role of the Diaspora. This is true of the rise of China, and equally so about the prospects for a renascent Africa. The discussions on the roles of the Diaspora, however, rest on a homogenizing narrative that prevents an understanding of the diversity that characterizes the global Diaspora experiences, or the capabilities of different Diaspora groups. This chapter's comparative analyses of the Chinese and African Diasporas show the need for incorporating this diversity in the analyses. Practically, the analyses indicate that the response of the state – or its lack of response – ultimately determines the effectiveness of the Diaspora and its contributions to the rise of nations.

Overall, the chapter has established the crucial role of the Diaspora to China's rise, and the limited contribution of Africa's Diaspora to African renewal. For comparative analytical purposes, the most important factor must be attributed to the socio-historical foundations of the Chinese Diaspora which have been historically and organically connected with the homeland, where their ties with the homeland's cultural bond have never been broken even after centuries of family settlement elsewhere. The rise of China in the recent decades and the economic and political role of Chinese Diaspora become mutually supportive reinforcement, rowing like two sides of the same coin.

The intense historical and national identity together with the Confucian family culture provided Chinese Diaspora with a basis for cooperation and solidarity in foreign lands and under hostile environments. This gradually generated distinctive Chinese Diaspora capitalism as a dynamic form of social institution characterized by entrepreneurial spirit and wealth creation mentality around family and social networks. Throughout a long historical evolution, the network-based Chinese Diaspora capitalism has been able to become an independent social, political and economic force which does not necessarily depend on the vicissitudes of external political constraints. In the past three decades transnational Chinese Diaspora capital and business networks, assisted by the homeland's proactive policies, have been playing an indispensable role in the economic rise of China and in connecting China with the rest of the region and the world. This has ensured that the influence of the Chinese Diaspora is felt throughout the region. Indeed in recent years the East Asian regional economic integration has been truly driven by overseas Chinese business networks linking the region with the economic growth and market expansion of mainland China (Li, 2007, Li and Zhang, 2008).

Similarly, the (historical) African Diaspora has been instrumental to the integration project of Africa. In part because of their disconnection with the homeland, and the desire for a reconnection with this imagined homeland, the African Diaspora provided the motivational basis, and the ideas for the African unification. Indeed and as was established, the very idea of African unity and integration was, and is, a Diaspora construct.

Unlike the Chinese Diaspora, however, the lack of an organic connection to a physical homeland, coupled with their structural location in the host country prevents any substantive role in the economic integration of the African continent. The recent attempt by the African Union to link with the Diaspora, and the growth of the second Diaspora – which unlike the historical Diaspora has organic links to the African continent – potentially provides new impetus and opportunities for a more concerted Diaspora involvement in the African renewal project.

In the final analysis, however, the Chinese experience shows that the ability of the Diaspora to contribute substantively to any project of nation building is fundamentally dependent on the structural position of the Diaspora, and equally, on the response by homeland states.

References

Alpers, Edward (2001) "Defining the African Diaspora", paper presented to the Center for Comparative Social Analysis Workshop. Los Angeles: University of California, October 25.

Asante, Molefi (2004) "Africa and its Diaspora: Forging Ideas of an African Renaissance", paper presented at the Conference of Intellectuals from Africa and the Diaspora. Dakar, October 6-9.

Barabantseva, Elena (2005) "Trans-nationalising Chineseness: Overseas Chinese Policies of the PRC's Central Government", *ASIEN – The German Journal on Contemporary Asia*, 96: 7-28.

Bolt, Paul J. (1996) "Looking to the Diaspora: The Overseas Chinese and China's Economic Development, 1978-1994", *Diaspora: A Journal of Transnational Studies*, 5(3): 467-496.

Bolt, Paul J. (1997) "Chinese Diaspora Entrepreneurship, Development, and the World Capitalist System", *Diaspora: A Journal of Transnational Studies*, 6(2): 215-235.

Borthwick, Mark (ed.) (1992) *Pacific Century: The Emergence of Modern Pacific Asia.* Boulder, CO: Westview Press.

Bridgwater, Pamela (2003) "The African Diaspora and Its Influence on African Development", remarks at Kentucky State University, Frankfort, Kentucky, March 28.

Chinese State Council, *Overseas Chinese Affairs Office of the State Council*, available at the website of the Central People's Government of People's Republic of China http://www.gov.cn/english/2005-10/03/content_74290.htm.

Damon, Allen F. (1991) "Financing Revolution: Sun Yat-sen and the Overthrow of the Ch'ing Dynasty", *The Hawaiian Journal of History*, 25: 161-186.

Deyo, Frederic C. (ed.) (1988) *The Political Economy of the New Asian Industrialism.* Ithaca, N.Y: Cornell University Press.

Drake, St Clair (1993) "Diaspora Studies and Pan-Africanism", in Harris, J (ed.) (1993) *The Global Dimensions of the African Diaspora*, second edition. Washington D.C.: Howard University Press, 451-514.

Elnur, Ibrahim (2002) "The Second Boat: African New Diaspora: Looking at the Other Side Of The Global Divide With Emphasis On Sudan", *African Issues*, 30(1): 37-41.

Evans, Peter (1995) *Embedded Autonomy: States and Industrial Transformation.* Princeton: Princeton University Press.

Goodman, David S.G. (1997-98) "Are Asia's 'Ethnic Chinese' a Regional-Security Threat?", *Survival*, 39(4): 140-155.

Harris, John (ed.) (1993) *The Global Dimensions of the African Diaspora.* Second edition. Washington D.C.: Howard University Press.

Hersh, Jacques (1993) *The USA and the Rise of East Asia Since 1945: Dilemmas of the Postwar International Political Economy.* New York: St. Martin's Press.

Jones, Leroy P. (1980) *Government, Business, and Entrepreneurship In Economic Development: The Korean Case.* Cambridge: Harvard University Press.

Koo, Carolyn (1995) "Tales of the Chinese Diaspora", *Institutional Investor*, 29(12): 220.

Kwong, Peter (1996) "The Chinese Diaspora", *World Business*, 2(3): 26-31.

Lever-Tracy, Constance, David Ip and Noel Tracy (1996a) *The Chinese Diaspora and Mainland China: An Emerging Economic Synergy*. London: Palgrave Macmillan.

Lever-Tracy, Constance and David Ip (1996b) "Diaspora Capitalism and the Homeland: Australian Chinese Networks into China", *Diaspora: A Journal of Transnational Studies*, 5(2): 239-273

Li, Xing (2007) "Conceptualizing East Asian Regionalism: From Japan-led 'flying-geese' to China-driven Integration", *CCIS Working Paper No. 3*, CCIS – Centre for Comparative Integration Studies, Department of History, International and Social Studies, Aalborg University, Denmark.

Li, Xing and Zhang Shengjun (2008) "China and Regional Integration in East Asia: Opportunities, Constraints and Challenges", *CCIS Working Paper* No.9, (Centre for Comparative Integration Studies, Department of History, International and Social Studies, Aalborg University, Denmark).

Mbeki, Thabo (2003) "African Diaspora in the 21st Century", speech delivered at the University of West Indies, Kingston Jamaica, June 30. Available at http://www.nathanielturner.com/africanDiaspora21stcentury.htm.

Nyíri, Pál (2001) "Expatriating is Patriotic? The Discourse on 'New Migrants' In the People's Republic of China and Identity Construction Among Recent Migrants from the PRC", *Journal of Ethnic and Migration Studies*, 27(4): 635-653.

Nyíri, Pál (2002) "From Class Enemies to Patriots: Overseas Chinese and Emigration Policy and Discourse in The People's Republic of China", in Pál Nyíri and I.R. Saveliev (eds) *Globalizing Chinese Migration: Trends in Europe and Asia*. Aldershot: Ashgate, 208-241.

Opoku-Mensah, Paul and Banjoko, Titi (2009) "Diaspora Philanthropy and the Pan African Agenda: The African Diaspora and NEPAD", in *The State of Philanthropy in Africa*, Trust Africa.

Opoku-Mensah, Paul (2006) "Civil Society and African Integration: The Challenge of Incorporating the African Diaspora", in *Transformation: Critical Perspectives in Southern Africa*, 61: 25-39.

Opoku-Mensah, Paul (2007) "The African Diaspora, Civil Society and African Integration", *CCIS Research Series*, No. 6. CCIS – Center for Comparative Integration Studies and Department of History, International and Social Studies, Aalborg University(http://vbn.aau.dk/fbspretrieve/13003220/CCIS_wp_no._6).

Prah, Kwesi (2000) "African Unity, Pan-Africanism and the Dilemmas of Regional Integration". Paper presented to the Southern Africa Regional Institute for Policy Studies (SARIPS) Annual Colloquium. Harare: September 24-28.

Prah, Kwesi (2006) *The African Nation: The State of the Nation*, CASAS Book Series No. 44, The Center for Advanced Study of African Society (CASAS), Cape Town.

Prah, Kwesi (2007) "Nationalism, Revolution and Economic Transformation", in Prah K. (ed.) *Afro-Chinese Relations: Past, Present and Future*, Book Series 45, The Centre for Advanced Studies of African Society (CASAS).

Smart, Alan and Hsu, Jinn-Yuh (2004) "The Chinese Diaspora, Foreign Investment and Economic Development in China", *The Review of International Affairs*, 3(4): 544-566.

Tu, Wei-Ming (1989) "The Rise of Industrial East Asia: The Role of Confucian Values", *Copenhagen Papers*, 4.89: 81-97.

Veney, Cassandra R. (2002) "The Ties That Bind: The Historic African Diaspora and Africa", *African Issues*, 30(1): 3-8.

Wade, Robert (1990) *Governing the Market*: *Economic Theory And The Role Government in East Asian Industrialization*. Princeton: Princeton University Press.

Wei, Chi Poon and Virginia Jing-yi Shih (2002) (co-chair of the project) *CHINESE OVERSEAS: Challenges and Contributions*, an Exhibit in Bernice Layne Brown Gallery, Doe Library University of California, Berkeley.

World Bank (1993) *The East Asian Miracle: Economic Growth and Public Policy*. New York: Oxford University Press.

World Bank (2007) *Concept Note: Mobilizing the African Diaspora for Development*, Capacity Development Management Action Plan Unit (AFTCD), Operational Quality and Knowledge Services Department (AFTQK).

World Business (2007) "The world's successful Diasporas", available at: http://www.worldbusinesslive.com/research/article/648273/the-worlds-successful-Diasporas/.

Yin, Rosanna Yin Lau (2001) *Coolies* (illustrated by Chris Soentpiet). New York: Philomel.

Zeleza, Paul (2002) "Contemporary African Migrations in a Global Context: towards building the black Atlantic", essay for the 10th CODESRIA General Assembly. Kampala, December 8-12.

Zeleza, Paul (2005) "Rewriting the African Diaspora: Beyond The Black Atlantic", *African Affairs*, 104(414): 35-68.

Chapter 5
Peak Energy and the Limits to Economic Growth: China and the World

Li Minqi

Introduction

There is a growing body of evidence suggesting that world oil production is likely to have peaked or will peak very soon. Moreover, studies have suggested that world natural gas and coal production could peak in about 2030. As fossil fuels account for about 95 percent of the world's commercial energy production (traditional biomass consumption is excluded), and to the extent that nuclear and renewable energies cannot expand at a sufficiently rapid pace to offset the decline of fossil fuels, the peak of the fossil fuels production will translate into the peak of the world energy production, with potentially devastating implications for the world economy.

Measured by purchasing power parity, China now accounts for 10 percent of world GDP, about half of the current size of the US economy. Under the current trend, China could overtake the US and become the world's largest economy before 2020. China's economic growth has been heavily energy intensive and arguably the single most important factor behind the rapid growth of global energy demand and greenhouse gases emission in recent years. China now accounts for 17 percent of the world's primary energy consumption and is set to overtake the US to become the world's largest energy consumer in one or two years. China has already overtaken the US to become the world's largest carbon dioxide emitter and now accounts for one-fifth of the global emissions. The coming world energy crisis is likely to have particularly severe impact on China's economic and social development in the coming decades.

This chapter attempts to develop a technical framework that would allow one to evaluate the potential implications of peak energy production on economic growth. The basic technique used is Hubbert linearization, which was used by American geologist Marion King Hubbert to predict the US oil production peak. The chapter applies Hubbert linearization to analyze not only the potentials of nonrenewable resources, but also the potentials of renewable resources and energy efficiency. The framework developed could be updated to evaluate the trajectory of energy supply and economic growth using new data that will be available in the future.

After considering the potentials of coal, oil and gas production, as well as the development potentials of renewable and nuclear energy, this chapter finds that the world economy will in effect suffer a permanent depression through the rest of the 21st century. China is likely to face an insurmountable energy crisis beyond 2020. Even with optimistic assumptions, drastic declines of economic growth rate and the eventual end of economic growth cannot be avoided.

Modern capitalism is an economic and social system based on the pursuit of endless accumulation of capital. Sustained economic growth is indispensable for the normal operations of capitalism. The Chinese ruling elites, in particular, have relied upon rapid economic growth to alleviate social conflicts and maintain stability. To the extent that resources depletion and the requirements of ecological sustainability impose severe (and possibly insurmountable) limits to future economic growth, fundamental social changes will be inevitable.

The next section gives an overview of the world's energy supply. The chapter then proceeds to discuss the potentials and limitations of oil, natural gas, coal, nuclear energy and renewable energies. The following two sections discuss the Hubbert Linearization technique, data sources, and present the projections of the world's and China's energy supply and economic growth in the 21st century. The last section concludes the chapter.

World Energy: An Overview

In this chapter, the primary energy supply is defined as the total energy supply from oil, coal, natural gas, nuclear electricity, renewable electricity and liquid fuels made from biomass. Traditional forms of energy, such as the burning of wood, cow dung, or other plant and animal residuals for household consumption, are excluded. Primary electricity (such nuclear, hydro, and other renewable electricity) is counted by their electrical energy content rather than "thermal equivalent".[1]

From 1980 to 2007, world energy consumption expanded by 63 percent, with an average annual rate of 1.8 percent. During the same period, world GDP (measured by purchasing power parity) more than doubled and grew at an average annual rate of 3.3 percent. World energy efficiency (ratio of GDP to energy consumption) grew by 45 percent, with an average annual rate of 1.4 percent.

Oil accounts for 38 percent of the world's primary energy supply. Coal, natural gas, nuclear energy, and renewable energies (including hydro electricity, other renewable electricity, and fuel ethanol) account for 31 percent, 26 percent, 2.3 percent, and 3.2 percent respectively.

1 Under the current technology, in electricity generation using fossil fuels, it takes about 2.5 units of fossil fuels energy to generate one unit of electrical energy. In term of energy content, 1 million tonnes of oil equals 11.63 trillion-watt hours of electricity. But in term of thermal equivalent, 1 million tonnes of oil is treated as the equivalent of 4.4194 trillion-watt hours of electricity.

From 1980 to 2007, China's energy consumption more than quadrupled and grew at an average annual rate of 5.6 percent. During the same period, China's GDP grew at an average annual rate of 10 percent and energy efficiency grew at an average annual rate of 4.1 percent. In 2007, China's energy efficiency was about 60 percent of the world average.

Domestic coal accounts for 72 percent of China's primary energy supply. Domestic oil production, domestic natural gas production, and nuclear and renewable energies (mainly hydro electricity) account for 10, 3.5, and 2.7 percent respectively. Imported energy (mainly oil) accounts for 11 percent.

According to the International Energy Agency (IEA, 2008), about 31 percent of the world's energy supply is lost in transformations and distribution. Final consumption accounts for 69 percent of the world energy supply. Industry (including non-energy use) accounts for 36 percent of the world energy's final consumption. Transportation accounts for 28 percent. Other sectors (agriculture, commercial, and residential) account for 36 percent.

36 percent of the world's primary energy supply is used for electricity and heat generation. But due to transformation and transmission losses, electricity and others (direct use of heat, wind, solar, etc.) account for only 20 percent of the world's final energy consumption (electricity accounts for 17 percent). 42 percent of the world's electricity is used in industrial sector. 57 percent is used in other sectors. Only 1.7 percent is used for transportation.

Coal accounts for 41 percent of the world's electricity generation. Natural gas, hydro, nuclear, oil, and others (biomass, geothermal, wind, solar, etc.) account for 20, 16, 15, 5.8, and 2.3 percent respectively.

Peak Oil

In 2007, the world's annual oil production (including crude oil, oil sands, shale oil, and natural gas liquids) was about 3,900 million tonnes, with a daily production rate of 82 million barrels.

52 percent of the world's oil is consumed in the transportation sector, 22 percent is used for industry (14 percent is used as chemical industrial inputs), 12 percent is used in agriculture, commercial and residential sectors, 6.5 percent is used for electricity generation, and 7.1 percent is lost in transformation and distribution. According to IEA (2008), oil accounts for 43 percent of the world's final energy consumption.

World oil production and the ultimate recoverable resource have been well studied and a consensus is now emerging that world oil production either has already passed the peak or will peak very soon. The US used to be the world's largest oil producer. Its oil production peaked in 1970. The two most important European producers, Britain and Norway, peaked in 1999 and 2001 respectively. Mexico, which was the world's fifth largest producer, peaked in 2004. Russia, the world's second largest producer, is likely to have peaked in 2007. A new study finds that Saudi Arabia's crude oil production may have peaked in 2005 (The Oil Drum, 2009).

Colin J. Campbell, an Irish petroleum geologist, conducted a detailed study of the world's oil discovery history and pointed out that the world oil discoveries peaked in the 1960s (Campbell, 2005). In a recent research report, the German Energy Watch Group argued that the world oil production was imminent (Energy Watch Group, 2007a). The Association for the Study of Peak Oil and Gas Ireland now estimates the world oil production peak to take place in 2008 (ASPO, 2008).

Dave Rutledge, Chair of the Division of Engineering and Applied Science at California Institute of Technology, studied the historical series of world oil and natural gas production and concluded that about one-third of the world's ultimate recoverable resources of oil and natural gas have already been exploited, implying a peak of the world total production of oil and gas around 2015 (Rutledge, 2007a).

In 2007, China produced 187 million tonnes of oil, with a daily production rate of 3.7 million barrels. China is now the world's second largest consumer. In 2007, China's daily consumption of oil reached 7.9 million barrels. Thus, more than half of China's oil consumption needs to be imported.

The consensus among the Chinese researchers is that the domestic oil production is likely to peak around 2015, with the peak production level unlikely to be above 200 million metric tons (Cui, 2008: 33).

Oil may be substituted by liquid fuels made from coal or natural gas. But both coal and natural gas are nonrenewable resources and the conversion processes result in large losses of energy.

Liquid fuels can also be made from biomass. But the production of bio-fuels has low energy returns and the expansion is limited by the availability of land and fresh water. If about 40 percent of the world's arable land is used to grow biomass, the net liquid fuels made from the biomass (after subtracting energy inputs used in the production) may be able to replace 20 percent of the world's oil consumption (Trainer, 2007: 75).

For personal transportation, transportation vehicles currently powered by gasoline can be replaced by electric vehicles, electrified public transportation, and electrified railways. But some major infrastructure transformations would be required to facilitate the electrification of personal transportation. It is very difficult or impossible to use electricity to power the heavy trucks, ships, airplanes, and various types of heavy equipment used in industry and agriculture. Electricity obviously cannot serve as chemical inputs.

About two-thirds of the world's oil demand (liquid fuels consumption in industry, agriculture, freight transportation on roads, and sea and air the transportation) may be considered to be "core demands" that cannot be substituted by electricity without major difficulties. According to ASPO (2008), by 2030, the world oil production is likely to fall by one-third from the peak level. Thus, beyond 2030, world economic growth could be constrained by severe bottlenecks in meeting the core demands for oil.

Natural Gas

In 2007, the world's natural gas production was about 2,900 billion cubic meters or 2,700 million tonnes of oil equivalent. 36 percent of the world's natural gas is used for electricity generation, 24 percent is used for industry (6 percent is used as chemical industrial inputs), 25 percent is used in agriculture, commercial and residential sectors, 2.9 percent is used in transportation, and 13 percent is lost in transformation and distribution. According to IEA (2008), natural gas accounts for 15 percent of the world's final energy consumption.

Gas-fired turbines can be turned on and off rapidly. Natural gas thus plays a crucial role in meeting peak electricity demand (when electricity demand is much higher than the average electricity generation flow) and making up for shortfalls that result from accidents, repairing of existing power plants, and intermittent supply. Both wind and solar are intermittent sources of electricity generation. In the future, as wind and solar become significant sources of electricity supply, there will be growing demand for natural gas as the main backup power.

Laherrere (2004) predicted that the world natural gas production would peak around 2030. Campbell (2005: 209-216) expected the world conventional natural gas production to peak by 2025, staying on a high plateau until 2045, and then decline precipitously.

China's current annual natural gas production is about 70 billion cubic meters or 63 million tonnes of oil equivalent. The Chinese researchers estimate that China's ultimate recoverable natural gas is likely to be 10-13 trillion cubic meters, or 9-12 billion tonnes of oil equivalent (Cui, 2008: 33).

Coal

In 2007, the world's coal production was about 6,400 million tonnes, or 3,100 million tonnes of oil equivalent. 65 percent of the world's coal is used for electricity generation, 19 percent is used for industry (1 percent is used as chemical industrial inputs), 3.7 percent is used in agriculture, commercial and residential sectors, 1.3 percent is used in transportation, and 12 percent is lost in transformation and distribution. According to IEA (2008), coal accounts for 9 percent of the world's final energy consumption.

In most countries, coal provides the "base load" supply of electricity (the constant electricity flow required for the normal operation of electricity grid). Coal accounts for about 80 percent of China's electricity generation. Coal also plays an essential role in the steel and iron industry.

Since 2000, global coal production has grown at about 5 percent a year, making a larger contribution to the net increase in global energy supply than any other energy source. The world's official coal reserves now stand at about 850 billion tonnes. However, Rutledge (2007a) estimates that the world's remaining recoverable coal is likely to be 440 billion tonnes. Under the current production rate, the world's remaining coal could last about 70 years. Energy Watch Group (2007b) estimates that the world coal production could peak in 2025.

Since 2000, China's coal production has grown at about 10 percent a year. China now produces about 2,800 million tonnes of coal, accounting for about 40 percent of the world's total coal production. According to China's Ministry of Land and Natural Resources, China's remaining recoverable coal amounts to about 200 billion tonnes (Cui ed., 2008: 33). Using China's official coal reserve, Tao and Li (2007) estimate that China's coal production could peak between 2025 and 2032.

Nuclear Energy

The generation of nuclear electricity uses uranium, which is a nonrenewable resource. According to Energy Watch Group (2006), the world's proved uranium reserves will be exhausted in 30 years at the current rate of consumption and all possible resources of uranium will be exhausted in 70 years. If nuclear energy is to be relied upon as the sole source of electricity generation, the rate of production would have to be increased by six times and the remaining uranium could only last about 10 years. The expansion of nuclear energy is further limited by the slow pace of building new nuclear reactors.

A few countries (the US, Britain, France, Japan, and Russia) have experimented with breeder reactors, which could potentially increase the lifetime of uranium resource by 50-100 times. However, the breeder reactors have serious safety problems, are expensive to build and maintain, and are susceptible to long shutdowns. The French Superphénix reactor, the world's largest breeder reactor, operated for less than one year during its 10 years of service (Heinberg, 2004: 132-139; Kuntsler, 2005: 140-146; Trainer, 2007: 119-124).

Nuclear fusion is the reaction that takes place in the sun and has been achieved by human beings in the form of hydrogen bombs. To use it for economic purposes, however, the reaction has to be controlled. To initiate a fusion reaction, temperature of 200 million degrees Celsius has to be reached and no known materials on earth are capable of containing such temperature. Scientists have attempted to confine the reaction through different processes. But each attempted process has so far required more energy than the reaction itself can generate and has succeeded in sustaining the reaction for no more than a fraction of a second (Heinberg, 2004: 157-160).

If successful, nuclear fusion has the theoretical potential to provide a virtually unlimited supply of energy. But it could turn out to be prohibitively expensive in economic terms. In 2006, the European Union, the US, China, India, Japan, South Korea, and Russia signed an agreement to launch an experimental nuclear fusion reactor (about one-sixth the size of a regular power station) that would cost 10 billion Euros, or about 50 times as expensive as a comparable coal-fired power station. The researchers hope that by 2045 they could start generating commercial electricity from nuclear fusion reactors (*Financial Times*, November 22, 2006, p. 2, "Ten-Year Quest for Safe Nuclear Power Launched").

Renewable Energies

Hydro electricity is currently the most important renewable energy, accounting for 87 percent of the total electricity generation from renewable sources.

Among the renewable energies, hydro electricity, tide, wave, and geothermal have limited physical potentials and are unlikely to become a worldwide major source of energy (Trainer, 2007: 107-111). Wind, solar, and biomass are the three renewable sources that have a physical potential to make a large contribution to the future world energy supply. Wind and solar are primarily used for electricity generation. Biomass is the only renewable resource that can be used to make liquid fuels.

Green, Baski, and Dilmaghani (2007) estimated the long-term physical potential of renewable energies. Using the same assumptions regarding land availability as those used by the Working Group III of the IPCC (Intergovernmental Panel on Climate Change), assume that 1 percent of the world's total unused land (or 390,000 square kilometers) is used to produce solar electricity, 4 percent of the world's total land with wind speed higher than 5.1 meters per second (or 1.2 million square kilometers) is used to produce wind electricity, and 60 percent of the word's cropland (8.9 million square kilometers or 890 million hectares) is used to produce biomass, the long-term physical potential is estimated to be 326-481 EJ (extra joule, or 10^{18} joules, 1 EJ = 23.88 million tonnes of oil equivalent).

In an earlier paper, Lightfoot and Green (2002) pointed out that the assumed available land could be significantly too high. Much of the land is in very remote areas. The land may not be suitable and may not allow access for maintenance. In deserts, sand storms and large amounts of dust can be particularly serious problems.

Wind and solar are intermittent energy sources. Given the existing electric grids, wind and solar electricity can penetrate up to 20 percent of the installed electricity generating capacity or 10 percent of the actual electricity production without causing serious problems. Beyond these limits, further increase in solar and wind electricity will have to require large-scale storage of electricity (Lightfoot and Green, 2002). The development of "smart grids" using update technologies could alleviate these problems but cannot eliminate them. There are serious difficulties to store electricity on very large scales and substantial energy loss will occur due to conversion inefficiencies (Green, Baski, and Dilmaghani, 2007).

Solar thermal technology allows solar energy to be stored as heat, and does not suffer as much from short-term intermittency. However, solar thermal electricity has substantial seasonal variations and the winter performance is particularly weak (Trainer, 2007: 43-57). In addition to the intermittency and variation problems, the

Table 5.1 Cost and price of electricity generation of 1 giga-watt power plant: coal, wind, wind offshore, solar thermal, and solar photovoltaic (in million dollars unless otherwise stated)

	Coal	Wind	Wind Offshore	Household Photovoltaic	Solar Thermal
Capital Cost[a]	2,058	1,923	3,851	3,370	5,021
Annual Fixed Cost[b]	206	192	385	337	502
Annual Fuel Cost	282[c]	0	0	0	0
Annual Profit and Taxes[d]	206	192	385	0	502
Capacity Utilization[e]	0.75	0.25	0.35	0.15	0.25
Annual Generation[f]	6,570	2,190	3,066	1,314	2,190
Economic Price[g]	0.106	0.175	0.251	0.256	0.458

Sources: EIA (2009a) and the author's calculation.

Notes: [a]Cost estimates are from EIA (2009a). [b]Assume depreciation and interest rate being 10 percent of invested capital. [c]Assume 40 percent generating efficiency, 1 tonne of coal = 0.5 tonne of oil equivalent, and price of coal = 100 dollars per tonne. [d]Assume normal pre-tax profit rate being 10 percent. Household photovoltaics do not make profits or pay taxes. [e]In 2007, the capacity utilization rates for coal, wind, and solar electricity in the US were 74, 23, and 13 percent respectively (EIA 2009b). [f]In giga-watt hours. [g]In dollars per kilo-watt hour. Economic price = (Annual fixed cost + Annual Fuel Cost + Annual profits and taxes)/Annual electricity generation.

manufacturing of the solar and wind equipment consumes massive amounts of nonrenewable mineral resources (Prieto, 2008).

Electricity generation from wind and solar remain more expensive than conventional electricity. In the future, when wind and solar become major sources of electricity generation, it is necessary for wind and solar power plants to earn normal rates of return on capital without government subsidies. Table 5.1 compares the cost and price of electricity generation from alternative sources. After correcting for capacity utilization and applying normal rates of return on capital, wind electricity is about twice as expensive as coal-fired electricity, and solar electricity is three to four times as expensive. High costs of wind and solar electricity will limit their pace of expansion once they become a significant part of electricity generation.

Biomass production is highly water intensive and could be limited by the availability of fresh water. It also requires large energy inputs and the net energy output of biomass may be much smaller than the gross output. When resource, storage, and grid constraints are taken into account, the long-term potential of the renewable energies could be reduced to 150-175 EJ (Green, Baski, and Dilmaghani, 2007).

Methodology and Data

This section explains the basic methodology used in this chapter and presents the data sources used to project the world energy supply in the 21st century.

Hubbert Linearization

"Hubbert Linearization" is a common technique used to predict the ultimate recoverable amount of a nonrenewable resource. In 1956, Marion King Hubbert, an American geologist who worked for the Shell Oil Company, predicted that the US oil production would peak around 1970, a prediction that was later confirmed by the actual trajectory of the US oil production (Heinberg, 2004: 87-92).

The basic assumption of Hubbert linearization is that the annual production trajectory of a nonrenewable resource can be described by a logistic equation. The annual production is likely to first grow at an accelerating rate. Beyond certain inflection point, the growth slows down. The annual production reaches the peak when about half of the ultimate recoverable resource has been depleted. After the peak, the annual production declines at an accelerating pace. But the decline slows down as the resource approaches complete depletion.

As the production level approaches the peak, a linear relationship is likely to be formed between the growth rate of the cumulative production of the resource (that is, the ratio of the current annual production over the cumulative production from all previous years) and the cumulative production. The horizontal intercept of the linear function would indicate the ultimately recoverable amount. This can be described by the following equation:

(1) $$Q_t' / Q_t = a - a\,(Q_t / Q_u)$$

Where Q_t represents the cumulative amount that has been produced up to year "t", Q_t' is the current annual production in year "t" or the growth of the cumulative production, "a" is the intrinsic growth rate that determines how rapidly Q_t grows or how rapidly the ultimately recoverable amount is depleted, and Q_u stands for the ultimately recoverable amount of the resource. Estimating equation (1) through linear regression would allow one to determine the value of "a" and "Q_u".

The peak year of the annual production can be determined by the following equation:

(2) $$Q_t = Q_u / \{1 + \exp\,[-a\,(t - t_m)]\}$$

Where "t" is the current year and "t_m" is the peak year. The peak production should happen when about half of the ultimately recoverable resource has been depleted (Korpela, 2005).

Hubbert linearization allows one to use latest available data to continuously update the estimated coefficients. The model usually delivers reasonably reliable results when the annual production approaches the peak or has passed the peak, and the accuracy of the model's predication tends to improve as more data have been accumulated over time.

Data Sources

Historical data of world production of oil, natural gas, and coal before 1965 are from Rutledge (2007b). Historical data of world production and consumption of oil, natural gas, coal, nuclear electricity, and hydro electricity from 1965 to 2007 are from BP (2008a). Renewable electricity generation data are from EIA (2009c). Fuel ethanol production data are from BP (2008b).

Historical data of world GDP are from Maddison (2003) and World Bank (2008). World GDP growth rates in 2008 and 2009 are based on the projections of the IMF (2008).

Oil

A Hubbert linearization curve is fitted to the world oil production data from 1983 to 2007, with an R-square of 0.96. That is, it explains 96 percent of the observed variations in historical data. The results suggest that the world's ultimately recoverable oil is about 310 billion metric tons and the world production should have peaked in 2008.

A Hubbert linearization curve is fitted to China's oil production data from 2000 to 2007, with an R-square of 0.95. The results suggest that China's ultimately recoverable oil is about 13 billion and China's oil production will peak in 2016.

Natural Gas

A Hubbert linearization curve is fitted to the world natural gas production data from 1997 to 2007, with an R-square of 0.94. The results suggest that the world's ultimately recoverable natural gas is about 400 billion tonnes of oil equivalent and the world natural gas production will peak in 2041.

China's ultimately recoverable natural gas is assumed to be 12,000 million tonnes of oil equivalent. Using this assumption, a logistic function is fitted to China's natural gas production data from 1980 to 2007. The results are used to project China's natural gas production.

Coal

A Hubbert linearization curve is fitted to the historical coal production data of the world (excluding China) from 1950 to 2007, with an R-square of 0.82. The results suggest that the world (excluding China)'s ultimately recoverable coal is about 580 billion tonnes and the world (excluding China)'s coal production will peak in 2019.

China's ultimately recoverable coal is assumed to be 250 billion tonnes (China's historical cumulative coal production has been about 50 billion tonnes and the remaining recoverable coal is assumed to be 200 billion tonnes). Using this assumption, a logistic function is fitted to China's coal production data from 1950 to 2008. The results are used to project China's coal production.

Nuclear Energy

The International Energy Agency projects two alternative scenarios of nuclear energy growth from 2005 to 2030. Under the reference scenario, nuclear energy is projected to grow at an average annual rate of 0.7 percent and under the alternative policy scenario, it is projected to grow at an average annual rate of 1.6 percent (IEA, 2008).

Given the uncertainty of the future prospect of nuclear energy and to err on the optimistic side, this chapter assumes that nuclear energy will keep growing from 2007 to 2100 at an annual rate of 1.6 percent.

China currently has a nuclear electricity generating capacity of 7 giga-watts. The Chinese government plans to expand the nuclear electricity capacity to 40 giga-watts by 2020 (Cui ed., 2008: 309). This chapter assumes China's long-term nuclear potential to be 200 giga-watts.

Renewable Energies

Green, Baski, and Dilmaghani (2007) estimated the long-term physical potential of renewable energies to be 326-481 EJ. This chapter uses Green et al.'s highest estimate, 481 EJ. It is rounded to 500 EJ or 12,000 million tonnes of oil equivalent.

China's long-term technical potential of hydro electricity is estimated to be 500 giga-watts or an annual generation of 2,240 trillion-watt hours (Cui ed., 2008: 34).

By 2020, the Chinese government plans to expand China's wind electricity generating capacity to 100 giga-watts and biomass electricity generating capacity to 30 giga-watts. By 2030, China's solar photovoltaic electricity generating capacity is projected to increase to 100 giga-watts (Cui ed., 2008: 308-309).

China's long-term onshore and offshore wind electricity potential is estimated to be 1,000 giga-watts (Cui ed., 2008: 273). This chapter assumes that China's long-term solar electricity potential is 1,000 giga-watts and biomass electricity potential is 500 giga-watts.

China's total potential electricity generation from nuclear and renewable sources amounts to 8,150 trillion-watt hours or 890 million tonnes of oil equivalent. This is rounded to 1,000 million tonnes of oil equivalent.

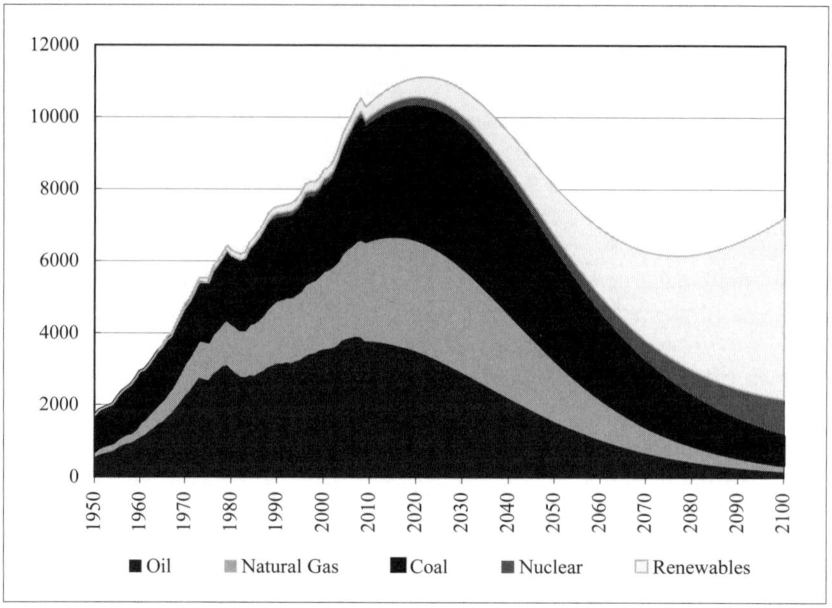

Figure 5.1 World primary energy supply (million tonnes of oil equivalent, 1950-2100)

Source: See the section on "Methodology and Data".

Peak Energy and Peak Economy?

Figure 5.1 presents the historical and projected world energy supply from 1950 to 2100. World oil production is projected to have peaked in 2008. World natural gas production is projected to peak in 2041. World coal production is projected to peak in 2029. Nuclear energy is projected to grow according to IEA's "Alternative Policy Scenario". Long-term potential of the renewable energies is assumed to be 500 EJ (12,000 million tonnes of oil equivalent). The world's total energy supply is projected to peak in 2029.

World GDP can be derived by multiplying world energy supply with projected energy efficiency. All economic activities have to consume some energy. Thus, in the long run, there is an ultimate limit to energy efficiency as is determined by physical laws. Lightfoot and Green (2001) estimated the long-term physical potential of world energy efficiency and concluded that in the long run, the world energy efficiency could reach up to 250 percent of the 1990 level.

Lightfoot and Green first estimated the efficiency improvement potential in each energy consumption sector (electricity generation, the transportation sector, the residential sector, the industrial sector, and the commercial sector) and then used the share of each sector in world energy consumption to calculate the weighted

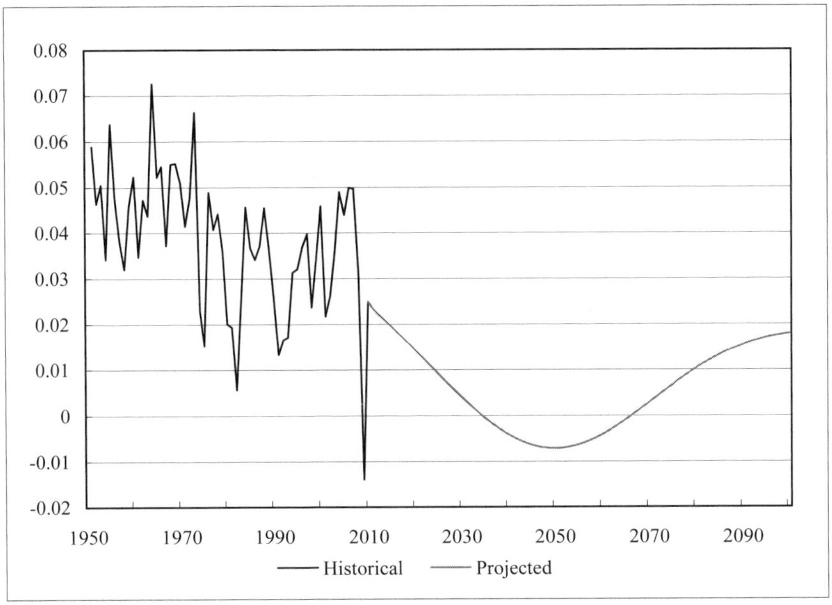

Figure 5.2 World economic growth: historical and projected (annual rate of change, 1950-2100)

Source: See the text of this section.

average, resulting in the world efficiency improvement potential. However, while Lightfoot and Green took into account the efficiency improvement potential in the process of electricity generation, they failed to take into account the efficiency improvement potential in the process of electricity consumption. Correcting for this error and making an upward adjustment of efficiency improvement potential in the electricity generation sector, the implied physical efficiency potential should be 430 percent of the 1990 level rather than 250 percent.

In addition, Lightfoot and Green also estimated that taking into account possible sectoral shift within the industrial sector that would reduce the share of highly energy intensive industries, the industrial sector energy efficiency could increase by about another 100 percent. As the industrial sector accounts for about 30 percent of the world's energy use, this implies a long-term potential for 15 percent reduction of world energy intensity or 18 percent increase of world energy efficiency.

In this chapter, the long-term world energy efficiency potential is assumed to be about five times the world's energy efficiency in 1990, or nearly three times as much as the current energy efficiency in Germany or Japan (currently the most energy efficient economies in the world).

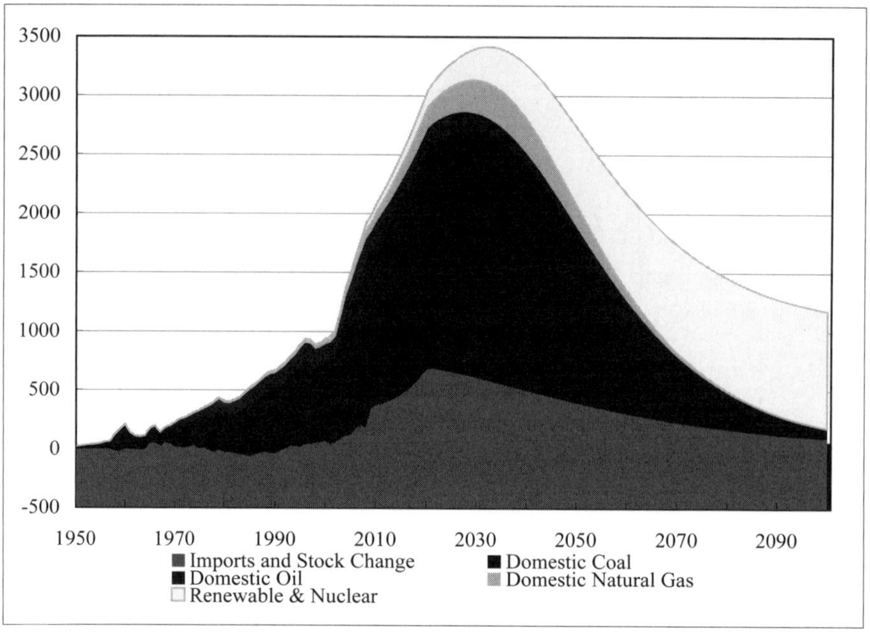

Figure 5.3 China's primary energy supply (million tonnes of oil equivalent, 1950-2100)

Source: See the section on "Methodology and Data".

Figure 5.2 presents the historical and projected world economic growth rates from 1951 to 2100. Based on this chapter's projections, after the current global recession, there is unlikely to be a meaningful global economic recovery. Global economic expansion will soon meet the constraints imposed by the declining world oil production. World economic growth rate sinks below zero after about 2050. The world economy will keep declining for about two decades.

To put the projections in perspective, from 1913 to 1950, a period that included two world wars and the Great Depression, the world economy grew at an average annual rate of 1.9 percent (Maddison, 2003). Between 1950 and 2008, the world economic growth rate had fallen below 2 percent only on three occasions, during 1974-1975, 1980-1982, and 1991-1993. These were generally considered to be periods of major world economic crisis (as well as political and social instability). Thus, if this chapter's projections are confirmed, then beyond about 2020, the world economy will in effect stay in a condition of permanent depression.

Figure 5.3 presents China's historical and projected energy supply from 1950 to 2100. China's coal production is projected to peak in 2030, oil production to peak in 2016, and natural gas production to peak in 2046. China's long-term

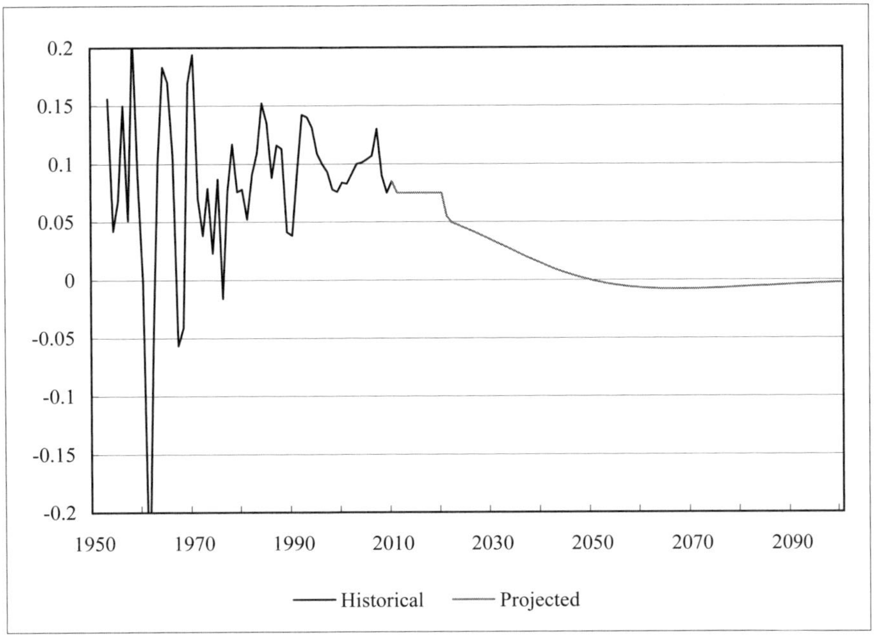

Figure 5.4 China's economic growth: historical and projected (annual rate of change, 1950-2100)

Source: See the text of this section.

potential of nuclear and renewable energies is assumed to be 1,000 million tonnes of oil equivalent.

China's energy imports are assumed to keep growing from now to 2020 to sustain rapid economic growth. The Chinese economy is assumed to keep growing at an annual rate of 7.5 percent from 2010 to 2020. By 2020, China's energy imports are projected to grow to near 700 million tonnes of oil equivalent, comparable to the current US energy imports. After 2020, China's energy imports are assumed to stay at 8 percent of the rest of the world's total fossil fuels production.

China's total energy supply is projected to peak in 2033. China's energy efficiency is assumed to converge towards the world average in the long run. Figure 5.4 presents China's historical and projected economic growth rates from 1951 to 2100. China's economic growth rate is projected to fall sharply after 2020. In the following decades, the economic growth rate falls steadily and approaches zero by 2050. Beyond 2050, the Chinese economy is projected to enter into permanent decline.

Figure 5.2 does suggest that the world economy will resume growth after 2070, though at comparatively slow rates. This reflects relatively optimistic assumptions about the potentials of renewable energies and energy efficiency. These potentials may not be realized.

This chapter's projections implicitly assume that different forms of energy can be substituted for each other. However, as is explained earlier, electricity cannot readily serve as substitutes for liquid fuels. Nuclear energy and most renewable energies can only be used to generate electricity. Thus, liquid fuels could prove to be a binding constraint on the world economy. In that case, the world economy may enter into permanent decline through the second half of the 21st century.

The projections have taken into account the constraints on world economic growth imposed by the depletion of the energy resources. But they have not taken into account the constraints imposed by other resources and the world's environmental capacity in general. In particular, the projected world fossil fuels production is solely based on considerations of resources depletion, but has not taken into account the requirements of climate stabilization. If those requirements are taken into account, the world energy supply may peak earlier and decline more rapidly after the peak.

Conclusion

This chapter's findings, if confirmed by the actual development of future events, will be of enormous significance for the global political and social development.

First of all, as the US hegemony is in irreversible decline, many have expected or hoped that China would replace the US to become the next leader of the capitalist world system, leading a successful systemic reconstruction. However, given the findings of this chapter, by the mid-21st century, the Chinese economy will probably find itself in permanent decline and China will be in no position to lead the restructuring of the existing world system.

Until now, the Chinese ruling elites have relied upon rapid economic growth to alleviate or divert various social conflicts and tensions. However, beyond 2020, as the Chinese economy falls into increasingly deeper economic crisis, it will become impossible for the ruling elites to contain the unfulfilled economic, social and political aspirations from the broad masses of the population. Thus, in all likelihood, economic crisis will be followed by political and social explosions.

Finally, the capitalist world system is one based on the endless drive for profit and capital accumulation. After centuries of ruthless accumulation, we have by now reached the point where the global ecological system is on the verge of total collapse, and further expansion of global material consumption is no longer ecologically possible. The global energy crisis and other aspects of the global environmental crisis represent the strong signals that the nature is sending to the humanity: the existing social system has reached its historical limit and the future survival of the humanity and the civilization depends on the building of a new, equitable, and sustainable society as soon as possible.

Bibliography

ASPO, Association for the Study of Peak Oil and Gas Ireland (2008) *Newsletter* 96, December 2008 <http://www.aspo-ireland.org/contentFiles/newsletterPDFs/newsletter96_200812.pdf>.

BP (2008a) *BP Statistical Review of World Energy* <http://www.bp.com/statisticalreview>.

BP (2008b) *Renewable Energy Section* <http://www.bp.com/sectiongenericarticle.do?categoryId=9023767&contentId=7044196>.

Campbell, Colin J. (2005) *Oil Crisis*. Brentwood: Multi-Science Publishing Company Ltd.

Cui, Minxuan (ed.) (2008) *Zhongguo Nengyuan Fazhan Baogao* (Annual Report of China's Energy Development). Beijing: *Shehui Kexue Wenxian Chubanshe* (Social Sciences Academic Press).

EIA, US Energy Information Administration (2009a) *Cost and Performance Characteristics of New Central Station Electricity Generating Technologies* <http://www.eia.doe.gov/oiaf/aeo/assumption/pdf/electricity.pdf#page=3>.

EIA (2009b) *US Summary Data-Electricity* <http://www.eia.doe.gov/overview_hd.html>.

EIA (2009c) *International Data-Electricity* <http://www.eia.doe.gov/emeu/international/>.

EIA, US Energy Information Administration (2009a) Cost and Performance Characteristics of New Central Station Electricity Generating Technologies <http://www.eia.doe.gov/oiaf/aeo/assumption/pdf/electricity.pdf#page=3>.

Energy Watch Group (2007a) *Crude Oil: the Supply Outlook*, October 2007 <http://www.energywatchgroup.org/fileadmin/global/pdf/EWG_Oilreport_10-2007.pdf>.

Energy Watch Group (2007b) *Coal: Resources and Future Production*, March 2007 <http://www.energywatchgroup.org/fileadmin/global/pdf/EWG_Oilreport_10-2007.pdf>.

Green, Chris, Soham Baksi, and Maryma Dilmaghani (2007) "Challenges to a Climate Stabilizing Energy Future", *Energy Policy*, 35: 616-626.

Heinberg, Richard (2004) *The Party's Over: Oil, War and the Fate of Industrial Societies*. Gabriola Island, B.C., Canada: New Society Publishers.

IEA, International Energy Agency (2008) *Key World Energy Statistics 2008* <http://www.iea.org>.

Korpela, Seppo A. (2005) "Prediction of World Peak Oil Production", in Andrew McKillop with Sheila Newman (eds) *The Final Energy Crisis*. London: Pluto Press.

Kunstler, James Howard (2005) *The Long Emergency: Surviving the Converging Catastrophes of the Twenty-First Century.* New York: Atlantic Monthly Press.

Laherrere, Jean (2004) "Future of Natural Gas Supply", Contribution to the Third International Workshop on Oil and Gas Depletion, Berlin, Germany, May 24-25, 2004 <http://www.hubbertpeak.com/laherrere/IIASA2004.pdf>.

Lightfoot, H. Douglas and Christopher Green (2001) "Energy Efficiency Decline Implications for Stabilization of Atmospheric CO_2 Content", Centre for Climate and Global Change Research, Report No. 2001-7, McGill University <http://www.mcgill.ca/ccgcr>.

Lightfoot, H. Douglas and Christopher Green (2002) "An Assessment of IPCC Working Group III Findings in *Climate Change 2001: Mitigation* of the Potential Contribution of Renewable Energies to Atmospheric Carbon Dioxide Stabilization", Centre for Climate and Global Change Research, Report No. 2002-5, McGill University <http://www.mcgill.ca/ccgcr>.

Maddison, Angus (2003) *The World Economy: Historical Statistics*. Paris: Organisation for Economic Co-operation and Development.

Prieto, Pedro A. (2008) "Solar and Wind in Spain and the World: Closing the Growth Gap?" 7th ASPO International Annual Conference, Barcelona, October 21, 2008.

Rutledge, Dave (2007a) "Hubbert's Peak, the Coal Question, and Climate Change", ASPO-USA Conference, Houston, Texas, October 19, 2007.

Rutledge, Dave (2007b) "Hubbert's Peak, the Coal Question, and Climate Change", Excel Workbook <http://rutledge.caltech.edu>.

Tao, Zaipu and Mingyu Li (2007) "What Is the Limit of Chinese Coal Supplies – A STELLA Model of Hubbert Peak", *Energy Policy*, 35(6): 3145-3154.

Trainer, Ted (2007) *Renewable Energy Cannot Sustain a Consumer Society*. Dordrecht, The Netherlands: Springer.

The Oil Drum (2009) "Saudi Arabia's Crude Oil Production Peaked in 2005", posted by "ace", March 3, 2009 <http://www.theoildrum.com/node/5154>.

World Bank (2008) *World Development Indicators Online* <http://devdata.worldbank.org/dataonline>.

Chapter 6
The Transformation of China: The Next between Internalities and Externalities

Li Xing

Introduction

China in the 20th century experienced a long turbulent period of social disintegration, regional warlordism, popular revolution, political chaos as well as a rapid transformative period of high economic growth and political rise on the global stage. Very few societies have been so radically transformed within one century as China has. Politically, the Chinese state and society transformed from a long period of an imperial system to a short-lived republic, and then from fragile and predatory warlordism to a revolutionary centralized socialist authoritarian state. Ideologically, Chinese value systems went through many iterations of a "great leap forward" from Confucianism to Marxism, from imperialism to republicanism, from feudalism to socialism and from collectivism to individualism. Economically, China underwent a state-led socialist industrialization project based on planned economy and collective egalitarianism, and then moved to an all-encompassing economic reform based on market mechanisms. The Chinese political and economic landscape had experienced repeated shifts from crisis and failure to very rapid growth and achievement.

The above radical transformations indicate the key feature of modern Chinese history, that being the search to ensure China's existence as a prosperous, strong nation and a united political entity, which has been a key concern for generations of Chinese in their struggles to find a solution for restoring their country's historical power status. A series of revolutions and modernization attempts, including the socialist project, suffered severe setbacks due to the challenges and constraints from both internal and external factors. Depending on how one assesses its successes and failures, contemporary China is remembered as having conducted historically unique experiments to skip over the stage of capitalism and bring about a socialist transformation, both in terms of social structures and the consciousness of the people. How can we comprehend and interpret these historical transformations shaped by fundamental changes? What are the internal driving forces and the external influences behind these transformations? And what have the consequential impacts been when internal transformations were triggered by external thrust, and vice versa?

For most of the 20th century Chinese development can be characterized as being driven by a duality of "challenge–response" interaction that, as one scholar explained it, exhibits "the combination of two fundamental dynamics: its endogenous forward drive and the exogenous shock treatment administered to it" (Tan, 1996: 242). In line with this thinking this chapter aims at providing a framework for understanding and analyzing the interplay between internal constraints and transformations and external responses and adjustments, and vice versa. The chapter has the following propositions, which are summarized and categorized in Table 6.1:

1. Before its collapse at the beginning of the 20th century, China's imperial system exhibited the classic symptoms of economic backwardness: political corruption, social debility and class exploitation, economic stagnation, negligible technical change, and heavy demographic pressure. The reality was a typical symptom of political–economic underdevelopment by any standard, which was explained by a number of theoretical schools of thought, such as *Asiatic Mode of Production*, *preindustrial stage theory, the state and social structure theory* and *the colonialism and imperialism theory*. The internal weakness was further deteriorated by the external pressure leading to the country's final collapse and disintegration.
2. Through sinicizing Western Marxism by accommodating the Chinese reality, the Chinese communists achieved state power in 1949. The Chinese revolution cut the root of the "old China" and created a socialist "new China" characterized by a historically unique experiment to skip over the stage of capitalism and bring about a socialist transformation of both the social structure and the consciousness of its people in ways that defied conventional ideological and political norms in established capitalist as well as socialist states. Externally, the "loss of China", together with the US defeat in two wars in Asia, had a shocking effect on the US-led capitalist system and contributed to the political economy of the rising Japanese and East Asian newly industrializing economies.
3. China's socialist period was characterized by state ownership, agricultural collectivism and welfare egalitarianism. Chinese socialism can be seen as an endeavor to pursue an independent and self-reliant development alternative. Chinese socialism was severely constrained by the US-led capitalist world order and it had to adjust to both internal constraints and external pressures. Nevertheless, the overall achievements of Chinese socialism laid a solid material and infrastructural foundation to China's comparative advantage in the post-Mao integration with the global economy. During the socialist period, Red China's attempt to "sinicize" socialism, although seemingly threatening, did not inflict any direct destructive impact on the capitalist world system.
4. China's post-Mao leadership undertook a modernization process through economic reforms aimed at sinicizing Western market capitalism by

> incorporating "Chinese characteristics" and by embracing market capitalism while incorporating China into the existing world system. China is now undergoing transformative changes through a series of processes of economic, institutional and ideological "passive revolutions". "Chinese capitalism", by combining market mechanisms with an active role of the party-state, is injecting impetus and opportunities into global capitalism while at the same time unleashing a "threatening" impact on the existing international order. Dialectically speaking, China's internal economic achievement and external dependence are two sides of the same coin creating both internal contradictions and external anxieties.

These propositions attempt to reveal the dialectical nexus between China's internal evolutions and the external influences inherent in the century-long "challenge–response" dynamism. Methodologically, the nexus is conceptualized by examining the internal and external interactions of socio-political and socio-economic developments from a relational–historical approach. *The relational approach* is seen as a way to study the interactive relationships in the process of societal development and social transformation through combining mutually-related internal and external factors. It implies that the "challenge–response" dynamism is always embedded in the multiple causalities leading to societal transformations. *The historical approach* on the one hand emphasizes that each socio-economic development, including politics, policies, institutions and ideas, should be understood within a specific historical context. That is to say, societal development and social issues are born with historical dimensions embedded in the transformative dynamism. On the other hand, the historical approach entails an analytical perspective that treats social development as a dynamic process. The relational and historical approaches are closely related and mutually dependent. The former emphasizes the *relation* and *interaction* among internal and external factors in the process, whereas the latter underlines the *transformative* and *dynamic* nature of the process.

The objective of this chapter is twofold: 1) to explore how external factors helped to shape China's internal transformations, i.e. how generations of Chinese have been struggling to respond to the external challenges and attempting to sinicize external political ideas in order to change China from within. One of China's most enduring features in the 20th century has been "an unending process of internalization of the external which we may call 'Sinification'" (Tan, 1996: 236); and 2) to offer a framework for understanding the factors and consequences of China's economic transformation from the broader dynamics of global capitalism. In many ways China's economic growth of the past three decades has been enabled and nurtured by the winding paths of global capital, while at the same time China's growth has heightened global competition, accentuated the inherent contradictions of capitalist development in other countries, as well as redefined the limitation of global capitalism around the world. Upon each of China's transformations, be it a rise or decline, the capitalist world system has had to adjust and readjust itself to the opportunities and constraints brought about by the global "China factors".

Table 6.1 The duality of internalities and externalities in China's century-long transformation

Key periods in China's modern history	The historical China 1840-1911 Development of underdevelopment	The revolutionary China 1911-1949 Sinicizing Marxism	The socialist China 1949 -1976 Sinicizing socialism	The capitalist China 1977 current Sinicizing capitalism
Main features of internal factors and transformations	• "Asian mode of production" • Community and family system • Despotic state with parasitic elite • Centralized governance • Economic self-sufficient with a closed market • Economical, technical backwardness • Political conservatism • Loss of cultural superiority after the Opium War • Social and cultural disintegration	• Semi-colonial status • Crisis of Confucianism • Nationalist revolution overthrowing imperial system • Inflow of Marxism-Leninism • Communist armed revolution • Anti-Japanese war and civil war • State reunification and independence • Victory of the Chinese Communist Revolution	• Uninterrupted revolution • Politics in command and mass mobilization • Class dictatorship • Plan economy and collectivism • Self-reliance and basic need approach • Common welfare and equality • Orientation in human resources • Basic achievement in socio-economic and socio-political domains	• Back to Marx's "stage" theories and redefining socialism • Economics in command • class and regional inequalities • Market economy and commodification • Capital accumulation and export-orientation • Dependence on foreign markets • Pragmatism, professionalism and elitism • CCP's internal adaptation and change • Emergence of civil society and NGOs • Environmental and social problem

Main features of external factors and transformations	• Rise of European industrializing power. • China's defeat in the Opium War – Enforced opening of China's trade and market • Western powers enjoying unequal treaties • Inflow of Western products and collapsing Chinese mode of production • Stimulating Chinese capitalism • Inflow of Western progressive ideologies	• China's anti-western imperialism by the Treaty of Versailles • The success of Russian Communist Revolution • The influence of Communist international • Japan's invasion and unification of internal forces • Civil war and American anti-communist China policy • US one-side support to the Nationalists	• The Korea War and Vietnam War • US as the guarantor for the region's security • Rise of Japan and the East Asian NIEs • Chinese socialism as ideological and socio-political challenges outside but not INSIDE the capitalist world system. • US containment policy both in Asia and Europe • US-China rapprochement to contain the Soviet expansionism	• Inflow of global FDI to China • Outsource of production to China • China as an engine for global growth and trade, commodity price, energy hunger, international aid, global environmental and security issues. • US concentration on anti-terrorism • China's influence in Africa and Latin America • Emergence of "Beijing Consensus" • Financial crisis and decline of US dollar • Rising role of Chinese yuan

The Development of Underdevelopment in China

Between the early 19th century and the victory of the Communist revolution in 1949, China exhibited the classic symptoms of backwardness: political corruption, social debility and class exploitation, economic stagnation, negligible technical change, and heavy demographic pressure. The reality China faced was a typical picture of political–economic underdevelopment by any standard. The questions are: how had this come about? What were internal and external constraints that brought about China's decline and underdevelopment? Were constraints more externally or internally caused? The decline of the Chinese civilization and its underdevelopment since the mid 19th century has been a subject of interest in social science and especially in the field of development studies. Different schools of thought have tried to offer explanations from different perspectives.

The classical Marxist conceptualization identifies East Asia societies with the *Asiatic Mode of Production* (AMP). The AMP states that, geographically, the landscape of Chinese traditional communities was dependent on irrigation systems which required a centralized authority to coordinate and develop large-scale hydraulic works; politically, the Chinese state was comprised of stagnant societies dominated by a despotic state class with a centralized governance; and socioeconomically, the Chinese economic bases consisted of economically self-sufficient families and village communities combining agriculture and handicrafts. The sustainability of the system was built upon loyalty to the state on the one hand and filial piety to the family on the other, which made political patriarchy and patrimonialism possible. Under this type of socio-political organization, the middle space between the state and family became so narrow that it was not possible to expect China (or any other non-Western, ancient society) to have had, or to have required, anything like the complex of attitudes, values, and institutions that are amalgamated and reified under the term "civil society".

The concept of the AMP endorses "the privileged position of Occidental over Oriental history: the dynamic and progressive character of the West versus the stationary and regressive features of the East" (Bottomore, 1983: 33). It perceives oriental society as stagnant "hydraulic society", unreceptive to the development of capitalist mode of production (Wittfogel, 1957). It argues that the Oriental pre-capitalist economic formations, together with their "primitive" societal forms and family- or clan-based social structures, were unfavorable for the emergence of the "capitalist mode of production", i.e. the existence of Occidental feudalism in politically independent kingdoms and cities was crucial for the growth of the production of exchange values and for the rise of a bourgeois class and industrial capitalism. The primary hub of this conceptual approach focuses on the constraints of the internal economic organization.

Another school of thought that also emphasizes the internal factors is *the state and social structure theory*. It is an attempt by China-scholars to explain underdevelopment in China specifically from the perspectives of its internal factors in relation to a number of features of the Chinese state and social structure. It stresses the social structure embodied by the Chinese family system, a conservative bureaucracy and ruling ideology, a parasitic elite, and a fatalistic attitude, etc., as obstacles to modernization (Ho in Lippit, 1980). The proponents of this theory suggest that the requirements of modernization were incompatible with the requirements of Confucian stability and the hierarchy system (Lippit, 1980). As with the AMP theory, the conceptual framework of this school emphasizes the malfunctioning of the domestic socio-political structure.

A more radical approach that targets the external factors is the thesis of *colonialism and imperialism*, which views underdevelopment as essentially an outcome of a historical process caused by Western colonial–imperialist expansion. It stipulates that external relations, such as trade and contact with the Western imperialist powers and Japan, tended to promote underdevelopment. In the view of this theory, underdevelopment is not an inborn characteristic of preindustrial societies but a consequence of a specific historical process. It argues that even though imperialist penetration did bring elements of modern economy to China, the impact was geographically confined and sectorally skewed to serve foreign interests (Esherick in White, 1982: 114). The reason why China was able to industrialize more rapidly since 1949 was because the "Communist revolution decisively broke the ties that chained China to the imperialist system" (Mould in White, ibid.: 114).

The most challenging arguments come from the culturalist school of thinking. Hegel, for example, at a time when the Western consciousness of the world created revolutionary history, saw China in the "Childhood of history"[1] (Hegel, 1837); and Marx, whose theories and insight inspired the Chinese revolution, described China as a society "vegetating in the teeth of time" and perceived in the Great Wall of China a metaphor for the universal resistance of non-European societies to change (Marx in Dirlik and Meisner, ibid.: 17). Their views were understandable because these perceptions of China, although premature, were the product of a comparison between the immobility of non-Western cultures and the revolutionary nature of Europe. What lay behind this viewpoint was the desire to establish a European model for other cultures to follow. To put China in the framework of the Weberian culturalist explanation, the failure of China to transition to the stage of capitalism was due to the fact that Chinese Confucian cultural values were not receptive to the development of capitalism in terms of creativity, competition and development. As seen in the other schools of thought, the theoretical paradigm of this approach likewise points to the limits of inner value systems. However, Weber's culturalist theory and method has been challenged both by scholars (Elvin, 1984) and

1 This is one of Hegel's metaphors, which is that, human being develops from "childhood" (East, or Asia), and then moves to old age (West, or Europe). The East is seen as the home of unreflective consciousness, like a child obeying his/her parents, in which individuality and subjective freedom are lacking. On the contrary, the Christian development of the Germanic world represents the old age history, i.e. the old age of spirit that is mature and strong.

especially by the rise of Japan, East Asian newly industrializing economies, and particular by the resurgence of China.

The introduction of these theoretical debates is aimed at highlighting the thesis of this chapter: China's century-long response to the internal as well as external constraints. It is to overcome these constraints, whether political, economic, cultural, or social, that the Chinese Revolution, both before and after the People's Republic, carried out historically unique attempts to transform China's society and the consciousness of its people in order to bring back China's historical status.

The Chinese Revolution in the Capitalist World Order

Since China's defeat in the Opium War and its final collapse occurring with the fall of the Qing Dynasty, Chinese academics and elites were deeply divided as to which direction China should move. There were mainly four schools of thought. The first school favored the restoration of traditional social structure, recovering China's historic power and expelling outsiders. The second school preferred a limited change, but was not interested in modern science and industry, nor was it interested in learning political philosophy and economic system of the West. Its only interest was Western weaponry technology and military training. The third school went to the opposite extreme. It favored total Westernization, and it was convinced that science and technology did affect values. People belonging to this school believed that it was impossible to borrow Western technology while maintaining Chinese ways of thinking and its outdated institutional structure. The most influential one was the fourth school: Marxism and Leninism.

Internalization of Marxism-Leninism

The Confucian cultural and value system developed over several thousands of years under feudal systems, while Marxism emerged in a European context in the 18th century. They appear to be unrelated both in timing and content; nevertheless, history brought the two together in China.

The post-Opium War challenges to the Chinese nation were dual: China had not only to build a modern economy, but also to create a new culture and value system in order to shape the direction of national development. The requirement of forming a new cultural identity became the goal for generations of Chinese reformers and revolutionaries because new value systems and attitudes are reconditions for the transformation of individuals as well as the material base of society, and economic development and culture are intricately interconnected (Kung, 1975: 219). China indeed needed a new comprehensive philosophical base, a new framework of understanding – a new Confucianism – and that was why Western progressive Marxism and radical Leninism found precisely this role in China.

During this period, different schools of thought entered China, including many foreign-inspired schools, such as Constitutionalism, Positivism, Marxism-

Leninism, Socialism, Liberalism, Darwinism, etc. It was during this period that the Marxist proletarian culture and class theory began to influence and inspire the worldviews of revolutionaries. Although the Chinese situation did not comply with the Marxist preconditions for the advent of socialism, such as a mature industrial base and a proletarian majority, nevertheless, there were many reasons for the attraction to Marxism-Leninism:

> It was an effective ploy to criticize the West from a Western point of view; b) it gave the Chinese a new methodological framework to understand their own past and foresee the contours of their future; c) it offered a conceptualized view of international reality. Lastly, it amply proved its anti-imperialist credentials-an important source of attraction-after the 1917 Bolshevik Revolution when the Soviet leaders denounced imperialism, unilaterally abolishing unequal treaties and relinquishing many privileges of tsarist Russia including extraterritoriality as well as their share of Boxer indemnities. (Kapur, 1987: 3)

Marxism-Leninism opened the horizons of Chinese progressive intellectuals and internationalized their conceptualization of China's domestic problems. The Marxist-Leninist teachings concerning colonialism and imperialism provided China with a radical approach viewing underdevelopment as essentially an outcome of a historical process caused by western colonial-imperialist expansion. Marxism, and especially Lenin's theory of capitalist imperialism, provided Chinese intellectuals with a partial theoretical framework as well as a psychological answer to their difficulties in finding the proper explanations and theories to address the failures of traditional Chinese culture and the humiliation suffered at the hands of the West (Peck, 1975: 73). It offered them a great source of inspiration to take positions and to analyze the world from different perspectives. China, as they saw it, was no longer the perceived center of the Earth surrounded by barbarians (China as the "Middle Kingdom"), but a society "that appeared more and more to be part of a world market of commodities and ideas" (Dirlik, 1989: x).

Nevertheless, it was the Chinese Communist Party (CCP) led by Mao that successfully linked the potential of the Chinese revolution to the worldwide proletarian movement and paved the way for the establishment of a populist tradition in the course of the national struggle for independence and prosperity. Since the founding of the Chinese Communist Party in 1921, the Chinese impact in both transforming and strengthening Marxism-Leninism was equally important. The Chinese view on its role in international affairs had changed from regarding itself as the center of the world and as constituting a universal authority to seeing that China's problem was part of the world's problems and that the Chinese revolution was relevant for the outside world.

Despite the fact that "there was precious little Marxism in Mao Zedong thought" (Gregor, 1995: 262), Mao was able both to combine learning with statesmanship, and Marxism-Leninism with China's reality. He seized this opportunity to sinicize the Chinese Communist movement by means of skilful redefinition and application of "class" and class politics.[2] Mao's strategy of "using countryside to surround city" turned the Chinese revolution into a successful peasant-based uprising. This is another indication of the "Chinese experiments with holistic transnational political ideas" (Tan, 1996: 247). No matter how significant Western progressive theories were in influencing the Chinese revolution, without Mao Zedong's adapting it to China's reality, Marxism-Leninism would probably have aroused only a few rebels. Although communist historians maintain that it is "the people who create history" and reject the great-man theory of history, there is no doubt that without Mao's contribution Chinese history would have run a different course (Chi, 1986: 296).

The "Loss of China" and the Rise of Japan and East Asian NICs

The communist victory in China in 1949 shocked the post-war US-led capitalist world order. This "loss" of China had a tremendous impact on American society (Thomson, 1992). From the President and government officials down to the media and ordinary people, Americans simply could not understand how a promising Chinese Nationalist government backed by modern US military support could be defeated by a Communist-led insurrection. The US perception of Mao and the new China as an anti-American force was largely misguided due to a lack of real comprehension of Mao's real sentiments and perceptions about the United States (He, 1994). Mao's major concern in his understanding and analysis of the United States was, in fact, always how to measure its power and influence on the survival and security of the new Republic. So while there might have been a chance after the Second World War and the Chinese communist victory for an American government to have developed normal relations with the socialist China, misperceptions got in the way.

The US government immediately responded to the "loss" of China by imposing military containment and isolation on Red China under the assumption that the containment of China could prevent the spread of revolution. For nearly a quarter of a century, the "loss of China" had a grave impact on America's policies in Asia, which were skewed by the fear of Communism, as were American politics, education, and society. This fear of Communism led the United States to fight two Asian wars with the goal of containing the Chinese revolution, i.e. The Korea War and The Vietnam War. The United States refused to recognize the victory of the Chinese communist revolution and US-East Asia relations became engulfed in years of blind and lethal zealotry.

The "loss of China" also contributed to the political economy of the ascendant Japanese and East Asian newly industrializing states thriving under American parenting (Hersh, 1993). Under American protection, external military threats and

2 Mao realized the power of hundreds of millions of peasants who could be converted to become part of the revolutionary army. The Chinese Revolution is in reality a peasant revolution rather than a working class one.

the internal danger of communist expansion were substantially contained in these two regions. In providing security, economic support and military aid to Japan and other East Asian states, the American goal was consequently to control and define their roles (including Germany in Europe) within the American-led alliance and prevent them from embarking upon an independent political and military course (Schwarz, 1996: 92-102).[3] The burden of the allied countries' military expenses was also greatly reduced by the American military presence. American military bases have been documented to have not only protected these countries but also to have provided them with economic benefits such as employment. Even today, the withdrawal of American military forces would be considered as a substantial economic loss.

America's long-term strategic interest in East Asia can be understood as having a dual objective: "watching" the role of Japan and "managing" the risk posed by the rise of China as a regional and global power. The American role and presence in this region as a guarantor of the balance-of-power are generally welcomed by these smaller nations. It is expected that in the foreseeable future the US will remain a key role player in East Asia, whether one likes it or not.

Chinese Socialism in a Capitalist World System

According to some scholars, the reason that China was able to industrialize more rapidly since 1949 was that the Communist revolution "decisively broke the ties that chained China to the imperialist system" (Moulder, 1977: viii-ix), and it cut the roots of a variety of complicated domestic constraints, such as localism, warlordism and foreign domination. However, like all socialist states, post-revolutionary China was still a constituent part of the "capitalist world system".[4] Would China be able to form an autonomous entity in interacting with the capitalist system while still avoiding the vicissitudes of vulnerability to the capriciousness of the larger capitalist bloc? In other words, would China be allowed to peacefully develop an alternative model and an independent path to social and economic development? The answer, as proved by the history, is no.

The Struggles and Constraints of Chinese Socialism

The history and trajectory of socialist states in the 20th century indicates that socialist movements worldwide, in the periphery and semi-periphery, all initially

3 It is recognized that the US post-war objective in East Asia, as a part of its global strategies, was to restore the functioning of the capitalist world system, which was fundamentally different from the fascist-militarist Japanese agenda during the Second World War.

4 Socialist countries, in the view of the World System Theory, are "state capitalism" because the state is the key actor in the capital accumulation process.

attempted to transform the basic logic of capitalism and establish an alternative mode of production, but ended up using socialist ideology to mobilize national industrialization in order to catch up with advanced capitalist states in the core.[5] Hence, seen from a world system perspective, socialist states were still situated within the interactions of the capitalist world economy, and their activities were very much constrained by the international system of the capitalist world economy (Chase-Dunn, 1999; So and Chiu, 1995). Socialist states, despite some socialist features, such as egalitarian distribution, employment security, comprehensive welfare provision, etc., were still integral participants in the model of *capitalist* accumulation. The history of Chinese socialism proved to be no exception.

It is necessary to point out that the setbacks of Chinese socialism must not be simply reduced to being ascribed to "utopianism" or domestic policy failures. This is because, in addition to internal difficulties, Chinese socialism encountered severe external challenges such as imperialist hostility, economic embargoes, and the deprival of access to capital and technology, diplomatic isolation and military interventions from the capitalist world led by the US. China also faced severe external constraints from the Cold-War world order, which in many ways influenced the choices and strategies of its socialist experiments as well as the course they took. The self-reliant strategy was a consequential choice of internal politics as well as external imposition. Even China's institutional set-ups were structured according to the need for survival in a persistent war situation.[6]

Thus, in assessing the merits and drawbacks of Chinese socialism, the analytical approach should not be only limited to the national level without also taking into consideration the external context. This applies also to the research of China's economic development – many academics tend to study socialist economies on a country-basis without acknowledging the fact that socialist states and their developments were an integral part of the capitalist world system. Their successes as well as failures were severely conditioned by the constraints and opportunities of the system as a whole. Many of China's development strategies and policy choices, such as the emphasis on heavy industries, large investment and human input into non-productive domains (defence industries) and tight political control, have to be seen in the way that these policies were more or less conditioned by the external environment: they were necessary sacrifices for the sake of national security and the survival of the socialist project. The need to develop industry as a basis of national defence loomed large and as such China's approach and

5 According to the World System Theory, countries are divided into "core, "semi-periphery" and "periphery" groupings. The core, also called the "First World", refers to the highly developed countries in the West that have a capital-intensive economy based upon importation of raw materials and exportation of finished goods.

6 The organizational logics of Chinese institutions (in Chinese "Dan Wei") have their roots from the war periods (the anti-Japanese war and the civil war). It was a decentralized system in which each unit/institution is supposed to survive on its own in terms of production, reserve, welfare, medical care, etc.

objectives were not very different from that of the Soviet Union, Japan and some other countries (Eckstein, 1977: 32).

As it is well known, the success story of Japan and the rapid economic development of some Asian newly industrialized countries (NICs) were largely based on an export-oriented strategy. It is widely recognized that the engine of economic growth in the East Asian model of development was attributable to the rapid growth of exports. Beginning in the 1960s, favorable conditions created opportunities for relatively low-cost industrial production to be integrated into the world economy through increased relocation of production by multinational corporations to low-wage countries. Due to the economic sanctions China was obviously denied access to all these benefits and was thus excluded from taking advantage of the favorable international development conditions during the upward phase of the world economy. Likewise, China would not have been able to pursue a development strategy based on export-oriented industrialization even if it had desired, nor was it able to adopt the import-substitution option due to the economic sanctions and embargo imposed upon it.

It is thus not exaggerating to posit that the rapid economic advance of China in the post-Mao decades is actually because of the "regaining" of these favorable international conditions. Dialectically, due to the international isolation that was imposed on China, and that forced it to adopt the alternative socialist development strategies of self-reliance and self-sufficiency, it was possible for China to use the socialist accumulative foundations to contain the distortions of external influences to a limited level. As a result of the socialist legacy, "China also stands out as the only developing country without any internal or external debts outstanding and a uniquely stable currency" (Bhattacharya in Bergmann, 1977: 228). It is forcefully argued by some scholars that some unique development strategies of Chinese socialism, such as economic growth, economic equity, employment, and economic self-reliance, provide good lessons for developing countries, especially with regards to promoting collective institutions, maximizing productive labor input, mass-based human development, universal well-being security, narrowing the differences between regions and between urban and countryside, and also between the divisions of labor, etc. (Weisskopt, 1980). Hence, China's overall socialist economic record was reasonably successful especially "when placed against the wretchedly low starting point from which China began its industrialization drive and the hostile international environment that so burdened the People's Republic in its early decades" (Meisner, 1999: 246).

In a nutshell, the economic success and comparative advantages generated during the decades of the Chinese socialist experiment laid a solid foundation and paved the way for Deng Xiaoping's open-door policy in integrating the Chinese economy with the world market. However, the latter course was not predetermined. The socialist achievements made China relatively stronger and equal in world market exchanges. The present contradiction between China and the West, especially the US, is that the latter wants to make sure that China competes in the world market according to the "established rules" because its comparative advantages could be used to break these rules. Therefore, it is ahistorical to stress the present success without giving a proper assessment of the contribution of the socialist achievements.

The Socialist Foundation for China's Economic Emergence

It is important to keep in mind that what the post-Mao regime has been doing since the end of the 1970s is not "economic reconstruction" but "economic reform" aimed at correcting the "irrational" part of the earlier economic policies. Hence, it is historically erroneous to ignore the *fact* that the achievements of Chinese socialism under political sovereignty, along with a major change in domestic class relations, laid the foundation for the economic progress achieved in the post-Mao era. What needs to be particularly emphasized is the importance of the success of land reform in the reconstruction of China (Hinton, 1998). Many positive democratic ideas, consciousness of political, economic and social rights generated from the Chinese revolution have penetrated into the people's way of thinking. For example, the current government development policy focusing on "harmonious society" is seen as the result of the popular pressure and resentment against social gaps and official corruption. Such a collective maneuver driven by public opinion indicates a great deal of courage inherited from the Cultural Revolution and represents. Hence, the theoretical and practical problematics that the Cultural Revolution struggled to resolve can transcend space and time and continue to yield insight upon reading in a new light (Li, Xing, 2001). The deep-seated revolutionary tradition will continue to play an important role in balancing market forces.

If we do not make a realistic assessment of China's socialist development during Mao's period, when it developed from a backward agrarian society to a major industrial power in the 1970s, we will not be able to understand the logic and limits of Chinese socialist development, and the problems inherited from that era (Selden, 1983). The effect of Chinese socialism can be obviously seen from the favorable position China had, when the economic reform started, in defining the terms and establishing the parameters of interaction with the capitalist world order. As one China-scholar observes,

> ... it [China] was not entangled in a complex web of external economic constraints which limited its freedom of action or skewed its decision in the interests of foreign powers or corporations. ... the establishment of a strong, autonomous state provided the political precondition for ensuring – with a margin for miscalculation – that international economic ties were more likely to be beneficial, as classical economic theory and modern development economics have promised. (White 1982: 131)

The Maoist independent and non-alliance foreign policy, armed with the aforementioned concrete advances in certain industries and military technologies, and assisted by its strong ties with the developing world that backed China's victorious re-entry into the United Nations as a permanent member of the Security Council, laid a solid foundation for its successful rapprochement with the United States and other core western powers. Consequently, the post-Mao regime was in a favorable position to negotiate political, economic and military relations with the core states of the world system on an either relatively equal or advantageous basis.

The success of the post-Mao market reform proves the fact that the fundamental changes and achievements during the reform period in the 1980s and the 1990s were a clear indication of the contribution of some aspects of China's socialist development strategies, especially in rural areas. For example, it has been recognized that China's village-township enterprises had played an important role in its economic growth during the reform period (Putterman, 1997). Township enterprises became, more so than the state sectors, the most dynamic engine of China's economic growth. According to a World Bank report, the growth and performance of China's township and village enterprises (TVE) was extraordinary: their share in GDP rose from 13 percent in 1985 to 31 percent in 1994; their output grew by about 25 percent a year since the mid-1980s; they now accounted for a third of total industrial growth in China; and for more than a decade TVEs had created 95 million jobs (World Bank, 1996: 51). Therefore, while criticizing the socialist period for its great upheaval, economic stagnation, the persecution of intellectuals and violent mass movements, we must recognize the dramatic improvements in the living conditions, development infrastructure, educational level and agricultural practices of China's rural population (Han, 2008). These improvements paved the way for the economic take-off in the beginning of the economic reform period because the reform started first in agriculture.

The Rise of China and the Existing World Order: Two-way Impact

Over the past decade China has been all over global media, much more so since 2008, which has covered Chinese events and issues with headlines ranging from the "Beijing Olympics", "global creditor", "global factory", "most polluted country", "resource hunger", "military superpower", to "democracy and human rights", "Taiwan-mainland relations", "Tibet and Xinjiang independence", and so forth. The sustained economic growth of China for the past three decades is claimed to be the biggest challenge to the existing world order since the end of the Cold War.

The Global "China Factors"

China's high economic growth of the past three decades has already made its economic impact felt worldwide:

1. The size of China's economy and its integration with the world economy have contributed to uncertainty about the global inflationary environment;
2. Its currency has been a subject of contention;
3. Its technological level has been substantially raised through massive investment in research and development (R&D);
4. Its increasing share of global trade has raised concerns for workers and firms in both developed and developing countries;
5. Its hunger for energy has led to the soaring increase of global energy prices as well as to resource competition and conflict;
6. Its formidable status as a new global creditor with the world's largest US dollar reserves, has equipped China with the potential capacity to "challenge US global financial leadership";
7. It has rivaled the United States and the rest of the developing countries as a destination for foreign direct investment; and the effects of its own overseas investments have begun to be felt across the world;
8. Beijing has become an "indispensable" force in international relations and global politics, playing decisive roles in solving regional and global problems;
9. Its economy has become the key engine driving regional economic integration in East Asia (Li, Xing, 2007a); and
10. Many other indications display China's global influence, including its enlarging involvement in the relationship with Latin America, its new activism at the United Nations, its representative voice in the WTO for the developing world, its close cooperation with the World Bank and IMF, and its efforts in promoting regional multilateralism and security through the Shanghai Cooperation Organization in central Asia, etc. As a result, China is increasingly seen as having the quality formerly held by the US as an "indispensable country" (Feffer, 2007).

To some scholars, the rise of China can be termed to be a "Beijing Consensus" (Ramo, 2004 and Li, Xing, 2007b), a notion coined to imply distinct attitudes to politics, development and the global balance of power; according to others it can simply be called the "Chinese model", a sinicized market capitalism termed "a socialist market economy with Chinese characteristics" implying an active role of the Chinese party-state in attaining macro-policy independence and socio-political stability. Both the "Beijing Consensus" and the "Chinese model" are being interpreted either as the rise of China's soft power (Nye, 2005) or as a serious challenge to the existing economic theories (Chow, 1997), as well as to international relations theories (Paltiel, 2005). Will we witness the emergence of "Chinese international relations theories" in the near future along with China's great economic and social transformation? The answer is that this is both likely and even inevitable (Qin, 2007).

What is the implication of the rise of China to the interests of the Western World at large and the United States in particular? What will be the backlash of the

US-led world order on China's internal evolution? Will a rising China be willing to be constrained by the established rules of the game set up and defined by the post-war world order? Or will it alter the rules or write its own rules in many areas, such as intellectual property rights, trade practices, state-market relations, military expansion, and inter-state relations? Opinion-makers among both realists and neoliberals provide very different analyses and policy recommendations in response to the rise of China. Realists stress the importance of understanding the world system as a zero-sum game, advocating prevention against the "coming conflict with China" (Bernstein and Munro, 1997 and Mearsheimer, 2001 and 2006). Whereas neoliberals emphasize the merits of an institutional approach to engage China so that it will be incorporated in international regimes and become a stake-holder in the existing global system (Ikenberry, 2008).

Challenges and Contradictions: Internal

It is foreseeable that in the near future China's import of natural resources, especially oil and gas, will have to be substantially increased, making China subject to the international energy market. The implication is seemingly clear that not only will the global commodity price and international geopolitical power relations be affected but also China's own internal evolutions, such as foreign policy thinking, foreign aid designing, arms sale considerations and compulsory expansion of its long-range naval power projection capabilities will be immediately impacted. There is a genuine consensus among Chinese leaders and scholars that energy has become a key strategic issue concerning China's economic development, social stability, and national security, and that the realization of China's key national interests[7] is highly dependent on the access to sufficient energy resources as well as the security of maritime transportation (Liu, 2006; Zhang, 2006). Therefore, relying on the external energy market can become a potential source of constraint as China strives to sustain the high economic growth rate.

In recent years we are witnessing rising incompatibility between the resurgence of Chinese nationalism and western reactions to China's ascendance. In many ways Beijing is indeed challenging, both politically and economically, the interests and intentions of the West. This opens opportunities for the regime to pacify domestic dissatisfaction and build new bases of legitimacy by using nationalism in the confrontation with external adversaries. Although resistance and antagonism toward the United States can be perceived among politicians, intellectuals and students, and so forth, the Chinese leadership is not very clear as to what is to be expected from the complete integration of China into the US-led capitalist world system. During China's socialist period, nationalism together with socialism was used to mobilize the people to make China into a self-reliant country. Now it

7 China's national interests are defined by the government as including sustained economic growth, the prevention of Taiwanese independence; return to as a global power status, and the continuous leadership of the Chinese Communist Party (CCP).

seems that nationalism and Confucianism are used to mobilize the country and people to restore China's "normal" great power status within the world order.

Due to the colossal rapidity in which China has experienced industrialization and urbanization in the past 30 years, the class structure of Chinese society has been dramatically transformed (Hart-Landsberg and Burkett, 2004; He, 2000), which has led to the historical and intellectual emergence of a third social force: civil society (Ma, 1994; White, 1994). The Chinese government has to not only accept both the concept and practice of civil society as an emerging independent social force, but also frame it or depoliticize it as a class-neutral entity. This is because in three decades the share of China's proletarian and semi-proletarian wage workers has increased substantially; and in the foreseeable future China's degree of proletarianization and wage level will be equivalent to the current levels of the semi-peripheral states in Latin America and Southeast Asia (Li, Mingqi, 2005: 435; 2008). Economic marketization has turned China's social and economic stratification into a "coat of many colours" (Unger, 1994). Ironically, many of today's contradictions in China's market socialism are of a class struggle in nature. Class divisions and struggles at the local, regional as well as national level will become the key sociopolitical problem affecting China's industrialization in the near and medium future. This reflects the true tenet that the means and ends of capitalism are not easily separated, and the more that economically successful methods of capitalism are utilized, the less socialist ends will be possible (Meisner, 1997; Weil, 1996).

China's remarkable economic achievement has been made possible by its growing integration with the capitalist world economy. Beijing's economic gains from the global economic transformation are inseparable from its increasing dependence on the global market. The approach and pattern of China's economic development increasingly resemble the East Asian NICs' model: deepening structural relations with Western industrial countries and dependence on foreign trade, investments and financing. If we look into China's "success" of economic growth, we will easily find that Western investors and private entrepreneurs have dominated the most dynamic sectors of the economy. In other words, China's rapid economic growth has been driven by exports with the assistance of foreign investments and joint-ventures. The ascendancy of an externally-oriented neo-liberal stratum will deepen Chinese dependence and reinforce the hegemony of foreign-linked groups, whereas the ascendancy of the nationalist sentiment will create ambiguous policies, which tend to define the terms and conditions of associations between public and private capital, both of internal and external investors as well as financiers. Market-driven growth encourages more concessions to induce capital flows and growth in unlimited possibilities of expansion and more structural changes to meet the demand of the overwhelming pursuit of external markets and resources. In addition, close integration with the world market is followed by the over-dependence of its productive forces on the fluctuations of the world market. It is already too late for Beijing to amend the defects of over-reliance on overseas markets. Millions of workers in the coastal provinces are depending on external trade and technology, thus intensifying the limitations on the Chinese state's capacities to pursue independent foreign policies. The current financial crisis (2008 and 2009) has indicted such vulnerability.

Therefore, some scholars (Shirk, 2008) see that the real danger lies not in China's external economic expansion, but rather in the internal insecurity of its leaders and potential social unrest stemming from the destabilizing effects domestically of economic marketization: massive social dislocations, rising unemployment, energy shortage, widening inequalities, environmental degradation, mass migration, ethnic tension, minority separatism, etc. The potential social and political costs of the contradiction inherent in China's transformation are extremely high. The separatist riots in Tibet in 2008 and in Xingjiang in 2009 were just two most recent examples.

Challenges and Contradictions: External

If the Maoist self-reliance and self-sufficiency path of development was projected as a potential development model and ideology, and the central goal of socialist politics was seen to challenge the inequitable hierarchy in the world economic order, such a socialist hegemonic project, although seemingly threatening, existed more or less outside the US-led capitalist world system. In other words, Chinese socialism was more an ideological challenge without being able to construct a sustainable alternative model to replace the capitalist world system. The rejoining of China to the capitalist world after restoring diplomatic relations with the United States, and especially after it started the economic reform since the end of the 1970s, was regarded as the most significant savoir of the capitalist world order because the core parts of the capitalist world system – the United States and Europe – were also much weakened by the long Cold-War competition with the former Soviet Union.

Many of China's contradictions in its external relations, especially in its relations with the West and the US in particular, lie in the two conflicting faces of China: entering the world capitalist market while preserving its "socialist" and national identity. A key contradiction arises between China's suspicion of the West and Japan due to historical experiences, and its intense desire to join in the club of Western advanced countries, and to borrow, learn and participate in trade and technology transfer, etc. With its sustained economic growth and rising military strength, China wants the West-dominated world order to acknowledge its "Chinese characteristics" in the process of joining the established capitalist world system. But this may cause serious contradictions with regard to China's internal political and economic structure in its interaction with the outside capitalist world. The current mixture of "neo-liberalism" and "nationalism" has caused ambiguity in ideology and policy planning. As a result, the Chinese Communist Party has to constantly adjust to changing realities to negotiate and renegotiate its political legitimacy (Sausmikat, 2006; Li, Xing, 2009).

Politically speaking, although China's post-Mao economic model of development is seemingly market- and capital-oriented seen from the basic features of capitalism, it is still minted with a distinct attitude to politics, development and the global balance of power, and focusing on market utilitarianism, institutional adaptation, performance orientation and social–political and technical innovations. It is driven by China's three-decade success in economic development, by a determinant desire of China to innovate an alternative development path, by a strong belief in state sovereignty and global multilateralism and by a strategy to accumulate the tools of "asymmetric power projection", i.e. how to achieve and maintain power in an asymmetric power relation to the remaining superpower and the transnational capitals. Such a model, ironically, can be viewed as a real menace because of its ambition to have access to a larger share of world wealth and resources as well as the potential for environmental problems. Ironically, such a "menace" exists *within* the mechanism of global capitalism! The "threat" of China's 1.3 billion people in resource consumption and wealth collection is much more real than Samuel Huntington's "clash of civilizations". The challenges of the Chinese model are putting into question not only the fundamental assumptions of western neoliberal economic theories but also the perceived causal linkages between economic modernization and western political democracy. Seen from the basic tenets of economic realism, trade, profit and security issues are more important to western national security and interests than moral issues regarding China's democracy and human rights.

While the West is salivating over the purchase power of 1.3 billion people, it forgets that a nascent ebullient capitalism often takes on rather wild features and may produce unexpected results. A free market economy in China drives people to seek every possible opportunity and means to earn a profit or just to survive. Seen from the Chinese side, many of Beijing's "misbehaviors" and China–West conflicts are actually the consequences of its economic marketization leading to the imbalanced priorities between human rights and capitalism, between the need for stability and the need of attracting foreign investment, between cheap labor and rapid export, and between economic liberalization and the CCP's political legitimacy. Seen from the western perspective, there is the wish to see the capitalist market economy demolish the Chinese authoritarian party-state on the one hand; but on the other hand, the rule-less profit-seeking practices of China's protocapitalism are highly harmful to western business interests and must be stopped through the authoritarian intervention of the Chinese state. The fact is that the West is increasingly losing political bargaining power to the extent that it is becoming addicted to the Chinese market. This has caused many policy failures in the West in attempting to combine "soft value issues" such as human rights, labour rights and Tibet independence, with "hard value issues", such as trade and profit.

While the "rise" of China has been generally viewed as providing global capitalism with potentially a "win-win" situation, it has also been seen by some as causing the relative "decline" of other export-oriented countries in East Asia and South America. China's capitalist growth strategies, measured by its growing share of imports globally (especially the US market) and of transnational capital (for example, FDI) have generated regional and global contradictions. According to the studies by some scholars, China's competitive advantages are weakening the relative monopoly of the existing semi-peripheral states in certain commodity chains by exerting pressures on their production cost and wage level (Li, Mingqi, 2005). The danger of *peripheralization of the semi-periphery* in the current capitalist world system is analytically theorized by one scholar:

> This has dangerous implications for the capitalist world economy. The semi-periphery plays the indispensable role of the "middle stratum" in the world system. A layer of the semi-periphery offers hope of "modernization", "development", and ultimately, upward mobility for the great majority living in the peripheral states. Should this layer disappear and be reduced to no more than a part of the periphery, the world system is likely to become politically highly unstable ... Peripheralization of the semi-periphery would deprive the capitalist world-economy of a major source of effective demand. Moreover, the peripheralized semi-peripheral states will inevitably face highly explosive political situations at home. The relatively more proletarianized working classes will demand semi-peripheral levels of wages and political and social rights. However, the peripheralized semi-peripheral states will not be able to simultaneously offer the relatively high wages and survive the competition against other peripheral or peripheralized semi-peripheral states in the world market. The entire semi-periphery will be threatened with revolution and political turmoil. (Li, 2005: 436-437)

It is unavoidable that China's capitalist growth strategy has generated regional and global contractions. China is being implicated as the cause of the problems of other countries and other regions: overproduction, decreasing regional wage rates, destructive regional competition for investment and resources, etc. (Hart-Landsberg and Burkett, 2004).

Last but not least, China's energy demand and energy diplomacy has great implications for global energy security. China's heavy dependence on global trade drives its mounting demand for resources to sustain its economic growth and to fuel its endless development projects. China has already become the world's largest importer of a range of commodities, from copper to steel and crude oil. Not only will global commodity prices and international geopolitical power relations be affected by China's energy demand, but so will China's international politics, such as foreign policy calculation, foreign aid design, arms sale considerations and the development of long-range naval power projection capabilities be closely connected with energy issues, forcing the current international energy regime to adjust its established rules of the game. This is because the international energy regime "is influenced not only by economic, political, and social factors of resource-rich countries but also by international political factors, particularly change in the international balance of power, adjustment of relationships among countries and changes to international rules (Xu, 2007: 6).

Since energy security has in recent years become one of China's top national security concerns, Beijing has a two-track strategy: 1) developing good relations with alternative regions which contain potential energy reserves, such as Africa and Latin America, through trade and investment; 2) preparing for technological advances and changes of climatic circumstances which will make maritime transport in the Arctic waters possible, linking the North Atlantic and the North Pacific in close commercial relations. It is expected that China, as a clear indication of involvement, will increasingly strengthen its political economy of international relations in the Arctic region and speed up its research through its polar research bases in Antarctica.

Conclusion

This chapter has attempted to construct a framework for understanding the nexus between the internalities and externalities in the process of China's historical transformations and its recent resurgence. Such an internal–external linkage intertwined with a challenge–response approach has a dialectical process of mutual generation: internal struggles were triggered by external challenges while internal transformations were responded to by external adjustments and accommodations. China's century-long internal struggles to overcome constraints on its development can be likewise paralleled by the continuous external responses to the "China factors". China's ability to successfully solve its internal development problems and manage external challenges will not only influence its internal stability, economic and political liberalization, and leadership but also affect regional and global security.

Historically China has been able to display the capacity of absorbing foreign ideas and influences as well as sinicizing and transforming them into an integral part of native value systems, such as the sinicization of Buddhism and Marxism-Leninism. Today it is still a question whether China will be able to sinicize capitalism and create a "socialist market economy". In recent decades economic growth has torn down much of the physical symbols of China's cultural history, but the Chinese people still remain an intensely historical nation with a strong and popular *nationalism*. Chinese nationalism is an integral part of the internalities of the driving forces that can be turned into a strong anti-west sentiment if the West refuses to accommodate or share leadership with China. The time was when nationalism was mainly led by the party and the state; today nationalists, assisted by modern technology and economic prosperity, are acting independently beyond the control of the state (Gries, 2005).

Currently we are witnessing an interesting situation facing China: due to its deep integration in the global capitalist economy, Beijing is gaining economic strength on the one hand but losing political independence on the other. In other words,

China's rise through active participation in the global political economy is, at the same time, being translated into greater vulnerability and dependence. Beijing's desire to retain its legitimacy through integrating the Chinese economy with the global market will make it politically vulnerable to internal economic setbacks and external pressures, thus endangering the preservation of its integrity.

In the past decades either fascination or irritation with China has always influenced Western scholarship and journalism, which often have produced intense sentiments ranging from excessive approval and unqualified optimism to unwarranted revulsion and deep pessimism. There were hopeful writings of confidence about China's "second revolution" during the most of 1980s; then there was deep antagonism toward China's lack of political reform following the June 1989 crackdown; and in recent years, there are exaggerated projections of China's threatening rise to superpower status. From time to time Western politicians and observers selectively use China's successes and failures to justify their existing theories and prejudices. A *correct* reading of the anxieties and contractions behind the rise of China is the way to understand the dialectical process of "mutual generation" and "mutual destruction" between domestic transformations and international premises. By doing so, a holistic understanding of China and its emergence can be formed.

References

Bergmann, Theodor (1977) *The Development Models of India, the Soviet Union and China*. The Netherlands: Van Gorcum & Co.

Bernstein, Richard and Munro, Ross (1997) *The Coming Conflict with China*. New York: Alfred A. Knopf.

Bottomore, Tom, Laurence Harris, V.G. Kiernan and Ralph Miliband (eds) (1983) *A Dictionary of Marxist Thought*. London: Basil Blackwell.

Chase-Dunn, Christopher (1999) "Globalization: A World-Systems Perspective", *Journal of World-Systems Research*, 5(2): 165-185.

Chi, Wen-Shun (1986) *Ideological Conflicts in Modern China*. New Jersey: Transaction Books.

Chow, Gregory C. (1997) "Challenges of China's Economic System for Economic Theory", *The American Economic Review*, 87(2): 321-327.

Dirlik, Arif and Meisner, Maurice (1989) "Politics, Scholarship, and Chinese Socialism", in Arif Dirlik and Maurice Meisner (eds), *Marxism and the Chinese Experience*. New York: M.E. Sharpe, Inc.

Dirlik, Arif (1989) *The Origins of Chinese Communism*. New York: Oxford University Press.

Eckstein, Alexander (1977) *China's Economic Revolution*. London: Cambridge University Press.

Elvin, Mark (1984) "Why China Failed to Create an Endogenous Industrial Capitalism", *Theory and Society*, 13(3): 379-391.

Feffer, John (2007) "China the Indispensable?" *Foreign Policy In Focus*, March 9 (http://www.fpif.org/fpiftxt/4070).

Gregor, James A. (1995) *Marxism, China, and Development: Reflections on Theory and Reality*. London: Transaction Publishers.

Gries, Peter Hays (2005) "Chinese Nationalism: Challenging the State?", *Current History*, 104(683): 251-256.

Han, Dongping (2008) *The Unknown Cultural Revolution: Life and Change in a Chinese Village*. New York: Monthly Review Press.

Hart-Landsberg, Martin and Burkett, Paul (2004) *China and Socialism: Market Reforms and Class Struggle*. New York: Monthly Review Press.

He, Di (1994) "The Most Respected Enemy: Mao Zedong's Perception of the United States", *The China Quarterly* (137), 144-158.

He, Qinglian (2000) "China's Listing Social Structure", *New Left Review*, 2(5): 69-99.

Hegel, Georg W.F. (1938) *The Philosophy of History*. Available at http://www.btinternet.com/~glynhughes/squashed/hegelhistory.htm.

Hersh, Jacques (1993) *The USA and the Rise of East Asia Since 1945: Dilemmas of the Postwar International Political Economy*. New York: St. Martin's Press.

Hinton, William (1998) "The Importance of Land Reform in the Reconstruction of China", *Monthly Review*, July-August: 147-160.

Ikenberry, G. John (2008) "The Rise of China and the Future of the West", *Foreign Affairs*, 87(1): 23-37.

Kapur, Harish, ed. (1987) *As China Sees the World*. London: Frances Pinter.

Kung, Chungwu (1975) "Cultural Revolution in Modern Chinese History", in Victor Nee and James Peck (eds), *China's Uninterrupted Revolution from 1840 to the Present*. New York: Random House.

Li, Mingqi (2005) "The Rise of China and the Demise of the Capitalist World-Economy: Exploring the Historical Possibilities in the 21st Century", *Science and Society*, 69(3): 420-448.

Li, Minqi (2008) *The Rise of China and The Demise of The Capitalist World Econmy*. New York: Pluto Press.

Li, Xing (2001) "The Chinese Cultural Revolution Revisited", *The China Review*, 1(1): 137-165.

Li, Xing (2007a) "Conceptualizing East Asian Regionalism: From Japan-led "flying-geese" to China-driven Integration", *CCIS Working Paper Series No. 3* by the Centre for Comparative Integration Studies, Department of History, International and Social Studies, Aalborg University, Denmark.

Li, Xing (2007b) "Paradigm Shift: From 'Washington Consensus' to 'Beijing Consensus'", in Kwesi K. Prah (ed.) *Afro-Chinese Relations, Past, Present and Future*. Cape Town: The Centre for Advanced Studies of African Society (CASAS).

Li, Xing (2009) "Why Is the Chinese Communist Party Able to Survive in an Era of Great Transformation?" *Kritisk Debat* 45.

Lippit, Victor D. (1980) "Development of Underdevelopment in China", in Philip C.C. Huang (ed.) *Development of Underdevelopment in China.* New York: M.E. Sharpe.

Liu, Xuecheng (2006) "China's Energy Security and Its Grand Strategy", *Policy Analysis Brief*, The Stanley Foundation.

Ma, Shuyun (1994) "The Chinese Discourse on Civil Society", *The China Quarterly*, 137: 180-193.

Mearsheimer, John (2001) *Tragedy Of Great Power Politics*. New York: W.W. Norton Company.

Mearsheimer, John (2006) "China's Unmerciful Rise", *Current History*, 105(690): 160-162.

Meisner, Maurice (1997) "The Other China", *Current History*, 96(611): 264-273.

Meisner, Maurice (1999) "China's Communist Revolution: A Half-century Perspective", *Current History*, 98(629): 243-248.

Moulder, Frances V. (1977) *Japan, China and the Modern World Economy.* Cambridge: Cambridge University Press.

Nye, Joseph S. (2005) "The Rise of China's Soft Power", *The Wall Street Journal Asia*, December 29.

Paltiel, Jeremy (2005) "The Rise of China as a Challenge to International Relations Theory", paper presented at the annual meeting of the International Studies Association, Hilton Hawaiian Village, Honolulu, Hawaii, March 5. (http://www.allacademic.com/meta/p70638_index.html).

Peck, James (1975) "Revolution Versus Modernization and Revisionism: A Two-Front Struggle", in Victor Nee and James Peck (eds), *China's Uninterrupted Revolution from 1840 to the Present*. New York: Random House.

Putterman, Louis (1997) "On the Past and Future of China's Township and Village-Owned Enterprises", *World Development*, 10: 1639-1555.

Qin, Yaqing (2007) "Why Is There No Chinese International Relations Theory?" International Relations of the Asia-Pacific, 7(3): 313-340.

Ramo, Joshua Cooper (2004) *The Beijing Consensus*. London: The Foreign Policy Centre.

Sausmikat, Nora (2006) "More Legitimacy for One-Party Rule? The CCP's Ideological Adjustments and Intra-Party Reforms", *ASIEN*, 99: 70-91.

Schwarz, Benjamin (1996) "Why America Thinks it Has to Run the World", *The Atlantic Monthly*, 277(6): 92-102.

Selden, Mark (1983) "The Logic – and Limits – of Chinese Socialist Development", *World Development*, 11(8): 631-637.

Shirk, Susan L. (2008) *China: Fragile Superpower*. New York: Oxford University Press.

So, Alvin Y. and Stephen W.K. Chiu (1995): *East Asia and the World Economy*. California: SAGE Publications.

Tan, Chung (1996) "Towards a Holistic Understanding of Chinese History", *China Report*, 32(3): 233-249.

Thomson, James C. (1992) "Americans and The 'Loss' Of China", in Mark Borthwick (ed.) *Pacific Century: The Emergence of Modern Pacific Asia*. Boulder, CO: Westview Press.

Unger, Jonathan (1994) "'Rich Man, Poor Man': The Making of New Classes in the Countryside", in David S.G. Goodman and Beverley Hooper (eds) (1994) *China's Quiet Revolution*. Melbourne: Longman Cheshire Pty Ltd.

Weil, Robert (1996) *Red Cat, White Cat: China and the Contradictions of "market Socialism"*. New York: Monthly Review Press.

Weisskopf, Thomas E. (1980) "The Relevance of The Chinese Experience For Third World Economic Development", *Theory and Society*, 9(2): 283-318.

White, Gordon (1982) "Why Did China Fail to Follow the Japanese Road?", in Manfred Bienefeld and Martin Godfrey (eds), *The Struggle for Development, National Strategies in an International Context*. New York: John Wiley & Sons Limited.

White, Gordan (1994) "Prospects For Civil Society: A Case Study Of Xiaoshan City", in David S.G. Goodman and Beverley Hooper (eds) (1994) *China's Quiet Revolution*. Melbourne: Longman Cheshire Pty Lid.

Wittfogel, Karl (1957) *Oriental Despotism: A Comparative Study of Total Power*. New Haven: Yale University Press.

World Bank (1996) *From Plan to Market: World Development Report*. New York: Oxford University Press.

Xu, Qinhua (2007) "China's Energy Diplomacy and its Implications for Global Energy Security", *FES Briefing Paper 13*, Friedrich-Ebert-Stiftung, Berlin, Germany.

Zhang, Wenmu (2006) "Sea Power and China's Strategic Choices", *China Security*, Summer: 17-31.

Chapter 7
Chinese Globalization: State Strategies and their Societal Anchoring

Stig Thøgersen and Clemens Stubbe Østergaard

Introduction

China is generally seen as one of globalization's great winners. It is the top destination of foreign direct investments and producer of a substantial proportion of the goods that are consumed all over the world. The general trends of globalization have coincided with and been reinforced by the country's own opening to the outside world, and the mental and material life of the Chinese population has been fundamentally transformed in the process. In the 1970s it was still a favourite Sunday pastime for local citizens to stand outside the Beijing Hotel to catch a glimpse of a foreigner, and in smaller towns a Western visitor could create a major traffic jam just by walking down the street. The shops exclusively sold Chinese goods, and Western cultural products were only allowed if they highlighted capitalist exploitation. The contrast to today is almost unimaginable. Foreign designer clothes, music and electronic goods are now all-pervasive in China. Hollywood blockbusters can be bought on DVD in the streets of Shanghai and Guangzhou even before they have been screened in the US and taxi drivers can tell you the names of all major football stars in AC Milan or FC Barcelona. Millions of Chinese have been abroad as students, businessmen, or tourists, and close to half a million foreigners live more or less permanently in China. All these changes have taken place within the short time span of 30 years, and they have turned China into a potent symbol of globalization's transformative power. In China, globalization is not just a fancy catchword in a neoliberal discourse, it is tangible reality.

In this chapter we will discuss how China has confronted the challenges of globalization. First we discuss a number of Chinese globalization strategies, partly to uncover what is characteristic or different about them, partly to find explanations for the advantages China has reaped from globalization. We look at the process behind formulation of policies in this field, and delineate seven broad state strategies which together touch on nearly all aspects of Chinese policy and foreign policy. Risks and problems abound, a number of them derive from China's continued status of developing country. Over the last five years a major attempt – headlined "the harmonious society" – has been made to attain balance, after decades of hectic concentration on economic growth. It brings to mind Roosevelt's "New Deal" policies in the US of the 1930s.

A deeper understanding of China's success relative to globalization then entails an analysis of the discursive and institutional methods the state has employed to anchor the many strategies in the population. In the next section we look at the Chinese globalization discourse and how a narrative has been constructed that fully supports China's integration in the world but at the same time emphasizes the need for a strong state to defend national interests. The final section will discuss policies aimed at embedding the party-state more solidly in society. Entrepreneurs, intellectuals, workers, and farmers have all been affected by economic reforms and globalization in different ways and the Chinese Communist Party (CCP) has designed a broad range of political mechanisms in order to tie particularly the emerging elites closer to the state.

Along the way, we relate to four overall ideas. Theorizing on the "competition state" stresses the primary need for the state to facilitate increased growth and national competitiveness (Cerny, 1997). The analysis focuses on this when it depicts particularly the Deng Xiaoping era's efforts to create a growth-enhancing environment through major structural reforms. The idea of the "development state", as we know it from other East Asian countries (Wade, 1990), is alive in the continued strong role of the state and in the many special institutional contexts created. Whether it be around the organization and capacity of the state, or about its embeddedness in economy and society (Evans, 1995). Visions of a possible soft balancing effort as the driver behind some of the strategies (Hurrell, 2006) are treated tangentially in discussion of China's comprehensive multilateralism and its symbiotic economic relationship with the USA. Finally, we also are mindful of the contradiction between China's historically based focus on maintaining sovereignty, and mainstream expectations that this would make it harder to benefit fully from globalization (Sorensen, 2001). These have not been fulfilled, and while one explanation may be China's pragmatism and increased willingness to negotiate sovereignty (Carlson, 2005), the analysis in the following shows other possible explanations.

Globalization Strategies of the Chinese State

Flower growers in the fertile Yunnan province register Valentine's Day and other days in the western calendar. They produce cut flowers, and the export markets fluctuate so much that a few years ago they chose to invite an expert from Beijing to understand globalization better. The man was Yu Keping, a notable defender of globalization, and no doubt he helped increase Yunnan's competitiveness.

Competitiveness has become a success-and-survival criterion for states, and politics is increasingly about creating conditions that will increase economic growth. There are many ways towards this, but China seems to have had a particular ability to turn the enormous forces of globalization to its own advantage. This was done through a cluster of state strategies, which are particularly visible over the last 15 years, though they were launched much earlier.

Some strategies are outward directed, others inward. Among the first are the emphasis on international organizations and multilateralism, together with marked trade liberalization. In addition to this, the red carpet was rolled out for foreign investors, while simultaneously a strong push was made to get China's own industries to go abroad, and to create China-based transnational companies with strong brands. The East Asian region had a role to play too – either as the vessel of choice, or as a means of rescue in case of need. Inwardly we have seen the transformation of the Leninist state apparatus into a modern regulatory state, but also the fight to transform a core area of globalization, the world of international finance, into giving a "lift" rather than presenting a threat to China. Industrial workers lost their privileges, and a new private economic elite was allowed to enter the communist party.

Intriguingly, as we shall return to later, until the first years of the 1990s the word globalization was only used about trends in capitalist countries, never about China itself. Only in 1993 researchers were able to stop using "internationalization", and begin using the G-word about what was happening to the Chinese economy.

An Early Start and a Proactive State

It is noticeable that China started out very early in its globalization efforts. With Deng Xiaoping's reforms a globalized behaviour commenced already in the early 1980s, i.e. before the existence of some of the most important aspects of global economic participation. It has been called a "virtual globalization". But it shows a clear will to push China towards globalizing, even without the pressures which forced western economies in this direction. The result is a flying start.

Paradoxically, the Cultural Revolution (1966-1976) may be a precondition for this early commencement. After a decade of experience with "self-reliance" and being cut off from the world, China was forced to rethink. It had learned what being cut off from international technological development meant. The 10 years of chaos had also removed most vested interests, by the unprecedented weakening of party and state apparatus. Many of the interests, which in other countries would have prevented the turn outward, were gone. The slate was fairly clean, and the intellectual advisors that Deng set to work in various new think-tanks could make an unbiased start. Ideas became very important, more so than material conditions. A central idea was that the struggle in the international system was no longer primarily a military one, but economic. For China, globalization was also associated with modernity, and thus part of the whole modern national identity envisioned for the country by the CCP. In any case, integration in the international economic division of labour was central to the courageous economic reforms under Deng.

Another characteristic was the attempt to keep ahead of events, to be proactive and selective in the shaping of globalization strategies. This has been possible inter alia because think-tanks and advisors spent more time analysing the complex and contradictory nature of globalization rather than taking positions for or against it. The broad mainstream of actors has accepted globalization as an objective fact and an inevitable trend in human development. They have seen it as a process, not a state, and thus something that can be influenced – on the basis of analyses of threats and opportunities. The top-down authoritarian system, with a modernizing party having a monopoly on power, has permitted faster decision-making and the possibility of a consistent, long-term policy. The process has also made it possible to give primacy to inputs from expert advisors, at a time of general professionalization and specialization in the formulation of Chinese policy (Lampton, 2001).

A third marked characteristic is the central role of the state in this model. The leadership has been able to maintain the necessary autonomy, towards both external and internal forces. It has increased the capacity of the state to produce broad-spectred strategies – with the right timing and sequence – to try and maximize the fortunate consequences of globalization and minimize the unfortunate ones. As market-reforms picked up speed, and the economy grew, it had to fight to keep in charge. This is part of the explanation for the historical and continuing efforts of the one-party state to keep its leadership monopoly and hold onto some Leninist tools like the right to appoint and rotate a long list of officials countrywide. At the same time there is a will to change the state. While reducing government intervention in general, the active role of the state is maintained in some issue-areas, so expanding its capacity to take on the many new tasks with which a globalizing market-economy presents a country.

Where and How Are Strategies Formulated?

It may be useful to sketch some main features of the complicated machinery which produces China's strategies of globalization (Prakash and Hart, 2000a, 2000b). Global processes affect the system from outside. It may be the pressure from global markets, or international forces like the protectionist trade-regimes in certain areas, in the textile sector for instance the former Multifiber-agreement. It can also be the pressure of other governments to adopt certain policies, for instance the US-led pressure for liberalizing, for which the WTO negotiations with China were used as a lever.

These external stimuli strike in a context of Chinese institutions, which to a certain extent are a product of historic development. The context encompasses the rules surrounding policy-making and the relations between various party and government institutions (Shambaugh, 2008). Here are also the social contracts or historical compromises which exist at any one time, whether it be "low wage, but social security" of the Mao-period, "high growth, but inequality" of Deng's time, or lately the "harmonious society" of the Hu-Wen leadership, with its emphasis on sustainability in a wide sense, including compensation to the losers in reform and globalization.

There are winners and losers within various sectors of the economy, firms and factors of production – and among the 30+ provinces. Winners are mobilized in coalitions in support of further globalization strategies. These strategies are shaped by the relative power of winners and losers, and their very varying chances for collective action. Lobbying and interest group behaviour are fairly new phenomena in a Chinese context, but spreading rapidly. Important players in the domestic accommodation to market-integration are first and foremost the various state bureaucracies (which should often be seen as representatives of sectors winning or losing from for instance globalization), but also larger firms, business associations and even NGOs. Foreign or transnational interest groups can also be active, e.g. the American Chamber of Commerce in Beijing, and so can foreign governments, as exemplified in the occasional pressure for revaluation of the Chinese yuan.

In the middle of all this, the preferences and resources of central decision-makers remain important – in spite of their taking part in an increasingly collective decision-making. In the final analysis they are themselves dependent on the acceptance of a broader circle, not an electorate, but a "selectorate", of perhaps 500 (Shirk, 1993). They sit in leading posts centrally and around the country, and represent sector and regional interests in a kind of "shadow pluralism" (White, 1993) The small core group of leaders are no more and no less elected than the corporate leadership of global banks or transnational companies, but their ideas, education and experience are important factors.

Ideas are not just found with decision-makers and think tanks. They also continually enter China, both as part of the discourse coming from the ever more concentrated global media-industry, and as part of the socialization China receives through international organizations (Johnston, 2009). China also attempts to establish discourses as part and parcel of its globalization strategies, for instance defending free trade, when the US or EU resort to protectionism under the effects of the financial crisis. Globalization affects China, but China also puts its stamp on globalization, the more so as it represents up to a third of global growth.

Seven Globalization Strategies

What strategies have been produced and how are they expressed in China's practice towards globalization? There are at least seven categories, and they are all buoyed by the will to use globalization to further modernization. There is a wide consensus that globalization is a precondition for the introduction of market economy and the establishment of modern business, finance and administrative systems.

Over-Involvement in International Organizations and Liberalization of Foreign Trade

It came as a shock when, in 1980, shortly after reform started, Deng applied for Chinese entry into the hallowed halls of global capitalism, the World Bank and the

IMF. But this was just the overture to a speedy change from near isolation to actual "over-involvement" in international organizations – relative to China's low level of development. China exchanged personnel with the World Bank headquarters in Washington, became its biggest receiver of development assistance, and was the subject of countless thorough, comparative reports which helped change institutions, influence ideas and transform leadership resources in China.

Simultaneously, China could influence international affairs through its participation in the more than 1,000 global regimes and groupings it took part in. This demanded tailoring domestic legislation to global regimes, as when WTO-membership in 2002 entailed revising 2,300 central laws and regulations and hundreds of thousands at provincial level. China bit the bullet and signed heaps of agreements about everything from security over trade to environment and human rights. In 1977 membership of non-governmental international organizations amounted to 71, in 1997 it was 1,163. There may still be a stretch from formal adaption to real commitment, but there can be no doubt about multilateralism being a centrepiece of Chinese foreign policy.

The aim of reforms and the open door policy was to become globally competitive and join the global march of technology. This meant a great trade liberalization, ridding the mighty state trading corporations of their monopolies, so foreign trade could be privatized and opened up (Naughton, 2007: 375). Liberalizing also meant strong unilateral reduction of tariffs through the 1990s, and the WTO-terms that China finally accepted after 14 years of negotiations with the US were demanding. China is now the third largest trading nation, with reserves over $2,000 billion. According to IMF, China in 2007 was the country contributing most to global growth, namely 27 percent. The growing reserves enabled China to extend a kind of consumer credit to an over-consuming US by buying Treasury Bonds and investing in other bonds. It is striking that China is now the biggest producer of ordinary consumer goods, just as Great Britain was 1850-1900, the US from 1900-1960 and Japan 1960-1990.

Red Carpet Rolled Out For Foreign Investors

Overseas Chinese were the first to discover the cheap, but well-qualified labour power to be found in the new special economic zones. Here foreign investors were given big privileges, but in a few delimited locations. With success, they multiplied and in 1993 there were already 8,000 zones, and they became magnets, also attracting Chinese firms wanting to internationalize and gain technological advantages. There was even Chinese capital illegally "round-tripping" abroad to get the favoured treatment. The many counties (2,500+) and cities over 1 million (170) strived to create the best investment climate. This competition took many forms: tax, infrastructure, cutting red tape, service-provision, reduction of environmental demands, etc. When the centre stops it in one area, it quickly finds new ones. There is still a danger of a "race to the bottom", damaging both the environment and worker safety.

But the growth premium of this strategy is huge. The idea was to get investors with technology to China, hoping that partnerships and gradual diffusion would then put China in the global march of technology. It has worked; rising sharply through the 1990s foreign investments in 2001 made China the number one goal. 400 of the worlds 500 biggest MNC's are represented in China and half a million enterprises have foreign capital. The Chinese government maintains a relatively strong bargaining position based on the size of the market, a strong state role and the chance to play the many interested parties off against each other.

China now has a role as integrator in many of the East Asian chains of production. It is highly conscious of the need to move from labour-intensive manufacturing, where other countries can soon compete, to the high-tech fields. Many of the closures ascribed to the American financial crisis and the resulting recession, were in reality a phasing out and consolidation in industrial sectors where small, low-tech enterprises – unable to live up to new rules on labour safety and environment – had to close. A sure way to attract knowledge- and technology-intensive investments is via political stability and stable policies. China is predictable and stable enough for long-term investors. As a footnote, it is worth remembering that foreign capital is less than 10 percent of total fixed investment, and that China's export dependency is far below the global average.

The Rudder of Macroeconomics and Streamlining the Ship of State

It is hard to steer an aircraft carrier with the rudder of a dinghy. Yet this was Deng's situation after he had bought political backing for his reforms by decentralizing authority to the provinces and their powerful leaders. This made the rudder smaller. The success of reforms, raging economic growth, made the ship larger. To ensure a regulatory state, able to handle globalization, some power had to be recentralized. Large fiscal reforms have given the central power a growing share of tax income, and a better base for macroeconomic management. A large reform of the central bank removed it from provincial interference, making it possible to lead monetary policy and efficiently control the problematic financial sector (Yang, 2004). The strangulating state owned enterprises were put through structural reforms, which did away with 2/3 of them and dismissed 45 million employees. Finally, the many regulating agencies necessary for a market economy were expanded in the course of the 1990s: whether it be patents, copyrights, labelling, environment, standards, quality-licensing, consumer-rights, etc. At the same time, there were drastic cuts in other parts of the state, the central administration being almost halved. Privatizing and outsourcing slimmed down the state. All part of the transformation of an old Leninist state apparatus full of the industrial ministries of a planned economy, into one suited for market regulation, but still able to handle the challenges of globalization.

Survival on the turbulent sea which globalization creates for a country, demands a trimmed and independent central leadership at the helm of macroeconomic management. China has several thousand years experience of central leadership, but in 1998 reinvented itself in the form of a modern regulatory state, which at arm's length can make a frame for the economy. Top institutions were the Ministry of Finance, the central bank, and two strong horizontally coordinating central commissions, the State Economy and Trade Commission and the State Development and Planning Commission. Later a new horizontal authority was added, the National Development and Reform Commission, and it has become the most important forum. The state is thus an integrated part of China's process of globalization, weakened in some areas and strengthened in others. It borrowed the global pressure to further its own transformation and modernization, and this made it easier for policy-makers to reshape the state-system to harbour, frame and direct the market.

Finance and Foreign Exchange – Difficult Waters, and Full of Pirates

China's participation in the global financial system has been compared to a boat setting out. There are two important questions: what is the weather forecast, and how well-built is the boat? The weather will likely be bad, because the strong speculative capital-flows of today are very destabilizing. The boat is not nearly as big and strong as those of the world's leading financial corporations. China's banks come from a past of politically directed lending, and are learning risk-management and profit-orientation. The building of a modern bank-sector is proceeding, but the shedding of old non-performing loans is not quite over. With the end of 2006 WTO-regulations opened China's market for international giants like Citigroup, Deutsche Bank, Mizuho Group, which have the expressed goal of penetrating the financial markets of developing countries. It remains to be seen whether reform of the financial system is sufficient for China not to be "taken over" or submerged in these powerful maelstroms. The present crisis has given it more time.

During this crisis, many international voices have proposed that the Chinese yuan replace the dollar as reserve currency. This is wishful thinking, it will be a long time before the yuan is ready for that. China has exercised great caution in changing its currency regime, based on the weakness of its financial system, the effects on employment, and the threat of destabilization if short-term speculative capital is admitted. But after 10 years of being firmly pegged to the dollar, with full convertibility on the current account of the balance of payments, it commenced a gradual revaluation against the dollar, using a basket of currencies. Over three years it appreciated more than 20 percent. A gradual strategy is inevitable, because China lacks many of the preconditions for letting the currency float freely, such as risk management-capabilities, development of the interest-rate market, and instruments and markets for hedging. The country got its first exchanges in 1990-1991, and equity-markets are underdeveloped and turbulent. With Shanghai and Hong Kong as financial centres, this is bound to change – and capital controls have been relaxed – but this is an area of state globalization strategy that is still evolving and in a complicated learning process.

Strong Attention to Human Resources

Public opinion as a whole is very favourable towards globalization, as described later. One reason is the global attitude reinforced by education, Internet, study abroad and travel. Another explanation might be the Diaspora of about 35 million. overseas Chinese. They maintain family ties, and the party and government have created organizations, stretching to the grassroots, to engage this Diaspora and obtain its financial and commercial support. Its very existence, and interaction with the home country, may have given greater familiarity with the world, a more cosmopolitan attitude, and an expectation that the surrounding world can positively contribute. Japan does not have a comparable Diaspora, and the contrast is evident: before the Internet and globalization, Japan's ethnocentric culture seemed to work, since then it has had a hard time keeping up.

For labour as a whole, the reforms have meant loss of privilege on a large scale. Allowing this can also be seen as a globalization strategy. The right to strike was struck from the Constitution in 1982, and with the Labour law in 1994, which for the first time permitted firing workers, their weight in political affairs weakened. Further, the socialist institutions, where the work unit was a small welfare state, and the commune gave a social and health security net, have been discarded. For a long time they were not replaced by a new institutional infrastructure, including a welfare system, independent courts for conflict resolution, collective bargaining, etc. Only in the last five years have there been new efforts in these areas.

Regionalism as a Strategy for Globalization: Due Diligence

Regional cooperation can be used to protect against some negative aspects of globalization. It can be the context within which effective regulation and institution-building is possible. And it can strengthen its members bargaining position in global multilateral negotiations, on for instance the rules of the international system. It can be seen as part and parcel of globalization, but is also in some scenarios an alternative, if globalization collapses due to protectionism in the industrialized countries.

For this and other reasons, Chinese decision-makers from the start of the 1990s became more interested in multilateral cooperation in Asia. The Asian financial crisis in 1997 gave further impetus. East Asia was "unorganized" compared to Europe and North America, and China used free trade agreements as the easiest means of increased cooperation. Beginning with Hong Kong, a cascade strategy would gradually encompass the entire region. This built on and extended the strategy of trade liberalization. Its culmination so far is "The Pan-Asia Trade Pact" which starts up in 2010. On top of being the world's biggest free trade area, it also includes military exchange, early warning on epidemics, and not least a large infrastructure program among members. It has primarily been negotiated between China and the ASEAN-countries. Agriculture and its bureaucracies do not count for much in Chinese domestic politics, but in a democracy the over 60 percent peasant population would quickly have stopped the important tariff reductions on imported agricultural products. In Japan, the exaggerated political influence of agriculture still prevents the country making similar free trade initiatives in Asia.

Getting One's Own Multinational Enterprises Out in the World

When Shougang (Capital Steel), one of China's largest state-owned firms, in 1993 used $120 million to buy the Marcona iron-mine in Peru, a trend started which has now matured. With foresight, Shougang even then also wanted to buy oil-wells and food-industries. Today, 16 years later, China is very active in this "Go Out" policy, pursuing markets, resources like oil, minerals and foodstuffs, but also technological and management innovation. By buying divisions of multinational companies, like Siemens, Leyland, Philips, IBM, Alcatel, or whole companies like Volvo, and so on, China seeks to internationalize its enterprises, learn branding, and rise in global industrial production-chains. Main actors so far have been large state-owned and strong private enterprises, but more recently a sovereign wealth fund, China Investment Corp has begun spending hundreds of billions becoming the world's fifth largest. In 2008 fusions and acquisitions amounted to $120 billion, compared to India's $21 billion and Russia's $14 billion.

Japan has since the 1970s had success coaching a national team of strong firms. After 30 years the country at the end of the 1980s had 20 of the worlds 100 largest multinational firms in Forbes' "Fortune 500". China has attempted to foster a team of 30-50 of the best state-owned enterprises, but after 15 years there is still a long way to go (Nolan, 2001). The reason for this lack of success can be found in the high-income countries, particularly the US. The appearance of gigantic oligopolies, through the many fusions of the 1990s, have given a few firms in each sector enormous market-shares, enabling them to dominate global networks. It is far more difficult for firms in developing countries to compete their way forward, than it was a decade ago.

What China Cannot Do – At Present

There is a lot China *cannot* do. With the WTO-agreement China relinquished almost all the instruments that over the last 200 years have been the core of industrial policy for a range of countries that fostered large corporations. This includes for instance protecting infant industry with tariffs, quotas and export-subsidies. Exposing producers directly to the forces of the world market is of course also a globalization strategy. It is the opposite of neo-mercantilism, namely market-expanding policies and administrative deregulation, that China heaves to at the moment.

This does not mean that industrial policy and development state strategies are excluded forever. The new National Development and Reform Commission (NDRC) begins to resemble the key institution for macro-economic leadership and reform-initiative, which China has been lacking. A pilot institution for the huge vessel, so to speak. State capacity is again being built up, central revenues are rising, after a decade of complicated economic transition from plan to market. This might open up for selective industrial policy, within WTO boundaries, for instance to ensure Research and Development capacity or to prevent untrammelled access for MNC's to penetrate China's economy. But there is a dilemma here, insofar as a bargain seems to have been struck with these transnational giants. A bargain under which China gets state-of-the-art technology, while the MNC's get market shares.

Navigare Necesse Est – But Check the Forecast, Look at the Charts and Listen to People with Experience

There are problems and dangers galore in sailing the stormy and tricky seas of globalization. Nonetheless, "sailing is necessary". Yu Keping draws up three primary negative effects to counteract: first, economic security is threatened if foreign capital gets control of key sectors, if foreign debt becomes too large, or the finance-sector weakened; secondly, the country's sovereignty may weaken, and with it the very ability to continue to independently shape and implement globalization strategies; thirdly, political values and culture may be endangered, and so traditional cultural values must be supported, while a vigilant eye is kept towards the export of especially Americanizing elements during globalization. China must "reject uncritically adopting western political systems and core political values" (Yu, 2004).

But domestic waters also present problems. Among the many problems facing helmsmen and their navigators four will be discussed here:

- The Chinese domestic market is still too small, making China dependent on for instance the state of the US economy. The market grows too slowly because the savings rate is high, due to the lack of a social security safety-net.
- The skewed development produced by "GDPism" and globalization has given China problems of polarization: income inequality starts to rise from 1984 and has only recently levelled off. The problem is being handled with a policy of redistribution similar to Roosevelt's "New Deal" policies of the 1930s. The latest, 17th Party Congress confirmed such a policy.
- China lacks important capacities in book-keeping and accountancy, as well as a further development of the legal system, so that it fully supports globalization. A recent policy change moves the handling of wages of local courts to the central level in Beijing. This removes a strong hold that local authorities had over local courts, thus increasing their independence.
- China still has to move away from the low end of the international division of labour. Resources and the environment suffer at this level, and there

are other countries with large reserves of labour-power. Going up the production chains, to more value-added, poses great demands on Research and Development, Science and Technology, and in the end reform of a still somewhat sluggish system of education. But volume in itself has already brought China to the forefront of several science-fields, and more will follow.

New Policies: Structural Reforms and New Deal (Harmonious Society, Sustainability)

Under the umbrella-term "the harmonious society" China has since 2003 been engaged in repairing some of the damages done under 25 years of "economic growth first" under Deng Xiaoping. Compensating losers after a hectic growth-spurt, the policy can be summarized like this:

1. More quality and balance in growth.
2. More equality between urban and rural China and between regions.
3. Sustainability in ecology and resource-use: i.e. recycling and energy-saving.
4. Full attention to innovation and technology, plus independent renewal.
5. A harmonic society: Transparency in administration and social justice.

Let us look at three issue-areas as examples: Land and agricultural policy, social security and pollution control.

Rural policy and the land question has been a focus of China's current leadership under President Hu Jintao and Prime Minister Wen Jiabao. A first move was reducing the tax burden by removing the agricultural tax from January 1, 2005. Health clinics for all 640,000 villages is a policy in the process of implementation, via an 87 percent increase in the health budget. Phase one ends in 2010 by which time a third of villages should have clinics. The nine years of compulsory education have been made free for so far 60 percent of the rural population, to include everyone over the next couple of years. From 2002 work commenced to build cooperative health insurance, with a contribution from the state. This is moving slowly, and is expensive, but it may be the first time in China's history that net resources are flowing from urban to rural areas over the government budget. Land policy has been a troubled issue. Local authorities' hidden land-transactions have cheated peasants out of the money due to them, whenever cities wanted to expand or local government wanted to attract enterprises. Legislation in 2008 ensured that collective sale of land can be direct and circumvent local authorities, thus ensuring that peasants are compensated sufficiently (and actually receive the money themselves). This removes the most frequent reason for often violent protests in the countryside, and creates income which will increase their purchasing power, thus raising domestic demand. A new agency has been created to monitor land transactions and it very sensibly has nine regional offices i.e. it is placed directly under the centre in Beijing and above the 30+ provinces, in the hope that it will be able to keep clear of local pressures and considerations. The new set of rules also gives better conditions for migrant workers, a more transparent rural investment and financing system, and a unified labour market for city and countryside with hopefully less discrimination.

Creating a new social security system is an immense task, which is slowly being undertaken. In all cities there is now a "dibao"-program, a minimum social welfare. It increases the monthly income of the person in question to 20 percent of the average income of the city. If you are over the dibao-limit, there may be other funds to draw on, like pensions, retraining-money, insurance, old age pension and other types of pension. Over the coming four years China lays the foundations of a modern social welfare system, with "dibao", welfare, health service and pensions for both rural and urban citizens. The declared target is to reach a full fledged welfare society in 2049. It will be very expensive, but at the moment the portion of GDP redistributed by the Chinese state is small in international comparison, the revenue is rising fast, and it is a very incremental reform. There is also much to learn from existing welfare states for instance in Northern Europe.

Pollution control has been increased. Environmental legislation is not the problem, but local implementation is. Central expenses on control and monitoring increased by 61 percent in 2007, but what was even more important was the introduction of the policy of making the performance of officials in relation to environment and energy questions part of the basis on which they were promoted. Only then are environmental considerations able to compete with the attention given to employment and growth. Monitoring is increasingly automated and centrally controlled, reducing the possibility of bribing one's way out of transgressing environmental laws. Small firms with wasteful production processes and little environmental protection are increasingly closed.

A number of these policies are part of what some term a third wave of restructuring. After the first one in the 1980s, when foreigners came in, the next one in the 1990s saw the transition from state to private industry. Now it is a consolidation into larger enterprises that is going on. Producers in the low end are forced to obey environmental and worker safety legislation. The result is more bankruptcies, the more so under the economic crisis which started mid-2008. Dismissed workers are expected to join the ranks of an expanded service sector, but with 40 percent of assembly-industry exports coming from Guangdong province, they cannot easily be absorbed and so up to 20 million migrant workers had to retrain or go to their home villages.

It is a paradox that China on the one hand has accounted for 75 percent of all poverty-reduction in developing countries over the last 20 years. On the other hand it has reached a situation where inequality resembles that of the United States. 10 percent of the population owns 45 percent of the nation's wealth (the top 1 percent own 35 percent), while the poorest 10 percent only have 1.4 percent of wealth. This gives some wrenching distortions of the economy (Bowring, 2008):

1. Private consumption as low as 40 percent of GDP.
2. Overconsumption for extravagant public building.
3. Excessive investment in luxury housing, and too little for lower incomes.
4. Corporations tempted to speculative activities to create profits for owners and shareholders.
5. Excessive investment in producing for well-off households.

The government has many countermeasures: social systems, more health and free education in the countryside so the need for saving is lessened; more infrastructure and agricultural price subsidies; support – to the tune of CNY920 billion – for rural households buying electronics and household appliances; more central control of important investment decisions by state-owned enterprises and local authorities; expansion of the service-sector, which in 2015 is expected to be 30 percent of the economy. A lot hangs on the efficiency of these measures: continued societal stability and China's continuing role as an economic locomotive in a situation where large parts of the world are still struggling with the ramifications of economic recession.

The Chinese Globalization Discourse

In order to facilitate the implementation of the globalization strategies discussed above, the Chinese state has thoroughly revised the narrative about China and the world which is presented in the media. During the Mao era the ideal was self-reliance, and the leading global powers, US and the Soviet Union, were generally presented as hostile to China. However, a crucial element in Deng Xiaoping's economic development strategy was to attract foreign technology and investments, and this called for a discourse that presented Chinese interaction with global capitalism in a much more positive light.

The starting point was the slogan of "reform and openness" (*gaige kaifang*), which explicitly identified an open attitude to the world as a crucial element in the reform process. Deng told the sceptics that an opening to the West in no way meant capitulation. In one of his famous metaphors he compared China in the late 1970s to a house with a stuffy atmosphere. It was necessary to open the windows and let in some fresh air, and there was no reason to worry about the few flies (i.e. capitalist ideas) that might slip in at the same time.[1]

The image reflects a recurrent theme in the Chinese debate: is globalization simply about intensified economic and technological interaction, or will political and cultural "flies" follow in the wake of the ever deeper integration into global

1 We have not been able to find out on which occasion Deng used this image, but it has consistently been attributed to him, both in China and abroad. The origin of other colourful expressions by Deng, such as "It doesn't matter if the cat is black or white as long as it catches mice" is, in fact, equally obscure.

capitalism? The special economic zones established on the Chinese coast in the early part of the reform period vividly illustrate the initial ambition of making the foreign influence useful to China while at the same time encapsulating and restricting it.

The term globalization (*quanqiuhua*) signals a world with much less solid national borders, so for almost a decade official Chinese media used the word exclusively about events taking place outside China. The *People's Daily* (*PD*) first mentioned the term already in 1986 but over the following 10 years hardly used it and almost only in connection with crises in foreign multinational companies or on the global financial markets. Globalization was constructed as something going on "out there" that was only marginally relevant to China.[2]

From around 1996, however, the *PD* increasingly talked about China as an integrated part of the global economy and its readers learned that this integration was an advantage both to China and to the world. In 1996 it brought an authoritative speech by Li Tieying who was then chairman of the powerful State Commission for Restructuring the Economy and member of the Politburo. Li explained how China had its natural place in the global division of labour as a producer of low technology products and as a promising market for foreign goods. The tone of his speech was optimistic and proactive: China could not develop without the world, and the world could not develop without China (Li, 1996).

When the Asian financial crisis started in 1997 the Chinese media started showing a more guarded attitude towards globalization, and since that time it was often described as "a double-edged sword", which held unlimited possibilities to China and other developing countries, but which could also lead to growing economic polarization and marginalization of countries that were not competitive. Also around this time, the *PD* consistently started to describe globalization as an objective fact, a historical tidal wave, which China must join. The rich nations had invented the game, and their rules were not always fair to China, but isolation was not an option (Gu, 1998). The problematic aspects of globalization were normally described as a condition common to all developing countries. The main danger was that only the rich, industrialized nations would profit and leave the developing countries behind in even deeper poverty. In such analyses, China consistently describes itself as part of the developing world, and little attention is paid to the internal competition *between* developing countries for foreign investments and export markets.

In 2001, as the time for China's entry into the WTO approached, the coverage of globalization peaked in the *PD*. The WTO could have had negative consequences for many Chinese, not least for the farmers, for whom many at the time foresaw there would be difficulties competing on the global market. In this precarious

2 The discussion of the official Chinese discourse is based on our reading of longer articles and a sample of shorter notices in the *People's Daily*. The selection of texts was based on a full text search on the term *globalization* (*quanqiuhua*) in the Chinese electronic version of the *People's Daily*: *Renmin Ribao dianziban 1946-2008*.

situation the official media promoted with great vigour a master narrative about globalization as an inevitable historical trend, which China must face in an open and proactive way. It was a dangerous process, but the strongest and most competent nation states, such as China, would be able to control it and tame the transnational actors. Far from reducing the role of nation states the intense global competition called for a strong state that could steer China safely through the troubled waters of global capitalism.

In ideological terms the CCP tried to make its globalization strategy compatible with its Marxist heritage by arguing that the main task of the Party in the present period is to develop the productive forces, and the best way to do this is by attracting foreign investments and technology. Therefore, it is not correct to see globalization as the final victory of capitalism. To the contrary, the intensified development of the productive forces is bound to sharpen the internal contradictions in the capitalist system and will in this way strengthen the socialist project in the long run (Knight, 2008).

While China's ever closer integration into global capitalism is presented almost as a law of nature, globalization processes in other fields than the economy are viewed with much more scepticism. When the *PD* mentions political globalization it is often in order to show how the concept is used as a cover for the promotion of Western interests, like when the USA used globalization as an argument for the intervention in Yugoslavia, or when Western lawyers argue for more supranational legislation (Huang, 1999; Shen, 1999). Such moves are seen as threats to China's main principle of national sovereignty and are therefore rejected. In the cultural field the *PD* prefers to use the term "diversification" (*duoyanghua*) rather than globalization. Cultural diversity should be protected and an Americanization of global culture avoided, so opposition in Europe, Asia and Africa against American cultural hegemony receives positive coverage in the official media.

While China's top leaders have expressed practically unanimous support for economic globalization, the country's social scientists and intellectuals have presented a much broader range of viewpoints. This is hardly surprising as anyone from neoliberals to traditional Marxists to new Confucians have joined the debate. Most of the burning issues discussed in the West have also been scrutinized in Chinese academic journals and on the Internet: is globalization fundamentally capitalist in nature? Will it increase social polarization? Will it mean global American dominance? Will the developing countries be left behind?

The academic debate is too rich to cover in detail here,[3] but there seems to be two main camps. The neoliberals are warm supporters of globalization and of China's membership of the WTO, which they see as the key to economic prosperity and, in the long run, political reforms. In the other camp we find what is often called the "new left" which is more focused on the social inequality and cultural and moral degeneration that they see as effects of foreign influence. This

3 Detailed introductions to the debate can be found in Yu, 2008; Knight, 2008; Bhattacharya, 2008; Garrett, 2001.

heterogeneous camp contains Marxists who see globalization as an updated version of imperialism, scholars inspired by Confucianism who support social harmony and classical Chinese values, as well as several other groups. Most debaters on this wing support a strong state and a very slow transition to democracy.

An interesting recent trend has been a more assertive Chinese approach to cultural globalization. Rather than imagining China as a cultural fortress, the Chinese are now more active in promoting values such as social harmony, loyalty and strong family ties as positive Chinese contributions to world culture. This idea has been taken up by some Western academics such as the political philosopher Daniel A. Bell (2008). The state has promoted this "going out" of Chinese culture through the establishment of Confucius Institutes with the task of promoting Chinese language and culture. At the time of writing (May 2009) there were already 328 such institutes extending Chinese soft power to 82 countries.[4]

State and Society in China's Globalization

The official discourse of China's role in globalization is matched by a set of policies aimed at embedding the party-state more solidly in society. China's market economic reforms together with the challenges that globalization generally poses to nation states could be expected to weaken the CCP's grip on political power. This has not happened, however, and one major reason is that the Party has been able to redefine its own role and link up with different social strata and groups through a broad range of mechanisms.

Private Entrepreneurs

Many observers have expected the new stratum of private entrepreneurs to present the largest potential challenge to CCP rule. By 2005 the private sector produced 71.2 percent of China's industrial output (Huang, 2008: 26) and it has long created most of the jobs, so the new economic elite can become a powerful opponent if it is not handled carefully. One move of the CCP in this field has been to accept managers and technicians as Party members. This has been possible since the 16th Party Congress in 2002 under ideological protection from Jiang Zemin's slogan about the "three represents", and the new recruitment policy seems to have targeted particularly managers of larger enterprises in the more prosperous parts of China (Dickson, 2007: 838). Successful entrepreneurs are now constructed as representing the "most advanced productive forces" and have also been given seats in People's Congresses and Political Consultative Conferences (*zhengxie*). At the grassroots level they have been encouraged to run for posts as village leaders. Many business associations also function as instruments of state corporatist control with the business community, although they in some localities

4 The Confucius Institutes have a central homepage: www.chinese.cn.

are more bottom-up in nature and actually articulate and defend the interests of their members (Zhang, 2007).

There are clear signs that these different measures have been successful. David Wank has shown how networks of officials and businessmen have replaced the traditional procedures of the planned economy. He found that the two groups had created a system of "commercial clientilism" that had reached a "stable equilibrium" reflecting "a convergence of interests" (Wank, 1999: 228).

Such networks are supported by personal relations. A large part of the entrepreneurs are former officials who have "plunged into the sea" of the private economy (*xiahai*), and they are therefore on the same wavelength as state and party representatives.

This is reflected in the surprising similarity in political attitudes between officials and businessmen. Bruce Dickson, who has investigated this issue for many years, finds a clear trend: China's capitalists are interested in preserving the political system in its present shape rather than in promoting democratic change, and they are, as a group, strong supporters of the CCP. On several issues they are actually more conservative than state and Party officials. They are more inclined to think that a multiparty system can lead to political chaos, and that society can be chaotic if everybody does not share the same thinking (Dickson, 2007: 851). Generally speaking the policies tying the economic elite closely to the state have thus been successful, although they have at the same time led to widespread favouritism, lack of transparency, and extensive corruption.

Intellectuals

Another potential challenge to the CCP could come from the intellectuals, who up through the 1980s were often quite pro-Western and critical of the Chinese political system. Their protests peaked during the spring 1989 demonstrations, when the student protesters came to represent everything that was young, progressive, and cosmopolitan, while the CCP leaders in charge of the suppression were cast as the old and conservative who were completely out of step with global trends. However, from around 1992 Party leaders slid out of their role as reactionary isolationists and promoted an image of the CCP as the main guarantee for China's continued integration on the global scene. People with higher education have benefited considerably from China's opening to the outside. They can travel all over the world to take part in conferences or on business trips, and they have access to practically all the information that is internationally available. Although the media, including the Internet, are censured, this has limited effect on the access to information of intellectuals who read foreign languages, and the academic debate is more open to critical viewpoints than the mass media in general.

Many Chinese intellectuals are involved in global networks, and as long as they stay clear of particularly sensitive political issues their living and working conditions are not fundamentally different from those of their overseas colleagues. At the same time, the CCP works hard to recruit intellectuals into the Party, and they have been quite successful, as reflected in the rising educational profile of Party members.

When combined with the fact that the intellectuals' income level has been raised considerably it is not surprising that most members of the intellectual elite are either politically passive or recommend slow and incremental political reforms. There are certainly individual intellectuals who stand up to the authorities, such as the rights protection lawyers who defend the interests of underprivileged groups (Fu and Cullen, 2008), but *as a group* the intellectual elite does not manifest itself as an oppositional force. Through its proactive response to globalization, the CCP has been able to conquer a position as the representative of international exchange and openness, and its globalization strategy has therefore contributed significantly to curbing the development of intellectual dissidence in the East European way.

Workers and Farmers

To China's industrial workers the changes on the labour market have meant a massive loss of privileges. Workers in state-owned enterprises used to enjoy lifelong employment guarantees, housing, pension and health care benefits, but much of this social security net has disappeared since the beginning of the reforms. Already in 1986 lifelong employment was replaced by individual contracts, and from 1995 massive lay-offs in state enterprises led to significant urban unemployment. Global competition is often used as an argument for low wages and hazardous work conditions, particularly for the estimated 170 million migrant workers who have turned China into "the factory of the world". Some scholars see a looming danger of a "race to the bottom" in which China will compete with other developing countries in offering the cheapest labour and lowest costs to foreign companies (Chan, 2003), while others are more optimistic (Liu et al., 2003).

A growing number of Chinese workers meet globalization abroad. According to official statistics there were one million Chinese workers who worked outside China in 2006. Compared to China's total population this is an insignificant number, and it represents only around one percent of all international migrant workers, but we should add to this figure the illegal emigrants who do not enter any statistic. China's entry to the WTO opened up for a new expansion in this field, and many Chinese local governments at county and provincial levels now try to solve their unemployment problem partly trough labour exports. As Chinese companies get increasingly engaged in mining and construction projects around the world the group of international migrant workers will definitely grow.

Although work conditions for both national and international workers are tough, it should not be forgotten that the new and much more open labour market has given many people a chance to earn a living and raise their own and their families' living standard. Maybe this is why Chinese workers rarely seem to blame globalization, or even the Chinese state, for their problems. Interviews indicate that most workers accept the rules of the global market economy almost like a law of nature, and that they tend to explain their problems on the labour market with their own lack of qualifications (Blecher, 2002). In this sense it can be argued that although the party-state has done very little to accommodate the workers, in contrast to what they have done in relation to the economic and intellectual elites, the ideology of global capitalism has been so pervasive that it has prevented major opposition from these former "masters of the country". There are, of course, numerous strikes and labour protests, but they are normally isolated cases rooted in local problems, and the state never allows them any opportunity to develop beyond that point.

China's farmers have not yet been exposed to the full pressure from global competition as they still enjoy some degree of state protection. When China joined the WTO many observers worried about the future fate of the country's many inefficient small-scale farmers, but over the last years the state has introduced a number of policies in order to boost rural incomes. The agricultural tax has been abolished, as mentioned above, and state price subsidies have also contributed to protect the farmers. The most sinister predictions have not materialized so far, but the fundamental structural problems involved in family farming on very small plots of land still exist.

In relative terms, there is no doubt that rural people have been the great losers in the reform process. Rural–urban inequalities have risen dramatically, and the social status of farmers is low. However, from the perspective of individual villagers things often look different. Based on conversations with village people over the years, we have the impression that many farmers, much like the workers, have seen at least some local families in their village succeed and "get rich first" and therefore tend to look for personal rather than structural explanations for their own poverty. There is widespread dissatisfaction and numerous protests in many areas, but like the industrial strikes they are mainly directed against local officials and address local issues rather than higher level policies.

The plans for improving social services that were discussed earlier in this paper can be seen as attempts at alleviating the problems that China's integration into global capitalism has brought to vulnerable groups among workers and farmers, and although it is still too early to gauge the effect of the reforms, they evidently represent a sign of increased attention being paid to non-elite groups.

Political Consultations

China's opening to the outside world has not only led to an increased exchange of capital, goods, and labour. Global political ideas and cultural trends have also found their way to the country, not least through new electronic channels of communication such as the Internet. It turned out to be impossible to keep the flies out, to use Deng Xiaoping's metaphor. The writings of practically all major modern and classical political thinkers have been translated into Chinese, and many people closely follow the political development, and particularly the elections, in Taiwan, Japan and the USA. There is a lively debate on the necessity of democracy going on in China (Yu, 2009), and in order to maintain legitimacy the CCP is constructing a model of political participation that is intended to give ordinary citizens some possibility for expressing their opinions about their own social and political environment – without moving any closer to a multiparty democracy.

The most celebrated reform introduced direct elections of village committee members and village leaders. Most observers agree that these elections have come a long way in terms of introducing democratic procedures, while it is more doubtful whether they have led to any major changes in the exercise of power (O'Brien and Han, 2009). Similar grassroots elections have been introduced in urban areas, but with less success, primarily because the residents' committees have less influence on local life than the village committees, which means that public interest in them has been limited. There have been some experiments with direct elections for the township level, but they have so far been blocked by the central authorities (Thøgersen et al., 2008). As an alternative to general elections there is now a trend to expand democracy inside the Party by giving local CCP members more influence on the selection of local Party secretaries and Party congress delegates. Such procedures are easier to control than general elections, and Party members are considered to be more politically mature and therefore more ready for democracy.

However, the political participation of ordinary citizens is also crucial for political legitimacy, and there are several experiments with different types of consultations in connection with political decisions. Public opinion surveys have become a popular tool for local leaders because such surveys inform the officials about what people want without forcing them to act according to the will of the majority. A somewhat similar idea seems to lie behind some local governments' practice of asking ordinary citizens to evaluate the performance of local officials. This is a way of getting rid of unpopular and incompetent cadres who would otherwise negatively influence the public image of the CCP.

Some of the most radical experiments with popular consultations have been carried out in Wenling in Zhejiang Province. Under the slogan of "deliberative democracy" panels with randomly selected representatives of the inhabitants of a town or a village have been asked to decide the priority of infrastructural projects and how the local annual budget should be spent. The pros and cons of the different projects are presented by experts, and the panelists can ask questions to these experts and discuss among themselves before a final vote decides the priority. The final decision over the budget is still in the hand of the local people's congresses, as stipulated in the law, but it would be difficult for congress delegates to disregard the decision of the panels, which are publicized by the local media.[5] The common feature in all these mechanisms is that they give people a voice and provide the leadership with information about public opinion without the CCP relinquishing the power to make the final decision. There are other experiments with expansion of democratic procedures in a "home grown" manner, as for instance in Shenzhen

5 For a full discussion of deliberative democracy in China, see Leib and He 2006.

recently with a system dividing political power in three columns, in a "checks and balances" like formation.

It should be kept in mind that these mechanisms still have the status of experiments. Most decisions are still made without consultations with local citizens, and it is difficult to predict the future of the different consultation methods at the national level. However, we may begin to see the outline of a model, which is not a parliamentary democracy, but which, in a best case scenario, will be able to take public opinion into consideration to a larger extent than is presently the case.

Conclusion

An early start on globalization meant a chance to think before the tsunami reached the shore, start up research projects, draw up plans, and have think-tanks analyse global developments and lay out options for the leadership. There have been reams of policy-papers and reports, and this may be part of the reason why the political leadership has avoided seeing globalization as a threat and falling back on short-term "solutions". Forewarned is fore-armed. Much has also been done to make public opinion positive to globalization. This effort has been aided by the absence of opposition parties wanting to cash in on globalization problems.

This lack of democracy is a point on which China differs. It is almost an article of faith in the OECD-countries that without democracy economic growth and innovation cannot last. Yet it has done so in China over 30 years or more. One explanation may be that the picture is not static, as we have seen. Finally, the democratization of information has assembled and articulated societal dissatisfaction, so that they pressure the leadership in the direction of institutionalized access to and possibilities for making it accountable. This is democratization with an unknown final destination, i.e. we should not expect China to move towards a Western model.

How does China's case fit with the theses laid out in the start of this chapter? There is no doubt that China fits the developmental state and competition state matrix quite well. Maintaining an important role for the state, and a significant state sector, with long-term goal-setting guided by a strong pilot-institution like the NDRC (see above). The trend is heightened under the restarted Keynesianism, which has worked to limit the damage wrought on the Chinese economy of the present global economic crisis. It appears that China's fast recovery in turn helped other economies pull through.

The ideas about soft balancing and "geo-economics" may need to be replaced by the concept of the appearance of a new, multinodal international system (Womack, 2009). Instead of the hierarchical system experienced so far, where all interaction passes through metropolis powers (think colonial times), technology and globalization have created a system with many nodes and many lines of communication. It can be compared with the build of the Internet. Regional powers like China, India, Brazil, Russia or South Africa get increased importance.

Because the system is no longer hierarchical – though still marked by asymmetry – dominance or hegemony are no longer viable strategies. They are replaced by soft power and persuasion. In line with this, China seems to have made a strategic choice to guard against global insecurities by seeking cooperation rather than dominance. Their success so far, particularly in the region, but also in its new global diplomacy, has in part been reached through accepting a number of binds, "pre-commitments", which limit the country's future options. At the same time, China upholds the international system as such, supporting multilateralism and international law, because China benefits greatly from the present arrangements.

This also means that the idea of Westphalian-type maintaining of sovereignty must be modified. While China has the attention to sovereignty characteristic of most of the world's states (based on their experience with colonial powers), it is beginning to be flexible. Sovereignty can to a degree be negotiated, as we see for example in connection with multilateral solutions and regional integration in Asia. The expectations China will be met with as a great power, and one aspiring to be a responsible power, taking part in the solution of global problems, will lead further along this path.

Precisely because China's economy is so exceptionally open, it affects the rest of the world in myriad ways. First of all, it produces development and reduces poverty – and thus instability – by functioning as an alternative growth locomotive to the United States. Growth in 2009 was estimated at above 8 percent, after reaching 7.9 percent in the first half of the year, and this helped pull the world out of recession. With its large foreign exchange reserves the country is a large scale creditor, investor, buyer, and development assistance donor. The amount of participation, and the many international ties, also will increase the likelihood that China's return will be peaceful. Growth and welfare are core national goals, and continued global market access thus essential. The plurality of international ties, and the size of the economy, makes it impossible to build on military might to ensure markets and raw materials. Even the United States, with 780 global military bases at an annual price of $100 billion, and a defence-budget 10 times China's, is finding it difficult (Johnson, 2009).

And so, what some have called "the BRIC scenario" (Brazil, Russia, India and China as major global players) is decidedly a possibility. Entailing a further development of the multi-nodal system this would be a world of reduced tension, where BRIC-countries and other regional leaders get increased interaction and importance, and where the United States and perhaps a better organized EU also are nodes. With or without an American–Chinese G2, there will be an increased role for the BRIC-countries with their ability under a multimodal system to connect directly, and with their common interests derived from being regional powers. As a group or as a phenomenon they will be an agent of change. Because, as Brantly Womack emphasizes, it isn't China but rather the whole of the multinodal system which challenges the unipole, the United States. China is just a leading representative of these changes, and the BRIC-countries themselves a kind of vanguard.

Bibliography

Bell, Daniel A. (2008) *China's New Confucianism: Politics and Everyday Life in a Changing Society.* Princeton, N.J.: Princeton University Press.

Bhattacharya, Abanti (2008) "Interpreting the Chinese Discourse on State in the Era of Globalization", *Strategic Analysis*, 32(4): 583-603.

Blecher, Marc J. (2002) "Hegemony and Workers' Politics in China", *China Quarterly*, 170: 283-303.

Bowring, Philip (2008) "China Can't Help", *International Herald Tribune*, 25 November 2008.

Carlson, Allen (2005) *Unifying China, Integrating with the World. Securing Chinese Sovereignty in the Reform Era.* Stanford: Stanford University Press.

Cerny, Philip (1997) "Paradoxes of the Competition State: The Dynamics of Political Globalization", *Government and Opposition*, 32(1): 251-274.

Chan, Anita (2003) "A 'Race to the Bottom'. Globalization and China's Labour Standards", *China Perspectives*, 46: 41-49.

Dickson, Bruce J. (2007) "Integrating Wealth and Power in China: The Communist Party's Embrace of the Private Sector", *China Quarterly*, 192: 827-854.

Evans, Peter (1995) *Embedded Autonomy: States and Social Transformation.* Princeton, N.J.: Princeton University Press.

Fu, Hualing and Richard Cullen (2008) "*Weiquan* (Rights Protection) Lawyering in an Authoritarian State: Building a Culture of Public-interest Lawyering", *China Journal*, 59: 111-127.

Garrett, Banning (2001) "China Faces, Debates the Contradictions of Globalization", *Asian Survey*, 41(3): 409-427.

Gu, Yuanyang (1998) "Jingji quanqiuhua yu 'youxi guize'" (Economic Globalization and the "Rules of the Game"), *People's Daily*, June 10.

Huang Nansen (1999) "'Rendaozhuyi ganshe' de shizhi" (The True Character of "Humanitarian Intervention"), *People's Daily*, June 3.

Johnson, Chalmers (2009) "How to Deal with America's Empire of Bases", available at www.countercurrents.org/johnson020709.htm.

Johnston, Alastair (2009) *Social States. China in International Institutions 1980-2000.* Princeton, N.J.: Princeton University Press.

Knight, Nick (2008) *Imagining Globalization in China. Debates on Ideology, Politics and Culture.* Cheltenham: Edward Elgar.

Lampton, David (ed.) (2001) *The Making of Chinese Foreign and Security Policy in the Era of Reform 1978-2000.* Stanford: Stanford University Press.

Leib, Ethan and Baogang He (2006) *The Search for Deliberative Democracy in China.* New York: Palgrave.

Li, Tieying (1996) "Zouxiang 21 shiji de Zhongguo yu shijie jingji de fazhan" (China on its Way to the 21st Century and Global Economic Development), *People's Daily*, November 15.

Liu, Minquan, Luodan Xu and Liu Liu (2003), "Labor Standards and FDI in China. Some Survey Findings", in Rana Hasan and Devashish Mitra, eds, *The Impact of Trade on Labor. Issues, Perspectives, and Experiences from Developing Areas*. Amsterdam: Elsevier.

Naughton, Barry (2007) *The Chinese Economy*. Cambridge: MIT Press.

Nolan, Peter (2001) *China and the Global Economy.* London: Palgrave Macmillan.

O'Brien, Kevin J. and Rongbin Han (2009) "Path to Democracy? Assessing village elections in China", *Journal of Contemporary China*, 18(60): 359-378.

Østergaard, Clemens S. (1995) "Economic Transformation in China: The role of State vs Market" in Laurids L. Lauridsen (ed.), *Institutions and Industrial Development: Asian Experiences*. Roskilde: International Development Studies, pp. 183-202.

Østergaard, Clemens S. (2008) *Kinas Eksperimenter. Reformer og Stormagtstatus? [China's Experiments. Reforms and Great-Power Status?]* København: Columbus (2nd ed.).

Prakash, Aseem and Jeffrey A. Hart (eds) (2000a) *Coping with Globalization*. London: Routledge.

Prakash, Aseem and Jeffrey A. Hart (eds) (2000b) *Responding to Globalization*. London: Routledge.

Shambaugh, David (2008) *China's Communist Party. Atrophy and Adaptation.* Berkeley: University of California Press.

Shen, Zongling (1999) "Ping 'falü quanqiuhua' lilun" (On the theory of legal globalization), *People's Daily*. December 11.

Shirk, Susan L. (1993) *The Political Logic of Economic Reform in China.* Berkeley: University of California Press.

Sorensen, George (2001) *Changes in Statehood. The Transformation of International Relations.* London: Palgrave Macmillan.

Thøgersen, Stig, Jørgen Elklit and Lisheng Dong (2008) "Consultative Elections of Chinese Township Leaders: The Case of an Experiment in Ya'an, Sichuan", *China Information*, 22(1): 67-89.

Wade, Robert (1990) *Governing the Market: Economic Theory and the Role of Government in East Asian Industrialization*. Princeton N.J.: Princeton University Press.

Wank, David L. (1999) *Commodifying Communism. Business, Trust, and Politics in a Chinese City*. Cambridge: Cambridge University Press.

Womack, Brantly (2009) "China between Region and World", *The China Journal*, 61: 1-22.

Yang, Dali L. (2004) *Remaking the Chinese Leviathan. Market Transition and the Politics of Governance.* Stanford: Stanford University Press.

Yu, Keping (2004) *From the Discourse of "Sino-west" to Globalisation: Chinese Perspectives on Globalisation.* McMaster University: Working Paper Series GHC 04/1.

Yu, Keping (2008) "The Developmental Logic of Chinese Culture under Modernization and Globalization", *Boundary 2*, 35(2): 157-182.

Yu, Keping (2009) *Democracy is a Good Thing*. Washington: The Brookings Institution.

Zhang, Jianjun (2007) "Business Associations in China: Two Regional Experiences", *Journal of Contemporary Asia*, 37(2): 209-231.

Chapter 8
Why is the Chinese Communist Party Able to Sustain its Hegemony in Eras of Great Transformation?

Li Xing and Peer Møller Christensen

Introduction

The Chinese Communist Party (hereafter the CCP) was founded on July 1, 1921 in Shanghai with only 12 founding members. After 28 years of ideological, political and armed struggles, the CCP finally founded the People's Republic of China in 1949. Today the party is the largest political organization in the world with more than 73 million members.

The CCP started as a Marxist-Leninist party in form, but a nationalist party in substance. The continuous legacy of Mao is due to his role as a nationalist leader in a hegemonic project more than as a Marxist leader in communist movements. Nationalism has always been an important element of the CCP's approach to maintaining political legitimacy and national unity. The CCP identifies and defines the national interest, and then safeguards what it can to defend that national interest in an endless endeavor to recover China's historical great power status.

Historically the CCP survived from numerous crises during the war period. Even after it became the ruling party following the establishment of the People's Republic of China in 1949, the CCP had survived from three major periods of crisis in which the legitimacy of the party faced unprecedented challenges.

The first major crisis was the 10 years of Cultural Revolution (1966-1976) in which political and economic radicalism and social chaos grew to include large sections of Chinese society and eventually brought the entire country to the brink of civil turmoil. Even before this crisis, the country had already experienced several mass movements, such as the Great Leap Forward and the Anti-Rightist Movement in the 1950s.

The second was the market reform since the end of the 1970s, which defined China's development in terms of economic growth and productivity and eroded the CCP's monopoly of political expression. The CCP's willingness to subordinate other values to rapid economic growth weakened traditional social cohesion and created new contending forces between the regime's pro-market policies and the population's acceptance of many socialist norms. Socialism's focus on workers' rights, common prosperity and state ownership clashed with the reform policies that emphasize market rationality, the suppression of labor unions, the dissolution of agricultural collectivism and the dismantlement of state-owned enterprises. Rampant official corruption, periodic bouts of high inflation and widespread unemployment illustrated the disjuncture between socialist ideology and economic reality. It was widely predicted that the political legitimacy of the CCP would eventually contradict the outcome of economic logic. Some even claimed and foresaw *The Coming Collapse of China* (Change, 2001).

The third crisis emerged in the aftermath of the tragedy of Tiananmen Square on June 4, 1989[1] in which the CCP's political legitimacy reached a dangerous low. Mainstream politicians and opinion-makers both in the West and inside China predicted an imminent collapse of the CCP because they believed the regime had forfeited its legitimacy to rule by using violence against its own citizens. It was expected that the CCP would crumble in a manner similar to that of its Eastern European counterparts. The party did not collapse, but the reform program was temporarily halted and China's relations with the West deteriorated. The 1989 tragedy unified the CCP on an extraordinary consensus that the political reform must slow down within a foreseeable future. The further deepening of the economic reform was seen as China moving towards performance-based legitimacy, or eudaemonic legitimacy.

However, contrary to the above predictions, what we are witnessing today is just the opposite: China's remarkable economic achievements are globally acknowledged. Nowadays China is one of the world's fastest-growing economies and has become a major player in international manufacturing and finance. From 1979 to 2007 China's real GDP grew at an average annual rate of more than 9 percent. According to the World Bank, China ranked second in contributing to world economic growth during the past two decades, and China's rate of contribution to global trade growth ranked among the world top three. Next to the United States China received more direct foreign investment than any other nation. Along with the United States China was unleashing a greater impact on global supply and demand than any other country. It is a fact today that China is becoming an engine of regional and global economic growth.

Right now, facing the on-going global financial crisis, both the United States and the EU expected a "responsible role" from China that holds the world's largest foreign currency reserve of $2,000 billion. This current financial crisis has clearly highlighted China's role in the reform of the international financial system and in the restructuring of the international financial architecture.

Most importantly, according to a series of worldwide country-based survey's of public opinion by *The Pew Global Attitudes Project* (2008) in recent years, more than 80 percent of the Chinese people expressed extraordinary levels of

---

1 It refers to a series of demonstrations in Beijing in and near Tiananmen Square mainly led by student activists and intellectuals between the period of April 15 and June 4, 1989. This event caused a short-term pause of China's reform program and deteriorated China–West relations.

The Chinese Look at Their Lives and Country

	Rating their country 2002	2008	Change	Global ranking*
Satisfied with country direction	% 48	% 86	*% pts.* *+38*	*#1*
Economy is good	52	82	*+30*	*#1*
	Rating their lives 2002	2008	*Change*	Global ranking**
Satisfaction with...	%	%		
Family life				
Very	13	14	*+1*	
Somewhat	69	67	*-2*	
Total	82	81	*-1*	*#29*
*Job****				
Very	6	4	*-2*	
Somewhat	57	60	*+3*	
Total	63	64	*+1*	*#34*
Household income				
Very	3	4	*+1*	
Somewhat	48	54	*+6*	
Total	51	58	*+7*	*#32*

*Based on the 24 countries in the 2008 Pew Global poll.
** Based on the 47 countries in the 2007 Pew Global poll.
***Based on respondents who are employed.

Questions 2 through 4. For full question wording and results, see the topline questionnaire in the back of this report.

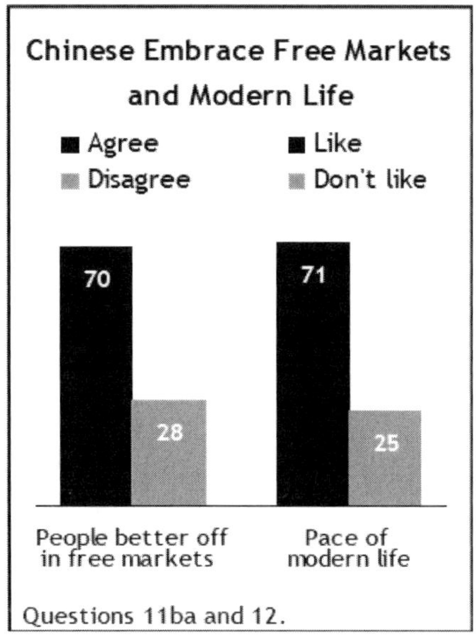

Figure 8.1 Chinese public opinions

Source: The Pew Global Attitudes Project 2008. The Pew Global Attitudes Project is one of the research projects conducted by Pew Research Center in Washington DC. It consists of a series of worldwide public opinion surveys that covers a broad array of subjects ranging from people's assessments of their own lives to their views about the current state of the world and important issues of the day. See http://pewglobal.org/.

satisfaction with China's development and economy in 2008 (see Figure 8.1). A majority of Chinese citizens were content with many aspects of their own lives, including their family life, their incomes and their jobs. A high percentage of Chinese embraced free markets and modern life following the transformation and growth of the economy (see Figure 8.1). But people also expressed their concern over corruption, inequality, inflation, environmental degradation, social welfare and health care in particular.

The above figures indicate that economic gains and rising living standards have indeed softened the social demand for political liberation and have created new legitimacy for the Party and state, even though the credibility of the Chinese government has come to rest on its developmental performance, a tendency which makes it politically vulnerable to economic setbacks.

The phenomena that, historically, the CCP has been able to recover from numerous crises and restore legitimacy are interpreted in various ways. Some take non-political perspectives pointing out the fact that historically and culturally, the long period of imperial rule together with the lack of a civil society and popular revisionist opposition made the party authoritarianism and strong-man leadership possible.

This chapter intends to provide a framework for understanding the historical and social background of the three crises, and the remarkable adaptability of the CCP to changing political and economic environments both at domestic and international levels. It attempts to explain the social background of the above-mentioned three crises, and describe how the CCP as an institution has been able to sustain its legitimacy through these crises. China's market reform in the post-Mao era and the new type of legitimacy and hegemony the CCP has achieved reflect some aspects of Gramsci's hegemony theory in which the post-Mao CCP leadership has been adapting themselves in a process of "passive revolution";[2] and the renewed hegemony is realized through a reconstituted "historic bloc"[3] on the basis of convergence of interests and through neutralizing the pressures of various contending forces that might otherwise trigger profound structural transformations.

The Historical and Social Background of the Three Crises

According to some Chinese scholars, the three above-mentioned crises have been caused by social contradictions within the Chinese society, and these social contradictions have shaped these crises as well as the adaptive reactions by the CCP responding to these crises. Wang Shaoguang (1995) has dissected the social background of the clashes and turmoil of the Cultural Revolution. He Qinglian (1998) has described the economic reforms as a process of "spontaneous privatization" of state-owned property, carried out by "power capital", i.e. individuals from the political power structure using their political power to transform state owned assets into their own individual property. Wang Hui (2003) has argued that the June 4th Incident in Beijing in 1989 was an inevitable measure from the Chinese leadership in suppressing the popular criticism of a comprehensive price reform. The adaptive behavior of the CCP has thus been a series of reactions to changing contradictions and patterns of power in the Chinese social fabric.

---

2 It is a notion used by Gramsci to refer to a style of state class politics which preserves control by a leading group on the one hand while instituting economic, social, political and ideological changes on the other. His original concept refers to the fact that the bourgeoisie class was capable of responding to socio-economic and socio-political crises by making necessary compromises and modifications as well as social reorganizations in order to reestablish and maintain its hegemony.

3 The concept refers to the capacity of a dominant group that is able to go beyond its narrow corporative interests, to exert a moral and intellectual leadership, and to make compromises (within certain limits) with a variety of allies and social forces. Such a broad union of social forces is termed by Gramsci as "historic bloc".

Two-line Struggle

According to Wang Shaoguang, the clashes and turmoil of the Cultural Revolution were caused by basic contradictions between two important social groups in the Chinese society, on one hand the party bureaucracy and party activists, on the other the marginalized layers of society consisting of intellectuals, former capitalists and landlords. In the Chinese political language, it refers to the long-lasting "two-line struggle" between the *Maoist socialist line* and the *capitalist revisionist line*. These social contradictions manifested themselves in the clashes between students stemming from these social groups who actually fought a basically rational fight for their individual and group interests. This was, according to Wang Shaoguang, the social basis of the struggles between different groups of Red Guards, which to outsiders seem very difficult to comprehend. The social contradictions, which actually formed the basis of the class struggle in Chinese post-revolutionary society, were especially sharp inside the educational system, where children from the social groups marginalized by the socialist revolution were discriminated against, while students whose parents were "advanced workers", i.e. members of the Communist Party, were favorized. When Mao appealed to the students to start a "cultural revolution", students with a "good family background", i.e. children of party members, immediately organized Red Guard organizations attacking "the usual suspects", former capitalists, landlords and intellectuals, in accordance with the pattern of most earlier political campaigns in post-revolutionary China.

Seeing the direction taken by the mass movement, Mao interfered, emphasizing that his main purpose of starting a cultural revolution was to criticize and fight "those inside the party going the capitalist road", i.e. the fathers and mothers of the Red Guard students. This message from Mao was well received by students whose parents belonged to the marginalized groups, and had been denied admittance to the Red Guard organizations because of their "bad family background". These students organized their own, alternative Red Guard factions, called "Rebel Organizations", fighting against the original Red Guard organizations. According to Wang Shaoguang, Mao almost immediately lost control of the mass movement, and the struggles continued between the two types of organizations, with each fighting, what Wang Shaoguang describes as, a rational struggle to defend or improve their respective positions in society. The discussions between these two different Red Guard factions were mainly centered on the definition of two basic concepts in the cultural revolutionary political discourse: "those inside the party going the capitalist road" and "class background". The Red Guards argued that, because of their upbringing in "good families" with a model worker or party membership history, they had inherited a revolutionary spirit, and could thus demand a strong position in society and preferential treatment. The rebels, supported by the cultural revolutionary wing of the CCP, questioned this "law of inherited political consciousness", and argued that they, not being spoiled by the privileges of party membership, could choose to distance themselves from their historical class background and become revolutionaries by conscious choice.

Furthermore, according to the Rebels, the parents of the original Red Guards had to be the individuals depicted by Mao as "those inside the party who go the *capitalist road*".

According to Mao's analytical conceptualization, the term "capitalist roaders" had two connotations: firstly, it referred to those who "held the red flag" and spoke the revolutionary language while supporting capitalist practices. Secondly and more importantly, it referred to people within the highest hierarchy of the Communist organization who "created organizational structures and promoted value systems that would allow the future generation to privatise property and subvert the collective power of the working class and peasants" (Petras, 1997: 446). Mao attempted to avoid the possibility that might lead the Chinese Communist Party, after assuming the vanguard role of the working class, into becoming a hegemonic class of its own (Li, 2001). This is because Mao had insight into the problem that after a long period of peaceful development, the CCP as the dominant organization of Chinese society could develop the tendency to design its own hegemonic project and to identify its own agenda and interests which did not necessarily correspond exclusively with those of peasantry and working classes. Under such conditions, the communist leadership would eventually become a new form of hegemonic class.

The struggles between Red Guard factions continued until the turmoil reached a level where the central leadership of the party, with Mao's consent, decided to use the military to quell the struggles, and many of the Red Guards and Rebels were sent to the countryside to learn from the peasants. Mao and the cultural revolutionary wing of the Communist Party had actually lost the Cultural Revolution, the Party had proved to be stronger than Mao and his followers had expected. The failure of the Cultural Revolution, and the political disillusioning of a great number of the Chinese population, did not manifest itself in full, until after Mao's death, when prominent members of the cultural revolutionary wing of the CCP were arrested and put on trial together with a number of their followers from all over the country.

Wang Shaoguang does not analyze the social background of the ending of the Cultural Revolution and the beginning of the period of economic reform leading to the development of a "socialist market economy". But from his analysis of the Cultural Revolution it seems to be obvious that the part of the leadership of the CCP, who had been attacked as the "capitalist roaders" by the Maoist line during the Cultural Revolution, had by then managed to establish a "historic bloc" between themselves, i.e. the party bureaucrats and the intellectual elites, who had been disillusioned by the social, economic and political turmoil caused by the Cultural Revolution and the persecution they experienced from the original Red Guard organizations. This historic bloc of social groups, which had been mutually antagonistic during the period of planned economy and the Cultural Revolution, were to become the main social forces behind the economic reforms, which led to the improvement of their social positions.

Seen from today's perspective, it is a paradox that the CCP led by such an elitist coalition is determined, in the name of the working class, to pursue its own hegemonic project in which many practices are actually injurious to the interests and welfare of the working class (Li, 2001). It was not until the market reform had torn down one sector after another of China's socialist economic base that people began to understand what Mao meant by "capitalist roader". At this point, it can be argued that Chinese socialism did not fall apart because of its demerits. Rather, it was intentionally torn down by members of its own elite who became increasingly pro-capitalist. The on-going marketization process was not the direct result of a massive revolution from below since the majority of the Chinese population obviously did not have the intention to totally destroy every aspect of socialism in spite of its many limitations and flaws. Rather, it was enforced by a "revolution" from above led by an elitist coalition that supported it, and benefited from it. This proves Mao's conviction accurate when he pointed out that the anti-socialist forces – capitalist roaders – existed right inside the central organization of the Party and state.

Real Capitalist Roaders

The "capitalist roaders" came to power after Mao died. They have indeed established themselves as today's compradors of "market socialism". The post-Mao leadership realized that the only way to maintain both their political power and economic interests was to transform themselves quickly into a new dominant class that could continue to rule through new class relations under the market economy. Breaking down the socialist economic system and replacing it with the market mechanism would enable them to become not only de facto owners of the means of production but also managers of the new economy. In this way they could capitalize on their official power while turning their bureaucratic privileges into economic advantages. At the same time they have resisted any political reforms under the banner of "maintaining social stability" because such reforms would challenge the status quo of their privileged position.

He Qinglian describes the marketization or commodification process of the economic reform in China as a process of "spontaneous privatization", indicating that the process was not only initiated by the central party leadership but also by individuals from the power structure, i.e. party bureaucrats or managers of state-owned enterprises using their political power, "power capital", to transform assets owned by the state into their own private property, by a process of "primitive capital accumulation". She explains the legal and illegal methods used by these power-holders in cooperation with friends, relatives and children to establish themselves as a new economic elite group – new Chinese capitalists – functioning in accordance with the new principles of socialist market economy. These methods include: using the double-track price system to extract surplus from illegal trade in raw materials and other products, a surplus which was then illegally channeled into newly established private enterprises; the "enclosure" movement whereby former collectively owned land was "enclosed" for the establishing of "developmental zones" and rented (de facto sold) cheaply to friends and relatives, who could then re-rent or resell this land at a profit; using the authority to conduct foreign trade to enrich themselves; by the means of so-called MBO (management buy out) granting each other cheap stocks in the companies they managed. The first step for these new capitalists was to transform their political power into direct economic control of economic units – state owned enterprises or newly established private enterprises. Having in this way established their economic position, they needed to consolidate their positions politically, actually regaining political power by means of their newly acquired economic power. The next step would therefore be to transform this new economic power into political power for themselves and their associates (friends and relatives). This was basically achieved when entrepreneurs, i.e. capitalists, in 2002 were welcomed as members of the CCP.

Alongside this development a new group of private entrepreneurs emerged, mainly intellectuals with technical expertise, who "jumped into the sea" (skipped their employment in state institutions and enterprises) and established new private enterprises. In this way a new economic elite was formed consisting of both former party bureaucrats and their families turned capitalists and intellectuals becoming new entrepreneurs. Both of these groups were allowed to become or stay members of the CCP, and thus gained considerable political influence, while the CCP gradually marginalized the former revolutionary classes, workers and peasants.

With the increase in the privatization process, the economic power of China's new bourgeoisie (middle class) is also growing (Han and Pannell, 1999). The situation is very ironic: the new capitalists today are politically stronger and economically wealthier than they were before the socialist nationalization in 1953. To protect their interest, they have raised the demand for political recognition and governing power. Besides creating their own types of associations, a large number of private capitalists have already entered People's Congresses and People's Political Consultative Conferences at different levels (Feng, 1999). The change of class relations constitutes and will sooner or later affect the existing political system and power structure. Today China's national labor forces are divided into formal contract and temporary workers with members of each group receiving differentiated salaries and welfare benefits. Even the Cultural Revolution would not have been "radical" enough to predict the degree of what is happening today: the widening gap between urban and rural living conditions, class polarization, rampant official corruption, massive unemployment, the return of drugs, prostitution and gangsters, child labor, primitive exploitation, and external vulnerability and dependence.

In June 1989 the crackdown in Beijing on campaigning students and sympathizers from all layers of society led to a temporary halt of the reform programme. The process leading up to the crackdown has been interpreted as an increasingly intensified struggle between on one hand "The Democracy Movement", i.e. students and other intellectuals struggling for democratization of China's political system and society, and a conservative Party leadership brutally using armed forces to defend its rule. In recent years, a new interpretation has been formulated in which the clash between military and demonstrators is seen more as a precondition for the continuation of the reform process initiated by the new Chinese economic elite in alliance with the Party leadership, and thus actually in accordance with the interests of the new economic elite. This interpretation was formulated by Wang Hui (2003) in China and was later presented to a broader Western audience by Naomi Klein (2007). The Democracy Movement in 1989 which started as a movement for improving living conditions for students and later included demands for a democratization of political life in China, gained support from major parts of the population of Beijing, angered by the inflation caused by initial price reforms and growing corruption. The criticism against corruption was not directed at plain bribery, but was mainly targeting the numerous examples of children of high-ranking party officials usurping state-owned wealth in the process described by He Qinglian as "spontaneous privatization" by "the power capital". According to the explanation offered by Wang Hui, the crackdown had the purpose to frighten the broad Chinese population from protesting against inflation and the new economic elite and thus clearing the road for a continuation of the reform process. This interpretation formulated by Wang Hui, who is usually characterized as one of the prominent representatives of the Chinese New Left, is supported by the Chinese economist, Sheng Hong, who by no means may be described as a left-winger. According to Sheng Hong (1996), the government led by Zhao Ziyang[4] in 1986 and 1988 made vain attempts to implement a comprehensive price reform with methods resembling "shock therapy". In either case the price reform and the inflation caused by them were met by popular protests forcing the government to abandon them. After the massacre, between 1989 and 1991, the government, according to Sheng Hong, at last succeeded in implementing a comprehensive price reform.

The Institutional "Passive Revolution" of the CCP

Examining the historical and social backgrounds of the crises experienced by the CCP helps us to understand the fact that the evolution of China's post-Mao development, whether political, economic or cultural, has been inevitably, in one way or another, linked to some of the historical and social bases originating from early crises and especially from the Cultural Revolution.

Under such conditions, crisis implies a necessity to reorganize society. In other words, a breakthrough in establishing a new order is not necessarily the outcome of the final collapse of the old one, rather, it is an outcome of social reorganization initiated or imposed by a dominant political force or a coalition of

4 He was the Premier of the People's Republic of China from 1980 to 1987, and General Secretary of the Communist Party of China from 1987 to 1989. He was a leading reformist.

forces. Social reorganization can be realized through passive revolution in which the survival of an existing order, albeit the emergence of a crisis, is made possible by the absorption of social contradictions which are not necessarily resolved, but are contained or transformed into becoming new forms of relations.

Thus, in an attempt to respond to the social contradictions brought about by the Cultural Revolution, the CCP initiated the economic marketization process, which in turn has also changed the social basis of the CCP. New legitimacy for the CCP has to be constantly regenerated and renegotiated through ideological adjustments and intra-party reforms (Sausmikat, 2006). According to this chapter, the party's subtle and persuasive uphold of control and legitimation throughout the above mentioned crises can be analyzed from, among others, two perspectives: 1) ideological and theoretical adaptation; 2) party cooptation and corporatism.

Sinicizing Capacity and Framing Power

"Sinicizing" (sinicize) refers to the process of transforming things (idea and concept) into Chinese-like ones or to change or modify them by Chinese influence. It can be argued that while the concept of political party in China was imported, the CCP is first and foremost a Chinese cultural product – it is a very different breed of political party from those in the West (Zheng, 2009).

During the founding period of the CCP in the early period of the 20th century, different schools of thoughts entered China including many foreign-inspired schools, such as Constitutionalism, Positivism, Marxism-Leninism, Socialism, Liberalism, Darwinism, etc. The CCP led by Mao seized this opportunity to sinicize the Chinese Communist movement through a skilful redefinition of "class" and sinicized the application of class politics.[5] For example, the Maoist's revolutionary strategy of "using countryside to surround city" turned the Chinese revolution into a peasant-based uprising. The Cultural Revolution can also be seen as a way of sinicizing socialist revolution, and establishing China as the center of socialist world revolution in opposition to the former USSR, then described as a revisionist capitalist society with hegemonic ambitions. Where the revisionists of the Soviet Communist Party emphasized "development of the productive forces", Chinese cultural revolutionary ideology emphasized revolutionizing superstructure, developing the relations of production, continuation of class struggle in the socialist society and permanent revolution, all with the purpose of preventing Chinese society from developing in a capitalist direction. This process of sinicizing has been a crucial element in China's revolutionary and post-revolutionary history.

5 Mao realized the power of millions of peasants who could be converted to become part of the revolutionary army capable of unleashing working class powers for great socio-political changes. The Chinese Revolution is in reality a peasant revolution rather than a working class one.

Political Discourse and Social Change

One of the unique features of the CCP's sinicizing capacity is its framing power. "Framing power" refers to the capacity of defining and redefining ideas, concepts, discourse, rhetoric which bear policy implication. Since the essence of social change lies in changing perceptions, and changing perception itself falls into the territory of framing, thus, the power of framing has strong effects on social change. The CCP's framing power undoubtedly reflects its ideological and institutional adaptation because political discourses are not only a way of expressing viewpoints but also a weapon to legitimize changes as the way they are meant to be. The CCP believes that framing an understanding in a particular way can lead to changes in the practices of an institution or a society as a whole.

The CCP is perfectly aware of the power of political discourse in connection with social changes because political discourse played an indispensable role in its victory in the revolution. In the past three decades of economic reforms, the CCP's sinicizing capacity and framing power has once again played its due role. Understanding the fact that the linkage between cognition/consciousness (language, concept and notion) and social change (politics, economics and policies) is established through the construction of language (argument, expression and explanation) which is embedded with powerful meanings and implications in social–political contexts, the CCP purposefully designed and formulated a particular set of explanations aiming to legitimize political and ideological revisionism and to defend the justification of reformist social–economic policies.

Understanding the great importance of promoting market capitalism without cognitive disconnection with the heritage of its political legitimacy of socialism, the CCP has been struggling to construct an awkward but pragmatic mixture combining socialist logo (socialist identity) on one hand and the market forces on the other. Such a mixture is clearly reflected in many language terms invented for theoretical finesse and ideological justification, such as "socialist market economy" or "market economy with Chinese characteristics", and "Confucian businessman", which are politically and economically contradictory but ideologically and theoretically useful for the new reality. The new reality is often coined with a number of sinicizing benchmarks, such as "adherence to the primacy of socialism", "supremacy of the leadership of the Communist Party", "adaptation of Marxist principles to the conditions of China", etc. These logocentric tenets are not just slogans, but they are imperative to the continuous legitimation of the CCP in face of the fundamental changes brought about by market capitalism.

One concrete example is that in order to ideologically justify the market economy in which the rule by capital and the exploitation of the working classes are accepted, the CCP has invented a theoretical justification which framed China's current development stage as "the primary stage of socialism" (rather than calling it the "primitive accumulation stage of capitalism"). It indicates the attempt of the CCP to withdraw from its previously sinicized conceptualization of Marxism and return to the classical teachings of Marx and Engels, who maintained that socialism must develop from the womb of highly advanced and productive industrial capitalism. The CCP argued that the authentic Marxist notion of socialism assumes basic preconditions for reaching socialism including the arduous industrialization process.

The CCP now claimed that China was still in a transition period from pre-socialist to socialist society and it was still in the stage of catching up with the missed accumulation of capitalism. On the basis of the new interpretation, the CCP argued that given the level of the productive forces in post-revolution China, the failure of Chinese socialism was due to the fact that transition to "fully-fledged" socialist relations of production had proceeded too rapidly, and China could not afford the socialist project without the stage of capital accumulation.

Sinicizing/resinicizing and framing/reframing have provided the CCP with both an image and an instrument: an image of implementing political measures that would improve the efficiency of the government – but not political reform; and an instrument needed to facilitate the goal of economic reform – but not western-style democracy with institutional checks and balances and popular voting. Political reform was conceptualized in narrow and technical terms referring to the implementation of measures that would improve the efficiency of the government and mobilize resources in order to let economic reform move forward. The collapse of the Soviet Union was concluded by the CCP to be the result of a long-term economic stagnation and a wrong-headed political reform with a wrong sequence – pursuing the political reform ahead of the economic reform.

Cooptation and Corporatism

Since the 1989 June 4th crisis, the CCP has been endeavoring to find strategies for a number of challenges to the party organization itself: how to liberalize the national economy without destabilizing the CCP-dominated political system? How to transform the party's organization and absorb new members in order to accommodate the new production relations? And how to balance the need to adapt to the new social, political and economic environment and the need to uphold the party's basic norms and tradition? One of the CCP's key strategies is cooptation and corporatism which are designed to help the party and the society to mutually adapt to each other.

Cooptation implies the active recruitment of new party members and the creation of new links with other emerging organizations. It aims to bring in new elites in the policy-making process, such as entrepreneurs and skilled experts, who may invigorate the party with new ideas and new goals. The CCP realized that the only way to maintain its political power and economic interests was to quickly transform the party into a new dominant productive force that is able to continue to rule through new class relations under the market economy. Breaking down the socialist economic system and replacing it with the market mechanism, although politically risky, can also enable the CCP to become not only de-facto owners of the means of production but also managers of the new economy. In this way they could capitalize on their official power while turning their bureaucratic privileges into economic advantages. At the same time they have resisted top-down political reform under the banner of "maintaining social stability" because such reform would challenge the CCP's privileged position.

Corporatism in the Chinese context refers to the central characteristics behind the so-called China's "socialist market economy", in which China has moved from a socialist planned economy with public ownership towards state regulation of a hybrid market economy with the existence of a large proportion of private economy that still remains much embedded in the party-state system that spawned it (Li, 2008). Chinese state corporatism can best explain the embedding features in the process of China's socio-economic and socio-political transformations through marketizing decision-making powers and commodifying public institutions (Wank, 1999). Corporatism has been playing a positive role in both encouraging marketization and decentralization of state capacities and public resources without falling into economic and social disembeddedment and maintaining the key ingredients of the "corporative relations" between the state and market that have led to sustained economic growth.

Class Politics

One of the core aspects of the CCP's hegemony is the effective application of class politics. "Class" has been a politically-associated concept ever since it became a socio-economic category when Marxism was introduced into China's modern revolutionary history. It played a central role in the series of political struggles within the CCP during the post-revolutionary period. Before the economic reform, the concept of class was not defined in the terms of classical Marxism (not in terms of ownership) but in terms of political criteria that were used to mobilize mass participation both in political movement and economic development.

The CCP now claimed that during the socialist period, it oversimplified societal complexities in many respects by reducing the multiple levels of social relations into the single dimension of class struggle. Although the reduction of politics to class relations was an effective political weapon during the armed revolution period in order to compress political struggles and to hold social complexities at arm's length, the question was whether such complexities could be encompassed in a simplified manner in post-revolutionary China.

Today, for the sake of accommodating economic modernization as the primary object, the CCP has had to abandon its class struggle tradition and banish class discourse from the official ideology in dealing with domestic and international affairs. The main objective of cooptation and corporatism is to turn the CCP organization into becoming inclusionary rather than exclusionary and to reinterpret a number of transformed social relations so that the CCP's new cooptation policy is politically and ideologically justified. The central point is to indicate the fact that the CCP also represents the interest of the newly emerged social groups of various kinds especially the new rich.

The CCP has found it necessary to transfer certain power from the political bureaucracy to those with technical and professional expertise (from "red" to "expertise")[6] in order to unleash the productive forces. Since the CCP has been promoting the reformist discourse – "science and technology are the prime productive forces" (not working class anymore), it states as a fact that the new technocratic-managerial classes are the leading productive forces for China's modernization project. These new classes consist of the same people who were the "red bourgeoisie", "class enemies" and "counter-revolutionaries" during the Cultural Revolution. Today they are becoming real bourgeoisie through the new production relations that make privatization possible. They are committed to economic development and market economy, but their loyalty to the party and socialism is questionable. They have the skills which are desired by party leaders to accomplish their new policy agenda. Their membership may lead to the rejuvenation of the party, but may also lead to destabilizing tendencies, such as increasing corruption and misconduct among party members. Paradoxically, the socialist period of China was one full of class politics but without real class divisions, whereas the reform period is one full of serious class divisions but with class politics becoming a taboo.

The situation is very ironic: the new capitalists today are much stronger and wealthier than they were before. To protect their interests they have raised the demand for political recognition and governing power. Besides creating their own types of associations, a large number of private capitalists have already entered various political representative organizations at various levels, such as the People's Congresses and People's Political Consultative Conferences. This increases party-market corporatism, and it also explains why China has been able to maintain consistency in economic policy.

Nowadays the CCP does not need to use coercive means to control society. Newly recruited party members are connecting the party with other organizations where they are also key actors. These newly emerged interest groups embedded with the CCP members allow the party to become the arbiter of competing interests in regulating conflicts of interests, channeling interest articulation and resolving problems. Therefore, linking with and accommodating emerging organizations gives the CCP a number of benefits in terms of information-receiving, depoliticizing and diversifying social conflicts, and strengthening state-market clientelism.

---

6 During the Cultural Revolution 1966-1976, "red" implied political attitude and class consciousness, whereas "expertise" referred to knowledge, expertise and skill. It was important that people with technical expertise must first and foremost adopt correct political and class attitude (red). In other words, "red" and "expertise" must be combined, but with the emphasis on the former.

Conclusion

The CCP's transformation and adaptation in the past three decades of economic reform has proved its capacity and resiliency in struggling to maintain the continuing domination of its ruling power. The CCP has been able to manage the changes brought about by the economic liberalization process as a proactive player throughout – an initiator, a planner, an organizer, an implementer. The resilient nature of the CCP implies that as long as the party is transforming and adapting itself in accordance with China's socio-economic changes, the basic structure of its dominion over the state and society will not be fundamentally altered (Zheng, 2009).

Thus, it can be well concluded that the CCP's capacity in maintaining social and political stability in the midst of recurrent crises is one of the strongest enduring features of contemporary Chinese political culture. In order to sustain its power and legitimacy without upsetting the market mechanism, the CCP has been adapting itself in a continuous process of "passive revolution" aiming to generate new sources of hegemony around a reconstituted historical bloc. Today, general consensus on the role of the CCP as the key stabilizer is shared not only by the CCP itself but also by the society at large. The adaptive behavior of the CCP can be analyzed as systemic behavior, i.e. the party as an institution with its own life trying to adapt to a changing environment by changing its own constitution and behavior and underpinning its survival using economic reforms in creating economic efficiency and authoritarian rule to maintain social stability.

This chapter attempts to show that analyzing the systemic behavior of the CCP as one of the key factors behind the rise of China is extremely important. But at the same time this analysis does not exclusively give a complete picture of the political and economic development in China, if the historical and social contradictions shaping the crises as well as the adaptive responses from the CCP to the emerging social contradictions are left out of the analysis. During the reform period, the social basis of the CCP has changed, and so has the pattern of social interests. Economic growth and social stability are intimately connected with the changing pattern of power relations in society, which is reflected in the pattern of relations of interests articulated and promoted in the actual behavior of the CCP. Analysis of social contradictions must, therefore, complement the systemic analysis of the CCP as an institution.

Historically China has been able to display a capacity for absorbing foreign ideas and influences and sinicizing and transforming them into parts of native value systems, such as the sinicization of Buddhism and Marxism-Leninism. Currently the CCP is attempting to sinicize capitalism and create a "market economy with Chinese characteristics". To which extent is the CCP willing to further modify the political system to make the economic system viable? To find the right answer is very difficult. But an open-ended answer is that if the CCP is able to create market capitalism with Chinese characteristics, it will be able to establish a political economy with very evident Chinese characters as well.

References

Chang, Gordon G. (2001) *The Coming Collapse of China*. New York: Random House.

Chen, Feng (1999) "An Unfinished Battle In China: The Leftist Criticism Of The Reform and the Third Thought Emancipation", *The China Quarterly*, 158: 447-467.

Han, Sunsheng and Pannell, Clifton W. (1999) "The Geography of Privatization in China, 1978-1996", *Economic Geography*, 75(3): 272-296.

He, Qinglian (1998) *Xiandaihua de xianjing*, Beijing: Jinri Zhongguo Chubanshe. (available in a German translation by Christine Reisner as: Qinglian He (2006) *China in der Modernisierungsfalle.* Hamburger Edition).

Li, Xing (2001) "The Chinese Cultural Revolution Revisited", *The China Review*, 1(1): 137-165.

Li, Xing (2004) "'From 'Politics in Command' to 'Economics in Command': A Discourse Analysis of China's Transformation, *Copenhagen Journal of Asian Studies*, 18: 65-87.

Li, Xing (2008) "Market Capitalism with Chinese Characteristics", *Kritisk Debat*, 44.

Klein, Naomi (2007) *The Shock Doctrine: The Rise of Disaster Capitalism*. London: Allen Lane.

Petras, James (1997) "The Chinese Cultural Revolution in Historical Perspective", *Journal of Contemporary Asia*, 27(4): 445-459.

Sausmikat, Nora (2006) "More Legitimacy for One-Party Rule? The CCP's Ideological Adjustments and Intra-Party Reforms", *ASIEN*, 99: 70-91.

Sheng, Hong (1996) "A Survey of the Research on the Transitional Process of Market-Oriented Reform in China", *Chinese Economic Studies*, 29(2): 5-38.

Wang, Hui. (2003) *China's New Order. Society, Politics, and Economy in Transition*. New York: Harvard University Press.

Wang, Shaoguang (1995) *Failure of Charisma*, New York: Oxford University Press.

Wank, David L. (1999) *Commodifying Communism Business, Trust and Politics in a Chinese City*. Cambridge: Cambridge University Press.

Zheng, Yongnian (2009) *The Chinese Communist Party as Organizational Emperor: Culture, Reproduction, and Transformation*. London: Routledge.

Index

References to footnotes are indicated by *f.* Page numbers in *italics* refer to figures, tables or graphs.

THE INTERNATIONAL POLITICAL ECONOMY OF NEW REGIONALISMS SERIES

Other titles in the series

Clash or Cooperation of Civilizations?
Overlapping Integration and Identities
Edited by Wolfgang Zank

New Perspectives on Globalization and Antiglobalization
Prospects for a New World Order?
Edited by Henry Veltmeyer

Governing Regional Integration for Development: Monitoring Experiences, Methods and Prospects
Edited by Philippe De Lombaerde, Antoni Estevadeordal and Kati Suominen

Europe-Asia Interregional Relations
A Decade of ASEM
Edited by Bart Gaens

Cruising in the Global Economy
Profits, Pleasure and Work at Sea
Christine B.N. Chin

Beyond Regionalism?
Regional Cooperation, Regionalism and Regionalization in the Middle East
Edited by Cilja Harders and Matteo Legrenzi

The EU–Russian Energy Dialogue
Europe's Future Energy Security
Edited by Pami Aalto

Regionalism, Globalisation and International Order
Europe and Southeast Asia
Jens-Uwe Wunderlich

EU Development Policy and Poverty Reduction
Enhancing Effectiveness
Edited by Wil Hout

An East Asian Model for Latin American Success
The New Path
Anil Hira

European Union and New Regionalism
Regional Actors and Global Governance in a Post-Hegemonic Era. Second Edition
Edited by Mario Telò

Regional Integration and Poverty
Edited by Dirk Willem te Velde and the Overseas Development Institute

Redefining the Pacific?
Regionalism Past, Present and Future
Edited by Jenny Bryant-Tokalau and Ian Frazer

The Limits of Regionalism
NAFTA's Labour Accord
Robert G. Finbow

Latin America's Quest for Globalization
The Role of Spanish Firms
Edited by Félix E. Martín and Pablo Toral

Exchange Rate Crises in Developing Countries
The Political Role of the Banking Sector
Michael G. Hall

Globalization and Antiglobalization
Dynamics of Change in the New World Order
Edited by Henry Veltmeyer

Twisting Arms and Flexing Muscles
Humanitarian Intervention and Peacebuilding in Perspective
Edited by Natalie Mychajlyszyn and Timothy M. Shaw

Asia Pacific and Human Rights
A Global Political Economy Perspective
Paul Close and David Askew

Demilitarisation and Peace-Building
in Southern Africa
Volume III – The Role of the Military
in State Formation and Nation-Building
*Edited by Peter Batchelor, Kees Kingma
and Guy Lamb*

Demilitarisation and Peace-Building
in Southern Africa
Volume II – National and
Regional Experiences
*Edited by Peter Batchelor
and Kees Kingma*

Demilitarisation and Peace-Building
in Southern Africa
Volume I – Concepts and Processes
*Edited by Peter Batchelor and Kees
Kingma*

Reforging the Weakest Link
Global Political Economy and Post-Soviet
Change in Russia, Ukraine and Belarus
Edited by Neil Robinson

Persistent Permeability?
Regionalism, Localism, and Globalization
in the Middle East
*Edited by Bassel F. Salloukh
and Rex Brynen*

The New Political Economy of United
States-Caribbean Relations
The Apparel Industry and the Politics
of NAFTA Parity
Tony Heron

The Nordic Regions
and the European Union
*Edited by Søren Dosenrode
and Henrik Halkier*

The New Regionalism in Africa
*Edited by J. Andrew Grant
and Fredrik Söderbaum*

Comparative Regional Integration
Theoretical Perspectives
Edited by Finn Laursen

Japan and South Africa
in a Globalising World
A Distant Mirror
Edited by Chris Alden and Katsumi Hirano

Development and Security
in Southeast Asia
Volume III: Globalization
*Edited by David B. Dewitt
and Carolina G. Hernandez*

Development and Security
in Southeast Asia
Volume II: The People
*Edited by David B. Dewitt
and Carolina G. Hernandez*

Development and Security
in Southeast Asia
Volume I: The Environment
*Edited by David B. Dewitt
and Carolina G. Hernandez*

Thailand, Indonesia and Burma in
Comparative Perspective
Priyambudi Sulistiyanto